D1709954

Coming
out of
the
MIDDLE AGES

中
CHINESE
STUDIES
▪ ON ▪
CHINA

Coming out of the MIDDLE AGES

Comparative Reflections on China and the West

Zhu Weizheng

Translated and Edited by
Ruth Hayhoe

M.E. Sharpe, Inc.
Armonk, New York   London, England

Library of Congress Cataloging-in-Publication Data

Chu, Wei-Cheng
    [Tsou ch'u chung chi. English]
    Coming out of the Middle Ages: comparative reflections on China and the
West / by Zhu Weizheng; translated and edited by Ruth Hayhoe.
        p. cm. — (Chinese studies on China)
    Translation of: Tsou ch'u chung chi.
    ISBN 0-87332-638-5
    1. China—Intellectual life—1644–1912. 2. China—Intellectual life—
    Occidental influences. I. Hayhoe, Ruth. II. Title III. Series.
DS754.14.C56 1990
951′.03—dc20   90-8161
                                                                         CIP

Printed in the United States of America

ED   10   9   8   7   6   5   4   3   2   1

Contents

Preface

In China one has to be extremely careful when committing thoughts to writing. Many years ago, when I was a pupil in primary school, I saw the following slogan posted all over the place: "Respect and cherish paper with words on it." My elders and betters explained to me that this was because once paper had words written on it, it came under the jurisdiction of deities. If it was soiled, thrown away or trampled upon, these deities would take their vengeance.

Later after I had entered the university and become an "intellectual," I experienced many campaigns of "thought reform" and in the process became aware of the aptness of this slogan of my childhood and the explanation provided for it. When you put black characters down on a white page, you must beware of the troubles this white page may bring upon you.

Take this situation as an example. You keep a diary in China, and what you have written in it is already forgotten, or perhaps you take notes on books you have read, a record specifically for your personal use, and subsequently you completely forget what you have written in these notes. It is entirely possible that some day these writings will suddenly become evidence that you have committed "crimes of thought." The very ordinary things that you originally wrote down are now subject to a "reading between the lines," and in them are found criminal thoughts that you could never have dreamed up, to be used as evidence of your crime of "slander" and of "vicious attack" on those in authority. Anyone who is accused of this kind of crime faces consequences that are far from pleasant.

In the early nineteenth century, a well-known Chinese thinker, Gong Zizhen, commented in one of his poems that he "avoided being present at certain events because he feared even to hear about the literary inquisition." This was one kind of response to the sight of many people who were punished by the loss of life and destruction of their families for books and articles they had written. The literary inquisition was a matter of being condemned as a criminal simply on the basis of individual thoughts one had written down on paper. This kind of thing has also occurred in the Western historical experience, yet contemporary Western readers will be strangers to it. If Chinese readers had been used to respect for individual privacy and for freedom of thought and expression from the time they were young, they too would no longer have any idea of what is meant by a literary inquisition.

However, even though Gong Zizhen has already been dead for 150 years, the literary inquisition that he so feared has not yet become something that is of interest only to a small number of historians in China. In writing diaries or letters, Chinese scholars and literary people have seldom revealed their inner world completely, except during a few short periods. Needless to say, in writing books and putting forward theories, it is even less possible to give direct expression to their ideas, since this type of writing is addressed to the public.

In addition to the cautiousness created by this environment, Chinese scholars carry certain burdens of their own—that is the fact that scholarly circles find it difficult to accept divergent voices, especially voices that are not in accord with the opinions of authority. Authority and truth are not the same thing, yet in China they are constantly made to appear the same. Therefore, those who are pursuing scholarly research have to be prepared not only to endure a harsh and solitary existence but also to face all kinds of pressures that have nothing to do with scholarship. This makes it particularly difficult to persist in independent thought.

In recent years there has been some improvement in China's scholarly atmosphere. The symbol of that improvement, to use the official term created by the authorities, has been a "loosing of the bonds." This term is a vivid one, amounting to an admission that Chinese scholars in the past had actually been tied with heavy ropes, just like convicts in prison. When prisoners have their ropes loosened, so that they can move their hands and feet a little, this is naturally an improvement in their treatment. Yet prisoners in loosened ropes are still prisoners. For scholarly research to develop in creative ways, the basic condition must be that it is not subjected to any pressure or interference not derived from scholarship itself. For scholars in China, this prospect remains a poetic fantasy.

When our colleagues overseas read scholarly publications that have appeared in China, they often feel perplexed. Why is it that such a wealth of material leads to such meager scholarly conclusions? Why is it that certain new and original opinions, which need to be thoroughly discussed and debated, are silenced before discussion has begun? This situation may well be due to the fact that these new opinions lacked profundity of thought, as has been suggested in the criticism of some scholars outside of China. But that is not always the case. Other critiques have made the point that pure scholarly work in China tends to exude an aura of despair or indignation. From this it may be possible to gain a better understanding of the reasons for this abnegation, in spite of the fact that scholars have a strong desire to speak out.

The volume on which this translation is based contains twenty-one articles. Most were originally written to record the results of my own thinking and so enable me to move ahead in my research. In other words, they were mainly written for myself to read, and I had no thought of publishing them. Later, due to unexpected circumstances, I agreed to put together this collection for publication and simply did a small amount of revision and retouching. The Chinese version was first published in 1987 by Shanghai People's Press.

Possibly because I originally wrote it for my own eyes alone—or could it be because I have long been used to the state of living in bonds and felt paralyzed by it—I was surprised to find when this small book was published that it was seen by friends in China and overseas as simply a direct description of my personal views. But is this really the case? I am convinced it is not. The content belongs purely to history. The problems that I have taken for reflection were discovered in the process of my work—they are all important questions, yet all need further and more profound investigation. I know that my own attitude to history is a rigorous one, yet I am also aware that the book has not been able to rise above the present style of Chinese scholarly writing. In my case, those articles that were not originally written for publication, and may appear very condensed, could all the more easily lead people to get a sense of the tendency for Chinese scholars to "understate their meaning."

Nevertheless, Professor Ruth Hayhoe of the Ontario Institute for Studies in Education and the University of Toronto felt that the book was worth introducing to Western readers. She was willing to undertake the task of selecting and translating much of its content from the perspective of Chinese-Western cultural interaction and comparative culture in order to make possible this English version. In this undertaking she was supported by her colleague, Professor Timothy Brook, also of the University of Toronto, who agreed to check the translation and references. I can only express my gratitude to both these friends for their good will. I must also thank Professor Lynn Struve of Indiana University for agreeing to check part of the translation. I am sure that Professor Hayhoe's elegant prose, which has been revised by these two historians of the Ming-Qing period, will far excel my original work. As for the content of the volume, I anticipate with eagerness both discussion and criticism from those who read it.

Zhu Weizheng, January 8, 1989
Toronto, Canada

Translator's Note

It has been both a pleasure and a challenge to undertake the translation of Professor Zhu's reflections on China's historical experience in coming out of the Middle Ages. All but one of the essays selected for translation are found in *Zou chu zhongshiji*, published by Shanghai People's Press in 1987. "China's Lost Renaissance" was written for a conference commemorating the seventieth anniversary of May 4th in Beijing in May 1989. In the original volume, the vignettes of Ming-Qing thinkers appeared directly after the lengthy opening essay, "Coming Out of the Middle Ages." For the English version I decided to put them into an appendix. I suspect they should not be read as simple biographical notes, but as profound and highly condensed reflections on the contradictions that were particularly acute for those living through such a historic transition as that from medievalism to the modern period. Thus their esoteric character may mean they appeal mainly to specialists in the period.

The volume overall is intended for a wide general readership, and with this in mind I have tried to provide translations for all specialist terms and the titles of the many Chinese works referred to. In most cases it has been possible to draw on the literature already available in English, but some have had to be translated for this volume. If these titles are not always felicitous, I ask for the readers' indulgence. It was a difficult task. A great deal of background reading was necessary for the work of translation, and one colleague suggested that I prepare a comprehensive English bibliography of relevant sources. Not being myself a Ming-Qing historian, I was not confident that my collection would be representative. Thus I have simply presented Professor Zhu's footnotes as he prepared them originally, with a few added explanatory notes to help the general reader. This seems true to the spirit of the volume, which was intended more as a set of wide-ranging reflections to stimulate new approaches to research than as a systematic scholarly account of the period.

Finally, I would like to pay tribute to the subtlety and richly allusive quality of Professor Zhu's prose, much of which I fear may have been lost in the process of translation, in spite of my best efforts. Some stylistic changes also seemed necessary to suit the Western reader. Sentences have been shortened, and paragraphing has been adjusted in some places. For example, the first lengthy essay originally had no paragraphing and was meant as a stream of consciousness piece. After some consultation with colleagues, I decided that paragraphs were needed in the later part of the essay, to assist the reader through a fairly demanding argument.

If the reader gains even half of the insights into Chinese culture that were my reward for the efforts at translation, I will feel the task has been worthwhile. For me, it is an honor to be the first to introduce to English readers fruits of scholarship carried out over many years that reveal a rare level of communion between Chinese and European thought.

Ruth Hayhoe
July 1989

Coming
out of
the
MIDDLE AGES

1 | Coming out of the Middle Ages: Historical Reflections on the Late Ming to the Late Qing

The Middle Ages had developed from raw primitiveness. It had done away with old civilization, old philosophy, politics and jurisprudence, in order to begin anew in every respect.[1]

Such highly flourishing civilizations entirely disappeared. What was this "gateway of death" that they passed through?[2]

1

China had a very lengthy Middle Ages. If one accepts the view that by the third century A.D. China had already entered the historical period of feudalism, that would mean that the beginning of the Middle Ages in China was at least two hundred years earlier than in Western Europe, and if one takes a widely agreed date for the end of Chinese feudalism—the early nineteenth century—it would mean that China's Middle Ages lasted for fifteen hundred years. In the history of human civilization, this is a very long period of time.

2

The concept of the Middle Ages is not purely one of time, it is also a spatial concept. It would be more appropriate to say it is a relative boundary on a space-time continuum. In the past, the disputes over the beginning of the Middle Ages have been a kind of see-saw battle. There were many reasons for this, but at the very least there is a common methodological failing here, which is that a Newtonian concept of time-space has, to a large extent, monopolized our discussions. Time is linear, in this conception, so that in describing the special characteristics of a period, it is either "progressive" or "backward." Space is conceived in a Euclidean way, so neglecting history's regional characteristics. We have exaggerated the temporal conception of imperial dynasties so as to encompass all of the spatial characteristics of a particular period in China, without placing any limitations on it. Of course some attention has been given to the special characteristics of the different races, yet we have overlooked the fact that these special characteristics can only be effectively explained from the perspective of a space-time continuum. Using the Han race as a reference point in any one period to measure whether other racial groups were "progressive" or "backward" can hardly be seen as any more accurate than using the old yardsticks of barbarian sinification which absolutized contemporaneity. In the past, Chinese historians have completely repudiated geographical determinism, yet it cannot be said that geographical environment is totally unimportant. To refuse for this reason to probe the space-time continuum of the movement of history has led to distortions. *The History of the Communist Party of the Soviet Union* (1938), which was the first to criticize geographical determinism, demonstrates its author's oppositional and inflexible logic on this point, whereas Engels at an early stage criticized the errors in this type of thinking.

3

If we were to take the perspective of a space-time continuum in exploring the history of the Middle Ages, might we not hinder an overall understanding of history? Is it not possible this would lead to some doubt over the very existence of a so-called Middle Ages? This would happen only if we neglected the methodological insights provided by Marx's study of the economic formation of capitalism. In his investigation into the capitalist mode of production, Marx took England as his primary example for theoretical elaboration "because a body, as an organic whole, is more easily studied than are the cells of that body. In the analysis of economic forms, moreover, neither microscopes nor chemical reagents are of use. The force of abstraction must replace both."[3] In other words, since England was typical of the capitalist mode of production of that time, like a body in which bourgeois society was already reaching maturity, its economic formation was particularly suitable for this kind of abstract analysis. Does that mean Marx refused to do microeconomic research? No, *Capital* starts with a kind of dissection of small cells under the microscope. Nor did Marx deny that other European nations or peoples were experiencing their own unique historical development. Both the preface and afterword of *Capital* emphasize this point. When Marx was discussing the social antagonisms of early capitalism in his actual research, he used France as the primary example, and when discussing remnants of early agricultural communal society, he took Russia as his example. Marx's sense of the importance of spatially distinct types within the same time period could be suggestive for studying the Chinese Middle Ages. I feel it is particularly important for investigating the culture of the Middle Ages. In comparison with political history, economic history, and the history of philosophy and literature, research into cultural history in China was interrupted for a long period of time. This means that many approaches to analysis and explanation are waiting to be researched from the very beginning. No matter how culture is delimited, all definitions tend to be reified abstractions. It is thus very easy to fall into the error of neglecting the space-time continuum. Take, for example, certain assessments of the status and use of Confucianism during the Middle Ages. In my view they not only neglect the temporal course of history but also fail to attend to history's spatial diversity, using a subjective perspective in place of scientific abstraction.

4

Within cultural history itself, an investigation into how Chinese culture came out of the Middle Ages is especially vexing and difficult. On the eve of the May 4th Movement, Lu Xun gave this description of the situation: "In China's social conditions one can see nine or ten centuries shrunk into one period of time: from Chinese pine torches to electric lights, from wheelbarrows to airplanes, from darts to machine canons, from not allowing presumptuous discussion of laws and principles to defending the law, from the savage mentality of carnivors sleeping in animal skins to human rights, from receiving spirits and worshipping the snakegod to suggesting that aesthetics replace religion, these phenomena all existed side by side.''[4] At a later point Mao Zedong made a similar observation. They both detected the relative character of contemporaneity, the objective existence of spatial diversity in one period of time. They felt that in reforming China, one could not neglect all the contradictions and conflicts among China's medieval and prefeudal cultures. Furthermore, it is impossible to deny the different temporal manifestations of spatial diversity, not only those beginning after the destruction of the Qing dynasty, but those well before the end of this dynasty. If one defines ''the early modern period'' as the period in which the capitalist mode of production and the corresponding relations of production and exchange became evident, then one cannot deny that in certain regions of China the sprouts of this development were already evident at an early period.

5

Certain Sinologists abroad reached the conclusion long ago that between the tenth century and the establishment of the Northern Song kingdom, Chinese society had already entered a ''preparatory early modern period.'' If we use our technical terminology, this would mean that an embryonic formation of the capitalist mode of production was already evident. During the 1950s some historians in China hinted that they had also accepted this view, but the result was that they were attacked for abandoning the true doctrine. They were suspected of ulterior motives in wanting to change what was supposed to be the lengthy period of Chinese feudalism into a much short period. I am not going to discuss this particular case now, but the problem still exists. For example, the British scholar Joseph Needham, in his monumental history of Chinese science, shows considerable sympathy for this view from the perspective of the issue of when the modernization of science and technology began. Since then, however, only economists have ventured cautious discussions of the problem of when the early manifestations of capitalism can be seen. Most tend toward a rather generous and elastic periodization, saying that the early manifestations of capitalism are found between the late sixteenth century and the late eighteenth century. This allows them to take shelter in the brilliance of the sacred canons whenever necessary, since the classical texts state that in the society of the Middle Ages capitalism was already present in embryonic form. This type of explanation, however, creates a problem for researchers into other aspects of history, if one tries to be consistent within Marxism-Leninism. If one accepts that politics are the manifestation of cumulative economic conditions and that social existence determines social consciousness, then even if the sprouts of capitalism never fully matured, they were still present from the Wanli to the Qianlong eras, a period of two hundred years, and did not wither or die, suggesting they must have had some effect on Chinese politics and Chinese thought over the period.

6

Of course, one can pay no attention to this issue, continue to quote the classics, and insist that it was English gunboats in the nineteenth-century Opium Wars that blew open the "five holes" in the door of China (i.e. the treaty ports), allowing the Chinese to discover there was a whole world outside. Perhaps some feel that putting it this way is a loss of face, that before the English gunboats had found their way around the Cape of Good Hope, China already had people who were fixing their gaze on the outside world. The debates go on over whether the first was Lin Zexu or Wei Yuan. It is difficult, however, to ignore the direction in which logical enquiry would take us; it is difficult for classical texts to silence the voice of history. Whether one pays no attention to considerations of face or tries to save face, there is only one conclusion that can be reached. That is that right up until the mid-nineteenth century, the commodity economy within Chinese feudalism was developing slowly on its own momentum toward capitalism. When one comes down to it, this is only a kind of hypothesis or possibility. A possibility is not the same as reality, and the use of daring hypotheses and careful testing was condemned at an early period as a method that opposed Marxism-Leninism. The basic requirements of historical materialism are respect for the objective facts of history. If, however, we show respect for the facts of history yet still maintain that English gunboats caused China to break out of the medieval wilderness and enter the gateway to modern civilization, then we cannot avoid a disheartening conclusion. The Chinese did not have the ability to forge ahead toward modernization themselves, but they had to ''be modernized.''

7

If this notion of "being modernized" accords well with historical reality, then no matter how depressing it may be, historical research would have to accept it. The problem, however, lies in the fact that good intentions and a strong dislike of medievalism cannot take the place of historial facts, but may well hinder a dispassionate investigation into history. However, the blame cannot be placed entirely on emotive approaches to knowledge. According to a widely agreed self-reflection, the tendency for historical research to be fragmented may also be at fault. Thirty years ago, it was generally agreed that the beginning of the "early modern period," and thus the end of the Middle Ages, should be fixed at the outbreak of the Opium Wars in 1840. No doubt there were adequate reasons for placing the boundary at this point, yet it has become a more and more unbridgeable gap dividing those who research the Middle Ages and those who research the "early modern period" into two separate forts. The barriers caused by this division of labor have become increasingly impervious, and few scholars on either side step over the 1840 line. Yet the logic of research demands that it be overstepped by both groups, even if this takes place mainly on the level of reflection. To demonstrate the necessity of the advance toward modernization, as we look back we inevitably criticize the closed-mindedness, muddle-headedness, and backwardness of the past. The practice of research on the Middle Ages, however, has been to take the rise and fall of dynasties as the main process to be observed. Since the civil war and foreign humiliation of the Qing dynasty took place mainly during its last seventy years, does that mean its previous two hundred years were ones of unmitigated brightness? If not, how was it that people of the Qing praised the peace and prosperity of the Kangxi, Yongzheng, and Qianlong reigns? Was it in fact a matter of each side blowing its own horn? There was no thought that there might be some shadings here, but it seemed both sides proved that on the eve of the Opium Wars, China was in a state of unusual stability, one that could not be disturbed except by a power coming from outside. If a society believes itself to be in a state of prosperity but is actually in a state of advanced decay, is there any way it can start "reforming itself" from within?

8

As luck would have it, the poet and thinker Gong Zizhen, who died on the eve of the Opium Wars, almost as if purposely to prove a point, called on the Qing rulers to learn the lessons of history a quarter century before the Opium Wars: "Rather than allowing someone in the future to bring about reform, would it not be better to do it ourselves?"[5] But in asking the question, he immediately gave a negative answer, saying it was already too late, as the Qing dynasty had entered its decline and these were just the last few rays of a setting sun. If one thinks about it, he said, there is almost no natural phenomenon that is not like a time of prosperity, yet a whole society from top to bottom is complacent; scholars, farmers, craftsmen, and merchants are indifferent, and even the thieves in the back alleys and bandits in the badlands do not care. "In these kinds of times, if scholars and ordinary people of ability appeared, then a hundred times as many vulgar types would step foward to supervise them, control them, and even kill them." "In killing them, there would be no need so much as to touch their necks or their backs, they would only have to kill their spirit and destroy in them the sense of indignation, the spirit of reflection, the desire for achievement, the spirit of honor, and the determination to concentrate their energies." "A point has been reached where all of human sadness, indignation, desire to achieve, sense of shame, desire to maintain honor, all of these sensitivities and ideals have been entirely stamped out. People do not desire to be killed, they constantly cry out for good government, yet they can't wait for peace and prosperity. Sooner or later a spirit of rebellion arises and they begin to call night and day for disorder. If this is the present situation, then can't we say that we are on the verge of disorder?" The fact that Gong Zizhen made these comments, of course, has made historians of the early modern period happy. Even though he died before the Sino-British Treaty of Nanking, they insist on making him the first of the poets of this period. Those researching the Middle Ages, however, have not felt he was worth the slightest attention. His intense expression of indignation was intended to stimulate the "self-reformation" of the Qing, and Dai Zhen and others had said similar things before him. Much earlier, scholars of the period of Huang Zongxi and Gu Yanwu had made even more concrete and practical suggestions for social reform. Thus we are still left at a loss.

9

In research, we cannot disregard the geographical dimension, but neither can we limit ourselves to it. Otherwise, just as the example above illustrates, in seeking a historical understanding of the same people in the same place at the same time, clear contrasts will emerge and it will be extremely difficult to reach agreement. This situation is not uncommon in historiography. For example, in the dynastic studies of the Middle Ages, every time the special conditions associated with dynastic change occured, the description of the attending contradictions and the proofs given for interpretations not only leave one at a loss, but also make one feel that to be a historian is to live constantly with doubt. The problem is not so much with gaps in understanding as with the fact that when looking at the same period and observing the same problem, there is no agreed interpretation. It seems to be a matter of not becoming a slave of the division of labor and not ignoring or passing over historical facts that lie off the well-trodden paths. A connecting link between the temporal and the spatial dimension should become mutually correcting in a research agenda. If one can break through the spatial boundary and use historical facts gathered wherever one can, one may be able to shake certain historical verities. After many mistaken years, Qing history is now finally being studied as a whole system, which cannot be arbitrarily chopped into two unconnected sections. This is a most fortunate turn of events for the project of seeking an understanding of the transition from the Middle Ages to the early modern period in Chinese history.

10

There is one more area that should not be neglected in research on either the Middle Ages or the early modern period, an area that has long remained unfamiliar. That is research on China done in Europe since the sixteenth century. Right up to the present we have been limited to the content of a few foreign works translated into Chinese for an understanding of what this body of scholarship reveals of the changing view of European scholars toward China over several centuries. Apart from knowing that Leibniz and Voltaire praised China, while Montesquieu and Hegel criticized China, we are almost totally ignorant of this body of scholarship. It is astounding that in research on world history done over a period of thirty years in China, the topic of how Europeans after the Reformation looked at China of the time has been left out of the field of vision. Surely, if world history is being studied from a Chinese perspective, this topic should not be neglected. Marx once said, "In a sort of a way, it is with man as with commodities. Since he comes into the world neither with a looking glass in his hand, nor as a Fichtian philosopher, to whom 'I am I' is sufficient, man just sees and recognizes himself in other men. Peter may establish his own identity as a man by first comparing himself with Paul as being of like kind. And therefore Paul, just as he stands in his Pauline personality, becomes to Peter the type of the genus homo.''[6] How do we know whether or not China was coming out of the Middle Ages at that time? How can we judge whether China of the era before the mid-nineteenth century was a ''progressive'' or a ''backward'' nation in the world of the time? Is there any reason we should not take the Western world as a point of reference?

11

If we look at our historical researches of the past, however, we find that there are serious problems with the point of reference we have chosen. The problem lies with the fact that we have gone against the criteria of comparative history established by Marx, that is, that we cannot be limited to taking a historical fact and contrasting it to a concept, but we must take a historical fact and contrast it with another historical fact. Before the late eighteenth century, so-called advanced capitalism had not yet appeared in Western Europe, not to mention the United States before the War of Independence, or Japan before the Meiji era, which means that this was simply a ''concept.'' If we therefore take this concept, which becomes reality only in the nineteenth century, to contrast with realities in China between the sixteenth and eighteenth centuries and make the judgment that China was then ''backward'' and had already stagnated to the point that its people could no longer tolerate the situation, can this be regarded as a scientific criticism? ''Marx treats social movements as a process of natural history. If in the history of civilization the conscious element plays a part so subordinate, then it is self-evident that a critical enquiry whose subject is civilization can, less than anything else, have for its basis any form of, or any result from, consciousness. That is to say that not the idea, but the material phenomenon alone, can serve as its starting point.''[7] In our research, we should take note of this comment of a non-Marxist on Marx's methodology.

12

If we try taking the phenomenon of a modernizing Europe to cast light on China of the same period, we will be surprised to find that people were doing the same thing two or three hundred years ago. In the seventeenth and eighteenth centuries in the intellectual and political circles of mid-Western Europe, those who were eager to see reforms in both the spirit of the age and the political system, including enlightenment thinkers, rationalists, agricultural reformers, opponents of absolutism, and opponents of the dictatorship of the Holy See, all from different perspectives and at different levels, took an interest in China. This interest was precisely the opposite to the kind of interest taken in the subsequent century in "educating" China by the colonizers. Its main focus was on taking China's "goodness and light" as a contrast to Europe's "ugliness." In their writings and speech about this distant and mysterious China, its politics were wise, its emperor was benevolent, its system was well regulated, its education was so advanced that those selected to rule, as both minor and important officials, had gone through rigorous examinations and were almost all philosophers. They knew how both to assist the emperor in pacifying the people and to represent the people in supervising the emperor. Thus China had already reached conditions that Europe of the Middle Ages could not dream of achieving— its population was myriad, its products were abundant, its life was prosperous, moral standards were lofty, culture was advanced, and the people enjoyed a life of happiness and contentment. So the story went. It is enough to delight those who argue that China's cultural supremacy from ancient times onward is the crown of world civilization and to infuriate those who are increasingly strident critics of Confucianism. It can also stimulate serious historians to proceed from initial surprise to deeper reflection. Surely it can give us some direction into how to research the way in which China came out of the Middle Ages.

13

In the seventeenth and eighteenth centuries, when the discussion of China's so-called advanced society had become modish in political and intellectual circles, even the Prussian ruler Frederick II, called by history Frederick the Great, became interested. He used a false name to publish a small volume entitled *A Report of the Chinese Emperor's Special Envoy to Europe, Fei Xihu* (*Zhongguo Huangdi fu Ou teshi Fei Xihu de baogao*). It was 1776, in the Qianlong reign, precisely the dark years when the cultural and intellectual policies of the Middle Ages were in their final decline, yet Frederick could take them as an example of "enlightened despotism." In fact he thought it was necessary to use the views of a fictitious Chinese envoy to attack the policies of the Holy See. This provides clear evidence that although China was backward and dark, in intellectual and political circles it was not seen as any worse than the various countries of Central Europe of the time.

If one single example seems to be inadequate as evidence, especially an example taken from the Kingdom of Prussia, which was considered backward at the time, then why not take as another piece of evidence the French advocate of agricultural reform, Turgot, who was commended by Marx? It so happened that in 1776 he was attacked and forced to resign as head of the Treasury because he had published a draft for reform that emphasized agriculture. Before this he had published a work that was to become famous: *An Investigation into the Accumulation and Distribution of Wealth*. He had taken China of the time as a typical example of an economy in which agriculture was the mainstay of production—using the economic model of his teacher, the advocate of agricultural reform François Quesnay—and his views had been challenged. For this reason, before he entered the cabinet, that is, before 1774, when he heard that two Chinese students who had been brought to France by the Jesuits to study for the priesthood were planning to return to China, he immediately gave them a table for economic investigation in the style developed by Quesnay, asking them to help by doing a detailed investigation into China's social and economic situation. We do not know the result of this, but we do know that Louis the XVI, who had appointed Turgot as head of the Treasury, imitated a precedent set by the Chinese emperor of a ceremonial "ploughing of imperial fields," and he was joined by the Austrian emperor in this comedy. For the emperor to carry out such a ceremony to demonstrate the importance he placed on agriculture was a tradition of China's Middle Ages. What does it mean, then, that an imperial ruler who was later to be sent to the scaffold by a revolutionary party had initiated it?

14

If we compare the attitudes and behavior of the two European princes, on the one hand, and the dictatorial style of the Qianlong emperor and his father, the Yongzheng emperor, on the other, one descriptive phrase comes to mind: it is like a small witch meeting a much bigger one. All were princes, all concurred in seeing themselves as sovereign rulers of their nations, yet the cultural policies used to maintain rule succeeded in China and failed in Europe. Why was this?

15

There can be no doubt that European views of China over these two hundred years were colored by a thick idealism, and the intention was clearly to use this foreign reference point to criticize their own weaknesses. There can also be little doubt that the main evidence for these views came from the reports of Western missionaries in China, especially the Jesuit fathers. For example, in the early seventeenth century the Dominican monk Campanella, in his *City of the Sun*, took China as an ally in setting forth his ideal of a nation ruled by philosophers. In this he was clearly inspired by his colleagues who had just managed to gain entry to the China mainland. If we imagine, however, that these idealized pictures were influenced by the excessive praise of missionary accounts, we would be mistaken. Anyone who has read the notes and letters sent by Matteo Ricci, Ferdinandus Verbiest, and other missionaries back to Europe, will discover just the opposite to be the case. In describing all that they saw and experienced in China, there were many surface impressions, yet their main concern was to vent their grievances on such matters as the malpractices of the officials, the corrupt habits of the people, the stubbornness of tradition, the opposition of "heretics," and how all these factors inhibited their work of preaching "the gospel." There was some commendation, but it was simply used to put Christians and Christian sympathizers into the best light. One cannot say that their descriptions of Chinese society and politics were not accurate, but they were certainly not idealized. Why, then, did Campanella, Voltaire, Leibniz, Locke, Quesnay, Turgot, and others use these reports as evidence to reach a very different sort of conclusion? The answer is simple—they were fed up with thinkers of the time who remained in the shadow of the Middle Ages.

16

The European view of China deserves further discussion.[8] Here I only want to use it as a reference point to show how, in the Western modernization process, there was one period in which humanity (of course that means certain persons) greatly admired the "Middle Emperor" on the other side of the globe. Those who were most entranced, such as Voltaire, even became indignant when other people made reference to certain evils in China, though his only counterargument was that "this great nation already had a history of over four thousand years." His craze for China even led him to say "when we minority peoples were gradually finding our way out of the Apenine jungles, the Chinese emperor was already ruling his nation like one family." Does this not have the flavor of the view that "the moon is rounder in China"? It could certainly have been criticized by neo-Confucian masters as a kind of "counting the records yet forgetting one's own ancestors." Nevertheless, everyone understood at that time, including such an inveterate rationalist and opponent of this view as Montesquieu, that Voltaire was taking China as a point of reference and using it to criticize all kinds of things in Europe, especially the chronic weaknesses that were hindering political modernization. For this reason even the influential official of the French court who persecuted Voltaire, in piling up charges against him, did not make disloyalty to his ancestors one of them. If we compare this with the fate of Chinese scholars from Paul Xu Guangqi onward who studied and talked about Western knowledge, the contrast is striking.

17

If we hold fast to a reference point that gives adequate attention to the relativity of the space-time continuum, we can then discuss the transition China made from the Middle Ages to the recent period. I am calling this historic transition a coming out of the Middle Ages. The beginning of the process, in my view, can be taken back to the late sixteenth century at the very earliest, what we are accustomed to calling the late Ming period. The end of the process, at the very least in my view, must be taken up to the eve of the founding of the People's Republic in 1949, that is, including the period that has been defined as a "semicolonial, semifeudal society." That means this process has gone on for three and a half centuries. But it is no longer than the parallel process in Europe. If one starts from the Italian Renaissance and goes up to the French Revolution, the European experience of coming out of the Middle Ages was close to 400 years. If one takes the beginning of the Industrial Revolution in England as the demarcating line, that is, the 1760s, it would still be a process of over 350 years. Even in the most advanced industrial societies there remain stubborn pockets of feudal thinking, as evident in the legal cases in certain states of the United

States over whether evolution should be taught in schools. Therefore we should be even less surprised that even though our Republic has strongly opposed feudalism since its establishment, remnants of feudal thought are still in evidence. After all, it has only been forty years that we have been seeking to destroy its foundations. Yet even though America has antievolutionists, Mormon believers, Indian reservations, and the descendants of certain European immigrants who still work by candlelight and dig their own wells for water, we cannot therefore make the judgment that America has not yet come out of the Middle Ages. Equally, just as Japan continues to have Shinto shrines, the mystique of the emperor, a patriarchal social system, traditional military arts, customs that allow the dead to control the living, upstart millionaires who blindly imitate feudal aristocrats, an extremely short-sighted medieval utilitarianism, and feudalistic gangsters who are extremely stupid yet make destruction their main aim, we cannot say that the whole society remains in the same condition as before the Meiji Restoration. By the same token, we cannot say that we ourselves have not come out of the Middle Ages because we still have vestiges of medievalism. In our discussion, however, the late nineteenth and early twentieth centuries will be taken as the boundary, for no other reason than it is dictated by the area of my professional knowledge and the context for reflection it has provided.

18

With the exception of a very few groups of people who may remain at the stage of a preclassical ancient society, at present all of the world's major peoples have already experienced their own Middle Ages. I stress the fact that it is their own, since history has repeatedly shown that all races have gone through the change process in distinctive ways, even though up to the beginning of the present century it seems that feudalism of some kind has been a stage all have had to pass through. Up to the middle of the last century Japan had already been modeling itself on China for over one thousand years, yet in their attitudes and the structure of their culture, the Japanese people remain very different from the Chinese. A commonality that surpasses these differences is achieved by human beings only as a result of using the process of abstract reflection over and over as a kind of filter. Yet if one takes a model as a kind of prototype, it becomes difficult to get clear insight into the facts of history. "Theory is gray, my friends, while the tree of life is always green.'' As we investigate the path taken by our people out of the Middle Ages, I hope we won't forget this Marxian maxim.

19

"The Middle Ages had developed out of raw primitiveness. It had done away with the old civilization, old philosophy, politics and jurisprudence, in order to begin anew in every respect.''9 We don't know whether Engels had looked at the brief history of the Qin dynasty two thousand years earlier when he wrote these lines, yet these words certainly sound like a critical commentary on the behavior of Qinshi Huang after he had unified the previous six states. From the time he conquered the Han to his victory over Qi, the Qin emperor took only ten years, a brilliant achievement from the point of view of ancient military history. Yet the fact that he turned six states into mere geographical names of the past and, with the connivance of their generals, totally destroyed 100,000 prisoners of war in one night, did not mean that he could wipe out the historical memory of the human mind, or a cultural atmosphere of contending philosophical schools that had developed over several hundred years. Li Si, who was clever at manipulating the ruler's psychology and outwitting his opponents, suggested to the emperor a so-called technique of pacification—to destroy all books, control education, and other such measures, ''to ensure that there will be no dissenting thought under heaven.'' Although the Qin emperor was soon overthrown himself, this great principle of medieval culture which he initiated, that is, finding ways to close the mouths of the people and allow no divergent thinking to develop in their minds, was taken up and used by rulers throughout the Middle Ages. From the Han through to the Qing, the statute books of successive dynasties have been repeatedly revised, the net of justice over the years has become more closely woven, yet the mutually reinforcing practices of using words as a means of punishment and using psychological techniques for conviction of crime have never been neglected nor abandoned. If you don't believe this, take a look at the dense and complex *Legal Code of the Qing* (*Da Qing lü*) or the even more frighteningly trivial and petty "substatutes.''

20

There can be no doubt that this unique medieval art of pacification gradually became less coarse and vulgar from the middle of the second century B.C.

on, as evidenced by the fact that Confucian techniques replaced Legalist ones in cultural policy, and this led to a whole series of reversions and variations. For example, one of the changes was that books were no longer banned and reading was encouraged, except that the only books available to read were the sacred texts and biographies of worthy men approved by the emperor with annotations made by his officials. For example, there was a change from officials being teachers to Confucian scholars taking on this role, yet these Confucian scholars were subjected to government investigation or examination before they were considered to have the qualifications necessary to become an education official. As another example, there was a change from forbidding all questions to allowing frank criticism, except that those who made the criticism had to gain a special right to speak and had to guarantee that "their thoughts would not go beyond certain limits." In spite of this, it should be said on behalf of cultural and intellectual development during the Middle Ages that certain paths were opened up. Yet the cultural history of the Middle Ages demonstrates that these narrow, winding paths were overgrown with brambles and, as Confucian technique became ever more practiced, intellectual and cultural life moved ever more toward a dead end. So what appeared to be the opposite direction of these changes turned out to be just a different policy used to embody the cultural principle that "no dissenting thoughts be allowed under heaven," one more case of all roads leading to the same destination. Early in the development of these changes, when Confucian technique was in the process of being raised to the status of an instrument of pacification, Gong Sunhong and Dong Zhongshu, from their separate perspectives of practice and theory, made an important contribution to this process. This contribution, to take a phrase used by Sima Qian and Ban Gu that can sum it up, was to "use Confucianism to decorate the historical record of political manipulation." In their actions they followed the Legalist principles of the Qin, including the terrible law of killing the whole clan of anyone accused of slander and of displaying in the city gate the corpses of any two or more persons caught discussing the *Book of Odes* (*Shijing*) or *Book of History* (*Shujing*). Yet in their speech they invoked the ancient laws of heaven. For example, Dong Zhongshu used the *Spring and Autumn Annals* to decide on a case.

21

There is one school of opinion that suggests that the Legalists respected officials and oppressed the people while Confucians put value on the people and held little respect for officials. I do not know whether there were Legalists or Confucians before the Qin unification, as this would suggest. If one takes classicists such as Dong Zhongshu and neo-Confucians such as Zhu Xi both as Confucians, then even if Confucius or Mencius were to come back to life, they might not recognize them. By the same token, if one takes the oppressive drilling of Zhong Tong, on the one hand, and the rigor of Yang Xun, on the other, and says they are both Legalists, then if Han Fei knew about this down below he would probably refuse to recognize them. It is true that Mencius made statements about valuing the people and giving little importance to officials. If therefore he can be seen as a populist, if indeed this came from his heart, that would only be due to the fact that he, as a noble in a situation of feudal princedoms, needed the people's labor to bring in the grain and to serve as soldiers. There are even some doubts over who he means by "the people." "It is not difficult to rule, if you do not offend the noble families." If you do offend the important families then you cannot become an official. Was not this negation also the legacy of Mencius? Nevertheless, in the first few hundred years of the Middle Ages, both Mencius's person and his books were nearly forgotten by all classical scholars except for the fact that he was counted as one of the Confucian school and occasionally mentioned. Certainly, no one paid any attention at all to his views about valuing the people and putting little importance on officials. When the time eventually came that he was remembered again, the situation was entirely different, and any despotic ruler of a small kingdom enjoyed enormous dictatorial powers. The first person who announced himself as the successor of Mencius, Han Yu, in speaking of the relationship between fatuous rulers and upright officials, insisted that "the officials' crimes must be punished so that the ruler's holiness can be vindicated." Later neo-Confucians, even though they acccorded Mencius second place after Confucius, were satirized for "respecting the ruler and repressing his officials and taking loyalty to the ruler's person as the key principle of education." Even Mencius's spirit of "showing contempt when speaking of important persons" was gone, so how can one speak of "populist thought"?

22

People always commend the willingness of Emperor Taizong of the Tang dynasty to accept remonstrance and Wei Zheng's direct criticism as a model of relations between ruler and official in the Middle Ages.

The purpose of this commendation is of course to exhort those in positions of rule to allow people to speak out and those below to have the courage to speak out, or, in other words, to develop a populist approach. Did the Middle Ages have any real democracy? Of course they did. Marx pointed out that democracy is a historical category. Within any ruling class there is a relative democracy, and social progress is manifested in a continued increase in the scope of democratic rights. From the kind of democracy that existed in the ancient slave society up to the kind of democracy established by the oligarchy of the bourgoisie in setting up republics in the early modern period there are exemplars. To imagine that autocratic monarchies mean that the monarch or his lords individually could do as they pleased would be a misunderstanding of common historical experience. Qinshi Huang, the founding emperor of the Qin, can certainly be called an autocrat, but were not his important policy decisions, such as to abolish enfeoffment, to establish the system of prefectures and counties, to put in place a legal administration, to reform the whole system, to melt down all weapons, and to banish books, all subject to imperial counsel, and did he not seek the opinion of high officials and advisers? It was only the final decision that the ruler himself took, and in taking that decision he did not need to follow majority views. For this reason he is regarded as an autocrat.

This kind of autocracy is a kind of consolidation of the will of the ruling group, although its basis is narrow and there are no fixed standards to bring restraint. It easily becomes a situation in which the ruler's view dominates, or he simply does as he pleases. If the ruler really lets go and behaves unscrupulously, however, this will bring disaster to those under his rule and cause harm to the ruling establishment, including the ruler's own family, since the resulting contradictions are likely to lead to the destruction of public order and the collapse of the dynasty. So it is essential for the ruling establishment to adopt some internal democratic norms, or perhaps one could say to regularize autocratic rule. From the Western Han period onward, different interest groups within the ruling establishment were continually in conflict and, in the process of struggle and compromise, certain standards emerged that had a restraining effect, including the selection process of officials, the assessment of the level of officials, the practice of supervision, the system of impeachment, petitions relating to policy decisions, the right to send back imperial orders, inspection, and ratification, and also including a system that used science and superstition in combination to determine the calendar and depended on astrological phenomena to reveal "Heaven's Will" to rulers and powerful officials. These standards were acceptable to both rulers and officials, so they can be called "government." The opposite is called "disorder."

Nevertheless, in the situation of the Middle Ages, when all important decisions were made by legitimate rulers or usurpers "who controlled the emperor and gave orders to those below him," the source of disorder always came from the small group at the peak of the ruling apparatus that was under least restraint. For this reason there was a council of officials who had the right to remonstrate with the ruler and could provide loyal criticism, only to regulate his morals and behavior to some degree and thereby prevent contradictions that would lead to an outbreak of disorder. Wei Zheng was one of these censors who had the special privilege of being called upon to speak out. He was unwilling to hold such a position and not use it, so he was courageous enough to rebuke Emperor Taizong to his face, a very rare occurrence in the Middle Ages. But this so-called act of direct remonstrance was actually protected by certain democratic norms within the ruling establishment. He was also protected by his special relationship with the emperor's family. As for Emperor Taizong, the fact that he allowed Wei Zheng to speak out and even put up with Wei Zheng teasing him about giving this direct criticism was rather unusual in the Middle Ages.[10] But was his supposed humility and willingness to accept this rebuke sincere? If so, why did he swear that he was going to "kill this country bumpkin" in a private moment of anger over Wei Zheng saying too much? Why did he later punish the dead by having Wei Zheng's tomb, with an inscription on it he himself had written, knocked over for some minor thing? Emperor Taizong was upheld as the "Heavenly Khan" by all the kingdoms in his periphery, and his period is certainly the one in which policy toward the "surrounding barbarians" was most enlightened throughout the whole of the Middle Ages. Yet the democratic relationship between this great ruler and his loyal official reached no higher level than this. Does not this ruler, who was surprisingly ahead of his times and truly had the character and morals of a populist, give us much food for thought?

23

Autocratic rule as a structure of government is like the head attached to the body of medieval social relations. From the Qin dynasty right up to the mid-Qing, it was overthrown many times in peasant rebellions, and many times attempts were made by "invading barbarians" to replace it. As a result, there were periodic times of anarchy that frequently led to the reinstatement of past feudal structures and caused the scholar officials of the unfortunate state to groan in amazement as they observed the place where the head had been lost. Maybe one could best compare this with the head of the cow demon king in the *Journey to the West* (*Xi you ji*)—where it was cut off, it simply grew back on the neck again!

In the history of the Middle Ages, there is no lack of examples of the peasants, who had suffered at the hand of feudal rulers, organizing rebellion and gaining political power. There are also plenty of examples of minority peoples who have preserved their own democratic tradition and who, on coming to power, keep their own system. But there is one type of example we cannot find. That is a situation where the rebels have not taken over the system of the oppressor and where the victors have not taken on the governing system of the vanquished. When the beggar monk Zhu Yuanzheng made a successful rebellion, he simply put in place a system of rule that outdid that of the Song and Yuan dynasties. When Hong Xiuquan, a primary school teacher from a tiny village, led the peasants and craftspeople in rebellion against the Qing dynasty, he completely forgot his own belief that "all people are equal before God" by the time he took over half the country, and in the stone city (Nanjing) he used a new name to restore an old system. As for victors preserving the political culture of their own race, most in the end see the system they themselves conquered as the best model. An example for this is the Qing dynasty. We can see that unless the social relations of the Middle Ages had already started to undergo a qualitative change, that is, the old body was already sick or dying, the autocratic system would either be given a facelift or be reformed in some partial way. There was no question of getting rid of the old and starting afresh.

24

For this very reason, the model of autocratic rule that I have been discussing was simply the concentrated expression of the general norms of social relations in the Middle Ages. I agree with the analysis made by Professor Hou Wailu in the early 1960s that China's feudal society, as it had developed by the mid-eighth century on the eve of the An Lushan rebellion, that is, at the so-called height of prosperity of the Tang dynasty, had already reached the highest point of its advance. On this point I can add some evidence from the perspective of cultural history, that is, the process of codification of the Chinese feudal system, which reached a turning point precisely in the early eighth century. The codification of the feudal system meant in practice a regularization through legal formality of the autocratic system of the Middle Ages. This was an extremely lengthy process, but it basically took its final shape in the period between the early Tang and the height of Tang prosperity. And what were the signs of this setting of the pattern? There were three books of "statutes successively formulated: In *The Tang Code* (*Tanglü shuyi*) were codes of criminal law and civil law, as well as official annotations that had legal force. In *The Tang Institutes* (*Da Tang liudian*) were codes regulating the organization of government and all sorts of systemic regulations. The *Rituals of the Kaiyuan Era* (*Da Tang Kaiyuan li*) took the form of the "five ceremonies" and contained cultural codes of an intensely religious character. These three books of statutes more or less cover all aspects of the social norms of the ruling classes under an autocratic system.

Therefore, it is no surprise to find that as long as there were no major changes in social relations, these basic principles and most of the related concrete regulations were taken over by generation after generation of rulers in the Middle Ages. It is equally surprising that right up to the Ming and Qing dynasties criminal law, civil law, laws relating to governmental organization, and the cultural legislation relating to religion all followed the patterns set by these three books of statutes, with minor changes in the detailed regulations. What is astonishing, however, is that the decline of China's Middle Ages stretched out over such a long period, in fact more than a thousand years. Of course the conservative character of the statutes meant the aspect of social relations that had congealed continued in existence in the standard form of laws long after a thawing process had begun to take effect. For this reason it is impossible to judge exactly when this long decline of the Middle Ages came to a final end. If the effectiveness of these books as a restraining power began to lose force in the sixteenth century, that would mean these principles and regulations had already been in effect for eight hundred years. How is one to describe a period of eight hundred years in which there was no change under heaven except with the term "the long stagnation"?

25

Nevertheless, we should qualify somewhat this professional estimation of China's Middle Ages. This so-called long stagnation in my view can only be used to describe the political system of the last half of the Middle Ages. It is not entirely suitable to depict the structure of social relations. In fact, from the mid-Tang onwards, the central concentration of power that characterized the autocratic system began to weaken, and the increasing localization of power that resulted from military governors setting up their own regimes may not have been as deleterious as has been suggested by most historians. From the Qin dynasty onward, China always emphasized unity and there were many benefits to unity. The greatest of these were the reduction in internal wars, the ease of interaction among regions and racial groups, and a relative social stability, all of which facilitated people's productivity and livelihood. Yet the other side of unity under autocratic rule was a control that stultified. Whether one considers economic development or cultural evolution, differences between different regions were an objective reality. This kind of spatial diversity was not merely the result of differences in environmental conditions but reflected time gaps in the level of social development.

What was the result of using the methods of political manipulation from above for the promotion of unity? Not only did the spatial and temporal gaps in economic and cultural development fail to disappear, they also hindered overall social development. Take, for example, the middle and lower reaches of the Yangzi River, especially the Jiangnan region in the lower reaches. From the Eastern Jin and the Southern dynasties (A.D. 470–589) on, this was the economic center of the whole nation, and in the Tang and Song dynasties it became even more the cultural center of the country. Nevertheless, from the time of the reunification of the Sui dynasty (A.D. 581–618), with the exception of the brief years of conflict between the Song and Jin dynasties and the early Ming, the political center moved more and more toward the north, resulting in a lopsided unification with a backward north ruling over a progressive south. There is no need to elaborate further. One only has to note the five hundred years in which Beijing was the capital of the Ming and Qing dynasties and the imperial governments of both dynasties depended for their revenues, including the grain tax, the handicraft tax, and commercial taxes, largely on the Jiangnan region. At the time of the Ming-Qing transition (the seventeenth century), over 60 percent of the land tax, which was paid in grain, came from the two prefectures of Suzhou and Songjiang. The Jiangnan region, whose main constituents were southern Jiangsu, northeastern Zhejiang, and southern Anhui, had a land area that was less than one-hundredth of the total land area under the Qing dynasty's control at the height of its power, and the prefectures of Suzhou and Songjiang were even smaller, yet they had to provide the economic support for the whole imperial government. On the one hand, this shows how advanced was the social development of the Jiangnan region, especially the southern part of the triangle of the Yangzi's lower reaches; on the other hand, it shows how the overcentralization of autocratic power led to the squeezing of economically prosperous regions to support the extravagances of the imperial house and the aristocracy, as well as the huge outlays needed by the imperial bureaucracy and the army.

This kind of contradiction, which caused the even greater strengthening of local forces in the Middle Ages and increased the centrifugal forces from the autocratic governmental system, was not necessarily a bad thing. It was to destroy the balance imposed through noneconomic factors and cause the social structure to switch from a passive to an active mode. It also forced the imperial government to strengthen its own centripetal force. Thus, to affirm the "long stagnation" of the political structure in the latter half of the Middle Ages is not to deny that there were changes in the social structure. If one suggests that the main reason for this long stagnation was that feudal society had an exceptionally stable structure, it would be most difficult to support this view against the historical evidence.

26

A problem closely linked to the issue of autocracy is the question of whether there were any independent individuals in the Middle Ages. Can this indeed be considered a problem? Certainly in Europe of the Middle Ages one cannot find any independent individuals; one sees either feudal serfs or their lords, vassals or suzerains, lay people or clergy, all of the former in relationships of personal bondage. Just as Marx said, "personal dependency here characterizes the social relations of production just as much as it does the other spheres of life organized on the basis of that production."[11] Yet in China of the Middle Ages, especially the latter part, the situation was not quite the same. With the exception of minority peoples, the system of serfdom had moved toward extinction very early, and the hereditary aristocracy of feudal states had also ceased to enjoy the kinds of absolute rule of the ancient feudal lords. The so-called extra-economic system of coercion reflected more and more the dual shackles of administration and blood ties. The system of rule by scholar-officials, however, which became increasingly ensconced in the late Middle Ages, meant that governmental leadership at each level was undertaken by officials directly appointed by the emperor. These local officials were limited both by the time span of their office and by the fact that they could not hold office in their own native place. In addition, they were subject to interference from the local gentry, so that their actual authority was far less than that of the most minor of princes in the ancient period. The elders of patriarchal clans or large families did enjoy privileges appropriate to their position within the clan, yet the relative level of this privilege was not entirely a matter of clan position, age, or experience. Their material prosperity and personal reputation were of even greater importance. As for religion, with the exception of minority groups and believers in foreign religions, most Chinese of the Middle Ages had no fixed set of religious beliefs, or perhaps one should say they had no one clear belief system. Even though Zhu Xi so energetically established himself as "a transmitter of Confucian orthodoxy" (*daotong chuanren*), privately he had a superstitious attachment to the ideas of the Buddhist monks and the Daoist teachers. This shows he was not sincere in his supposed devotion to Confucian teaching. For this reason, if one takes the relations of personal bondage characteristic of medieval Europe as a model to interpret Chinese medieval social relations, one will find it incompatible with Chinese reality.

27

If China's Middle Ages are to be compared, then, with the darkness of the European Middle Ages, the relations of personal bondage in the Chinese case were not nearly so congealed nor nearly so obvious. Of course, the reasons for this are complex. Since land could be bought and sold in China from an early period, family property could be equally divided, scholarly honor could be won by personal effort, family status could rise and fall, privileges could be attained or lost through official manipulation, and social status could be decided through the favor of the monarch. Therefore in the human relations of medieval China there was a certain kind of equality; at least everyone had an opportunity to pursue power and wealth. If this seems strange, one must remember it was only a surface phenomenon and a very superficial one at that. If one probes beyond this surface appearance to a deeper level, one soon realizes things were not as they appeared.

According to medieval custom, the "people" were divided into four categories: scholar gentry, farmers, artisans, and merchants. Of these four classes, only the leading class, the gentry, were able to attain social mobility through the imperial examination system. The term gentry (*shi*), according to an official definition from the Han dynasty, meant those who were thoroughly familiar with the past and the present, able to discriminate what could and could not be done, and able to take responsibility for affairs. If we use a modern term, this would mean intellectuals, who are versed in history, able to distinguish truth from falsehood, and competent in getting things done. This type of person originally made up a small percentage of the four classes of people. To gain the qualification of a scholar gentleman in the Middle Ages, one had to go through unified examinations organized by the government. These examinations were divided into several levels— at the lowest level one had to pass the prefectural examination organized by the educational official of the province to qualify as a *shengyuan*, popularly known as *xiucai*, and get oneself on the rolls as one of the literati. The farther up one went on the examination ladder, the more difficult were the examinations and the greater the competition. At the highest level, the *jinshi*, where the examination was held only every three years, about one hundred or two hundred people were lucky enough to succeed each time. What percentage did they constitute of all the literati, or even of the examination candidates? How many in a thousand or indeed in ten thousand? I don't know. What I do know is that those lucky enough to get this opportunity and become so-called culture heroes made up a tiny proportion of the four classes of people. If one takes this very small proportion and makes a conclusion about overall human relations to the effect that relations of personal bondage in Chinese society were weak or nonexistent, the least to be said is that one has not taken into account the relative quantitative-qualitative dimensions of the situation.

28

In the late Qing and early Republic, Zhang Taiyan made a slip in his estimation of this issue. All the problems that have arisen since with the intellectuals have constituted a sort of counter evidence to his view, as the question of proportion that I have raised has been disregarded. It is true this proportion was very tiny, yet it did exist. Since it existed, and indeed persisted for such a long time in the latter part of the Middle Ages, doubtless there must be some explanation. Don't we like to talk about the headrope of the fishing net and how when it is pulled up all the meshes are opened? The headrope is really the rope that controls the meshes. In the *Book of History* (*Shang shu*) one finds the expression, "If the net is pulled up by the headrope, everything will be in order." So one can see how ancient this metaphor is. "What is close at hand becomes the stuff of parables." If an ancient metaphor still seems fresh in the present, this certainly indicates there is both an ancient and a contemporary explanation.

Although the relative size of the headrope to the net is very small, it can still regulate the whole net; although all the net's meshing constitutes a large proportion of it, if one opens or closes any one mesh, it will not have any effect on the net as a whole. Such was the ruling system of the Middle Ages; if it was not the dictatorship of one leader, it was an oligarchy. If one looks at numbers, the relative size of the oligarchy to the population was tiny, yet because they had the power to control the whole feudal net, they could affect the way in which it was imposed upon society. How, then, can one consider only the issue of numbers and ignore the fact of the existence of this group? Those who were able to pass through the ever narrowing gates of the official examination system and make an assault on the doorway to power and wealth are the precise evidence of the ruler's dictatorial grip over the net itself.

When Emperor Taizong of the Tang saw the first group of new *jinshi* who came into his court to offer thanksgiving, in a moment of self-forgetfulness he divulged this secret: "All the heroes under heaven have come into my trap!" There were only thirty persons in that group of *jinshi*, yet Tang Taizong could see how he could use this tiny number to control the policies of all intellectuals in the country and gain success thereby. Nevertheless, the cleverness of Tang Taizong and his successors had its limits. He never thought about the fact that when he linked the ancient principle of "those achieving excellence in study becoming officials" with an examination system that had the appearance of equal opportunity, he had instituted a factor that would undermine the status quo he had struggled to preserve.

29

Can this be denied? In the early part of the Middle Ages, in the process of a centralization of power, the ruling autocracy continuously attacked the hereditary aristocracy and local despots. (They also drew support from the leaders of related clans and families.) Yet in a situation where the legitimation of the ruler depended on hereditary talent being recognized, the political privileges of the aristocracy could not be eliminated. The system of nine grades of rank instituted in the Wei and Jin dynasties set the pattern for the leading clans and families and preserved the hereditary privileges for the sons of families of power and influence to become officials. This point has already been demonstrated by historical research. Following the unification of the Tang, the southern scholar families lost most of their hereditary rights to act as advisers to the government, but the privileges of the great northern families continued as before. Although Tang Taizong used the incident of the *Genealogy of the Clans* (*Shizu zhi*) to frustrate and restrain the old aristocratic families, the direct purpose of this was nothing more than to force them to admit that the new aristocracy of the royal house was on an even higher level, that is, to force them to recognize that there should be a direct ratio between power and the quality of one's hereditary position.

But there was an unforeseen element in this situation. He restored the civil service examinations with the simple intention of trapping the more competent scholars from less prominent families. This he indeed succeeded in doing, yet the long-term effects were opposite to his intention. In the early Tang, the examinations for selecting officials were divided into six sections, and two of these were the most important: the *mingjing* (understanding the classics) and the *jinshi* (a broader examination testing ability to write prose and poetry as well as classical knowledge). Since the important northern clans of Qin, Lu, Cheng, and Zhu were all called *mingjing* clans, that is, they used their cultural level to demonstrate their aristocratic quality, naturally this *mingjing* section preserved the special powers of the sons of their families and assured them a place in government. Is not this the very meaning of the notion of privilege as "special powers" (*tequan*)? If one allowed other coveters of power to enter into an open competition, then the notion of privilege could only revert to its original connotation, which was the right to make sacrificial offerings to the gods. The sons of the old clans who enjoyed high position and comfort and could barely tell the difference between pulse and wheat if they saw them growing of course could not be expected to compete openly on the basis of talent with commoners.

The result was that in only one generation the *jinshi* section took precedence over the *mingjing* section: So "thirty was old to become a *mingjing* while fifty was young to become a *jinshi*," as the saying went. Scholars of humble origin had thus gained an absolute preponderance in the competition. Once one had become a *jinshi*, the right to official position was established. Even the most ancient and distinguished of the old clans had no way of resisting the beguilements of the prospects open to the *jinshi*. In the period of Tang Xuanzong, the celebratory feasts for the new *jinshi* became the favorite setting for the old aristocracy to select sons-in-law, which is just one more evidence of the situation. Cultural level would no longer be dependent on hereditary factors but would be attained through individual accomplishment. If one could demonstrate, through a legally established process, that one had the ability to serve in government, once taken into the system one could become the candidate for the head of a ministry, province, or prefecture. This in itself contributed to a kind of repudiation of privileges gained entirely on a hereditary basis.

30

There can be no doubt, however, that the autocratic system not only failed to get rid of the hereditary aristocracy, but in fact constantly manufactured new aristocratic groups. This is evident in that, in every dynasty and generation, the families of meritorious officials gained a hereditary position. At the same time, there is also no doubt that in the latter half of the Middle Ages, with the exception of the ruler's person, there was a continuing trend toward a loosening of the linkages between heredity and power. In the Northern and Southern Song and the Ming, it is well known that if even the relatives of the emperor wanted to intervene in government yet did not have positions as scholar-officials, this would be regarded as illegal. In the Liao, Jin, Yuan, and Qing dynasties, due to the ruling traditions of the minority groups, it was inevitable in the early period that there was some restoration of aristocratic government, yet subsequently in each case the scholar-officials were restored to power. The Khitan, Jurched, Mongol, and Manchu peoples all made exhaustive efforts to avoid a decline in power and set up racial barriers on all sides. The imperial aristocracy of the

Qing were especially thorough in this regard, with such policies as the establishment of garrison duty by the Eight Banners, the system of dual official appointments (one Manchu and one Han), the practice of holding high policy councils in the shaman temple where only Manchus could worship, the practice of using Manchu terms for all noble titles, forcing the Han to adopt the clothing and hairstyle of the Manchus, the forbidding of intermarriage between Manchu and Han, forbidding the bannermen to give up military life and compete in scholarly examinations, and not allowing the Han any reflection on history. These things were like a hedge between the races, and a way of forcing the Han to assimilate to the Manchus.

Of course, this policy had some effects. The endless disturbances around the time of the 1911 Revolution over the pigtail, and the fact that even the head of the Confucian clan (the *Yanshenggang*) used the famous menu called "the Manchurian Han banquet" specially created by the court, were evidence of the success attained in converting the Han to Manchu customs. An even stronger evidence was that the atmosphere of scholarly life as well as popular thought experienced a repression more severe than at any earlier period of society. The kind of literary inquisition that enveloped the whole eighteenth century was so intense that in the subsequent period even the teahouses of county towns had signs posted up warning people "don't discuss national affairs."

But did the Qing aristocracy achieve its purpose? Unfortunately, the contingents of cavalry from the Eight Banners who were posted in all the important positions around the country were soon following the old and unsuccessful ways of the Xianbei aristocracy and the system for military settlement (*fubing*) they had created. They became corrupt and scattered to such a degree that they could not fight, and the imperial government was forced to rely on the Army of the Green Standard and local Han militia groups in putting down peasant rebellions. Warriors or officials who had come from rich Manchu families, even though they set themselves above Han officials of the same station, for the most part could only display their talent in committing all kinds of outrages and in arranging to hold office without doing any work. They mostly became the stooges of scholar-officials who had come up through the civil service examinations or of the secretaries under them who had rich local experience. In the final analysis, every arrangement for preserving aristocratic government was frustrated by the subjective tendencies of the aristocrats themselves.

31

The Qing Empire was the last power structure to preserve the forms of rule of the Middle Ages. Does the end justify the means, or is one's purpose unable to legitimate the methods adopted? Fifteen years ago the noted Japanese social activist Ikeda Daisaku and the British historian Toynbee in their famous exchange over "prospects for the twenty-first century," put forward these two opposite propositions. Neither, in my view, is suited to explaining the history of the Qing dynasty. Personally I lean toward Toynbee's view that "if the point of departure is wrong, one certainly will not arrive at a correct outcome." Toynbee thought, however, that in the final analysis the point of departure and the outcome would be in accord, that is, if one has a certain kind of intention, one will have a corresponding kind of outcome, or, as the saying goes, "if one plants rose seeds, one gets flowers, and if one plants bramble seeds, one gets thorns." This does not seem to me to be the case. In fact, one can find examples of just the opposite in Qing history, and these are by no means exceptional situations.

The rulers of the early Qing, including the comparatively progressive Dorgon, Shunzhi, and Kangxi, also the rather conservative Oboi group and Yongzheng, all felt that it was necessary to rely on military power to ensure that the whole Manchu race continued to live off their spoils, and that this would strengthen the basis of existence for the imperial aristocracy. Who was to know that the long-term results of this were to be just the opposite of these short-term utilitarian intentions? Did their policy that the bannermen on garrison duty could not go outside of their military quarters to earn a livelihood result in their children carrying on the style handed down to them of courage and setting great store by martial qualities? Were they prepared to place their lives in danger and to make sacrifices for the sake of these spoils? On the contrary, the result was that the whole Manchu race became parasitic, the upper classes relying on exploitation for their livelihood and the lower classes surviving on the small share the plunder left over for them. Corruption and laziness and a kind of Ah Q–like[12] ineffectiveness was endemic, characterizing the whole minority race from the leaders of the bannermen down to the slaves in a situation that coincides exactly with a point made by Marx to the effect that the race that oppresses another race is the least free. In this case, the means made the end legitimate and normal, but the means also caused the end to diverge in perverse directions. This is a contradiction, yet it is also a fact.

32

I have already made reference to Yongzheng above. This third ruler of the Qing dynasty had only thirteen years as emperor (1722–1735). Yet if one compares him with either his father or his son, both of whom held power for a cycle of sixty years or more, his thinking and behavior deserve special attention. The stories about him are so numerous that it is difficult for historians to take all details into account in their analyses, and popular novelists have been only too ready to make up weird and bloodthirsty tales about him to satisfy the curiosity of readers. Yet in the midst of all these dubious tales, there is one story that cannot be doubted, that is, that this dark horse seized the position of heir from among all the sons of the imperial household. Kangxi died very suddenly, and just as suddenly Yongzheng took over the imperial position on the basis of an edict of succession, causing astonishment throughout the country at all levels. Rumors abounded—that he had killed his father, that he had changed the will, or that he had committed many other immoral acts. In spite of all this he became emperor, and without hesitation he used his power to strengthen his own autocratic position.

The means he used were ruthless enough. If anyone—no matter whether brother, cousin, relative by marriage, high official, contender for imperial power, military supporter, official in office, or gentry in a remote area— posed an obstacle to him, he immediately took steps to eliminate that person. In killing them he did not ask whether there was any evidence of their guilt but only set out to destroy root and branch. The scope of his clean-up campaigns mainly embraced the imperial clans of the Eight Banners and the major and minor aristocracy. This took the attack on the aristocracy even further and led to expansion of the scholar-official ruling system. Also, it got rid of some long-standing abuses of the later Kangxi period. But can one for this reason deny that his point of departure was a despicable lust for power? Can one therefore defend this route to dictatorship? "Evil" intentions may have "good" outcomes, but one cannot step onto the swampy ground of defending the despicable psychology of despotism just because of an objective historical assessment of the results.

33

Vico, the Italian historian who lived in the same period as Yongzheng, stumbled into this very swamp. Precisely in the third year of

Yongzheng's reign (1725), when Yongzheng was seeking to strengthen his autocratic position and turning his attack on both his political enemies and his loyal officials, on the other side of the globe Vico published the first edition of his *New Science*. In it he made a full affirmation of the autocratic system of rule. Vico believed that history had witnessed three types of political rule—theocracy, the dictatorship of heroes and aristocrats, and humane government. An autocratic system of government and a free commonwealth were both forms of humane government in his view. What was his rationale? Vico argued that the foundation of a humane system of government was the principle that all people were equal before the law, since all people were freeborn in the cities. "The autocratic system of rule makes it possible for the people and their officials all to be equal before the law and concentrates all military strength in the autocrat's hands, allowing autocrats to give priority to governing the people." Vico came to the conclusion that "Autocracy is the form of government best adapted to human nature when reason is fully developed."[13] Vico's logic had its historical sense, since in Europe autocracy was a kind of transitional form that led many countries out of the darkness of the Middle Ages, and there was a certain necessity about it. Yet surely this objective function of autocracy cannot be taken as evidence of its reasonableness and its suitability to human nature. If this were really the case, then in the Chinese Middle Ages those rulers who broke historical records for their autocratic behavior, from Qinshi Huang to Yongzheng, could all be called humanists. Unfortunately, although Vico did some research on Chinese history through the writings of the Jesuits, he gave no credence to their descriptions and dismissed China under the Qing dynasty as "a dark little chamber," summing up Confucian philosophy as "a vulgar morality." Otherwise, if he had floated over the ocean to China and presented to Yongzheng this hymn of praise to the humaneness of autocratic rule, he might have been able to gain the emperor's favor and escape being so impoverished all his life.

34

Thirty years after Vico's *New Science* was published, the citizen of Geneva, Rousseau, wrote his famous *Discourse on the Origins and Foundations of Inequality Among Men*. Had he read Vico's book or not? I am not clear on this. But he clearly opposed Hobbes's arguments in support of despotic rulers in *Leviathan*, and he had certainly read the Jesuit accounts of China. While he did not believe them as earnestly as did Voltaire, neither was he as skeptical as Vico, but rather he took the position of suspending judgment. In this book he only made reference to China in a footnote: "China seems to have been well observed by the Jesuits."[14] Nevertheless, in his vigorous attack in the book on the system of autocracy, not only was he opposing Hobbes and Vico, but he seemed to be directly commenting on China of the time. Let me quote from a section that Engels also once quoted. Like Vico, Rousseau believed that all people are equal before a despotic ruler, yet his logic was precisely the opposite to Vico's. "This is the last stage of inequality and the extreme term which closes the circle and meets the point from which we started. It is here that all individuals become equal again because they are nothing, here where subjects have no longer any law but the will of the master, and the master any other rule but that of his passions."[15] Whose logic best reflects the real picture of the medieval system of autocracy? Vico's and Hobbes's, on the one hand, or that of Rousseau, on the other? The revolutionary activists of the late Qing gave an answer to this through their practice. When all kinds of Western ideas flooded into China, they all spontaneously gave their allegiance to Rousseau, and all became fervent disciples of "natural rights." Doesn't this fact clarify the issue?

35

Did these young advocates of natural rights in the late Qing all understand this concept? By no means. Among them were not a few who had only come to know of Rousseau through Western books translated from Japan. In their view, since the system of autocracy was the chief culprit in human inequality, it was only necessary to move this large stone out of the way and "natural rights" could be revived and the evolution of the nation realized. This was the view behind the reasoning that "once the Qing emperor is overthrown, everything will go well," which was prevalent at the time. This vain hope inspired the struggle to overthrow the autocracy. When the 1911 Revolution made the Qing emperor a prisoner in the Forbidden City, however, grim reality destroyed these poetic dreams. Where were natural rights then? Where was the democratic republic? "Unmeasured amounts of money and blood had been exchanged for a false republic."[16] But could Rousseau be blamed for this? "Despotism . . . would finally succeed in trampling on both the laws and the people and establishing itself on the ruins of the republic. The times leading up to these final changes would be times of troubles and calamities.''[17] Are not these Rousseau's very words, and do they not provide a vivid image of the future fate of the ''Republic of China''? The Chinese are accustomed to equate monarchy with dictatorship, since up to the present century the only form of autocracy they had experienced was the medieval form. But the history of the republic provided a counter example, which proves that the medieval type of autocracy is not necessarily causally linked to the name of emperor or monarch. In fact, Qinshi Huang first established his dictatorial rule, then adopted an imperial name. Therefore, it is not a problem of whether or not there is a monarchical name, but whether or not medieval society has undergone a fundamental transformation. In this respect, not only Rousseau, but even the defenders of autocracy—Vico, Hobbes, and others—all left behind meaningful insights. For example, Vico used the account in Tacitus's *History* of how autocratic governments in Rome were established one after another to reach the conclusion that citizens in free political entities all seek personal advantage, treating government as something foreign to them and remaining ignorant and indifferent. ''Thus in that citizens have become aliens in their own nations, it becomes necessary for the monarch to sustain and represent the latter in their own persons.''[18] There is no need to point to Marx's commendation of Vico's analysis; one only has to look at the history of the late Qing and early Republic to see that this analysis seems to be a prophecy for China.

''Citizens become aliens in their native land.'' This phenomenon described by Vico was realized in an explicit way in China under the Manchu rule. It so disturbed the young Lu Xun that he gave up his studies of medicine and turned to literature, as everyone knows. But where did this phenomenon begin, and how did it develop? If we seek the answer to this purely on the conceptual level, it is hard to avoid coming up against Confucius himself. The teaching he passed down to the effect that ''if one is not in high official position, one has no right to reflect on the responsibilities involved'' gave enormous psychological comfort to scholars who were seeking personal security yet felt a sense of guilt about this. Historical evidence abounds on this point. Yet not all scholars believed in this Confucian precept. The ''proscribed party'' (*Danggu*) of Eastern Han scholars, those who participated in the imperial student movement (*taixuesheng yundong*) in the two Song dynasties, members of the Donglin Society in the late Ming, and those who were part of the resistance movement in the early Qing are all counterexamples.

What about the other three classes, the peasants, craftspeople, and merchants? Peasants and craftspeople had few opportunities to express their political views and were part of the so-called silent majority, yet if one looks at the occasional times when historians recorded how these groups were forced to take arms against dictatorial rule, from the late Qin right up to the late Qing, you can easily see that they were by no means indifferent to national affairs. As for the merchant class, even though they were constantly derided for looking to profits and forgetting principles, from the time that Qinshi Huang wanted to make connections with the rich widow of a merchant up to the Ming dynasty, when merchants regularly used their economic strength to indicate support or opposition to the government, it is evident that they did not behave as if they were aliens in their relations to government. Nevertheless, just when China was about to come out of the Middle Ages, that is, the seventeenth and eighteenth centuries, the atmosphere of scholarly and popular life seemed to change, in a direction that suggested a lessening of concern for government.

The upper echelons of the scholars were clearly divided into two groups. One group promoted Song neo-Confucianism (*lixue*) and seemed to give positive support to the Qing government—people such as Li Guangdi and Xiong Cili—though this was a false Confucianism that curried favor with the rich and powerful, as the emperor himself often pointed out in the scorn he heaped upon it. Another group promoted Han learning, which concentrated on textual criticism—such scholars as Hui Dong, Dai Zhen, and Qian Daxin. Yet, as Zhang Taiyan pointed out, this was also a passive response to the Qing policy of keeping the people stultified. "If your family is wise, you will expend your intelligence on explaining the classics and in this way avoid death." There were scholars, such as the Tongcheng group and the Yanghu group, who boasted that they were doing pure scholarship and did not limit themselves to the Han and Song schools. In fact, however, in their studies of content and style in writing, if they were not pandering to Song neo-Confucianism, then they were imitating the "Three Sus,"[19] and their political leanings were mainly toward the currents of the false Confucianism.

Merchants apparently really were seeking profit and forgetting principles. This was especially the case with the great merchants who used the opportunity of the government opening wide the door for the sale of official positions and titles to purchase positions and engage in bribery, that is, using official positions to protect commercial interests, establishing monopolies in the sale of certain goods, and stealing from the imperial treasury to get rich. For the most part they could only be called parasites on society, just the opposite to their contemporaries in France, the bourgeoisie of the third echelon, who dared to oppose the privileged classes.

The peasants and craftspeople remained the latent revolutionary force, and during these two centuries all uprisings or disorders arose under the guise of religion, as if one could only draw the people together through religious ties. This included the famous Taiping Rebellion, of course. In this period there was not one peasant uprising of any size that resembled the situation before the seventeenth century, when a leader like Li Zicheng could directly denounce a tyrannical government and stir up the people to a mood of opposition to dictatorship. What now had this function was religious heresy or even peculiar superstitions, indicating that the level of consciousness of the most oppressed among the peasants and craftspeople had dropped considerably. How had this situation come about? Could it be that what Lenin called the "disease of political indifference" was already an epidemic in China?

37

The contrast above already makes it clear that to understand this general indifference to matters of government, one need not go looking for the causes in the precepts handed down by the early philosophers. In the conditions of illiteracy and semiliteracy that prevailed through most of the Middle Ages, it was all right for people not to know the teaching of the *Book of Odes* and of Confucius, but they could not afford to remain ignorant of what could endanger their very existence in their immediate surroundings. In the time when autocrats instituted governmental terror to enforce the silencing of all voices, with the exception of a tiny number of censors who had been given the special privilege of speaking out by imperial decree, and even that line-up of "gentlemen" who devoted all their energies to governing the people tremblingly avoided "reflecting on responsibilities beyond their position," what could be expected of the "ordinary" or "uncivilized" people who were qualified only to be ruled? The disease of political indifference was clearly the daughter of governmental terror.

The Middle Ages did not lack excellent means for manufacturing an atmosphere of terror. I won't go back too early, but just consider two emperors who were greatly admired by the emperors of the early Qing: the Taizu emperor and his son the Chengzu emperor of the Ming. While both were uneducated blockheads, they were skilled emperors, particularly expert in manufacturing governmental terror. Ming Taizu, whose background was one of banditry, adopted the style of his bandit predecessor the Gaozu emperor of the Han, and in his later years killed huge numbers of worthy officials, with two important cases involving several tens of thousands of people, a fact that is well known to everyone. Just take, for example, the method he invented for punishing corrupt officials—removing their skin while they were still alive, stuffing it with straw, and hanging the stuffed bodies at the gate of the yamen for public viewing. This was terrifying enough that six hundred years later the villages of Jiangnan still commonly use the phrase ''strip off the skin and stuff it with straw'' as a form of curse. As for Ming Chengzu, never mind the fact that he initiated an armed rebellion and seized the imperial position from his nephew; he also killed all of the officials whom his father had arranged to support his nephew and who refused to take his side, and he thought out a poisonous plan to humiliate their women by arranging for ten to twenty strong young Hans to rape each of them in one night. This was the recompense he gave to these loyal officials and filial sons. The cultural level of the father and son was in the end so low, however, that while they were good at manufacturing tangible forms of terror, they were less adept at intangible ones. Though they enthusiastically revered Zhu Xi, their methods were still very crude. Whoever dared to criticize the Master Zhu was arrested, put into a straitjacket, and made to hang in public as a warning to the people. To succeed with physical abuse yet fail to penetrate the psychology of the people certainly went strongly against the teachings handed down by Confucius and Zhu Xi. The result was that after these two died they were succeeded by profligate sons, who did not even have the patience to read through Zhu Xi's notes on the Four Books. They managed to develop a system of spying yet were even less successful in dealing with problems in the world of mind and spirit. In this respect their performance was greatly inferior to that of Yongzheng and Kangxi three hundred years later.

38

Although the Yongzheng emperor and his father, the Kangxi emperor, were Manchus, they had a thorough knowledge of Han culture, and especially of the many techniques it provided for domination. Just consider the quality of their calligraphy, the fact that they were able to compose several pieces of doggerel, and that they could have discussions with scholars on certain problems within the classical texts. One can see immediately that their grasp of Han culture was a cut above that of Ming Taizu and his son. And how about their state of mind? Here the differences are even greater. Their jealousies, cold-blooded cruelties, and hypocrisies certainly outclassed those of Ming Taizu and his son, Ming Chengzu. The reason for this is straightforward. They did not forget that they had been leaders of the oppressed people before becoming rulers of a united empire. As leaders of an oppressed people, they feared that the more they became familiar with Han culture, the more they were likely to be assimilated to the Han, so they made an increasing number of religious distinctions between Han and Manchu. As rulers of a united empire, however, the more they became experts in techniques of domination, the more clever they were at exercising autocratic power, and indeed the more able they were in instituting governmental terrorism, particularly intangible forms of terrorism.

39

Historians have done considerable textual research into how Yong-zheng dealt with political enemies or "meritorious running dogs," and the textual criticism done by the famous Ming-Qing historian of the 1920s, Meng Sen, is most successful in revealing the real face of his techniques of power. If one compares the way Wang Xifeng depicts the wide-ranging capability of that group of mothers-in-law in the *Dream of the Red Chamber* with Yongzheng's skill in using techniques of power, they fall far short of Yongzheng's wizardry. The ways in which Yongzheng dealt with his brother's apparent ambitions, or the way he dealt with the worthy official who helped him in his plot to seize the succession, was to entrust them with important responsibility, purposely give them a difficult problem to solve, ask them to punish one of their supporters accused of plotting, induce them into making errors, force them to confess their mistakes, humiliate them before the people, publicly show mercy and forgiveness yet privately collect information against them, then find a handle against them, hand them over to the law, frame up charges against them, establish all of the "ten unforgivable crimes," and pretend to be merciful but actually deal with them severely. To put it simply, it was to lift them up to heaven and then place them back on earth. He had the names of his own half-brothers Yinyi and Yintang changed to Aqina and Saisihei, which mean "dog" and "pig" in Manchu. How can one avoid being reminded of the measures taken by Ming Chengzu against such loyal officials of the previous court as Tie Liang? Yongzheng used ninety-two charges, all of them unclear or uncertain, to cause Nian Gengyao to commit suicide, and while Nian was still in prison before he died, Yongzheng sent instructions to him forcing him to admit that he was being dealt with "leniently" in this kind of death, for the sake of protecting the leaders of his whole clan. How can one not think of this character as even more hypocritical than Ming Chengzu, and even more of an expert at intrigue?

40

Yet this kind of accomplishment was still a tangible form of terrorism. In attacking his potential enemies and killing meritorious officials at the same time, Yongzheng did not forget to cast a sidelong glance at the scholars who placed themselves somewhere between the court and the common people. Even though his head was crammed with the superstitions of Shamanism, Lamaism, and the Buddhist and Daoist monks, just like his father Kangxi, he knew how to "use the Han to control the Han," and Song neo-Confucianism was an extremely useful instrument to this end. One can see that he had learned a lot from the theories of Zhu Xi, as there were two techniques that he was particularly adept at: one was insisting that good "reasons" be given for killing someone, the second was "turning a person's own method back against them." Wang Jingqi was the first person sacrificed in one of Yongzheng's literary cases.

Another incident relates to the Hanlin expositor, Qian Mingshi. He was a well-known figure in the literary world of the time. Simply because, following the bad habits of the literati of the time, he had dedicated a poem to the illustrious achievements of Nian Gengyao, he was accused by Yongzheng of "using poetry to flatter evil doers." Apart from the fact that he lost his official post and was forced to return to his home county and placed under surveillance, Yongzheng wrote with his own hands the words "an offender against the Confucian code" (*Mingjiao zuiren*) and ordered two local officials to inscribe them on a board and hang it over Qian's door. At the same time he ordered all the government officials who had come for the *juren* or *jinshi* examinations to write a piece of poetry excoriating Qian Mingshi "to warn against obstinacy in evil ways and to make sure that all scholars under heaven are aware of what is strictly forbidden." Yongzheng himself called this "using literature as the law of the land, as a warning for people and officials." Intellectuals throughout the land, whether in the court or among the public, were given a severe warning as to how far they could go.

Xie Jishi, the imperial censor for Zhejiang, brought a lawsuit against Tian Wenjing, the governor of Zhejiang, accusing this provincial military leader of taking bribes and bending the law. This was originally within his authority as a censor, so he could be said to be carrying out the responsibilities of his office and to be loyal to the emperor. Who was to know that when this came to Yongzheng's attention, he would become furious. "Tian Wenjing has been impartially upholding justice. As for accepting bribes and bending the law, we can guarantee that no such thing has happened. We don't know what was Xie Jishi's motive in only impeaching Tian Wenjing among all the high provincial officials." In fact Tian Wenjing was a spy leader, whom Yongzheng had sent down to the Jiangnan region with the responsibility to keep an eye on the scholar-officials and literati. As for the accusation of taking bribes and using his position for private gain, he only had to be loyal to his ruler, and what was to hinder him in this? After all, when Han Gaozu heard that Xiao He was keeping himself from any corruption, he was uneasy, but when he saw that Xiao He was accused of taking bribes and bending the law, he was very pleased. Who could fail to understand the hidden meaning here? Unfortunately, Xie Jishi forgot this lesson, and for being faithful to his post he was removed from his post and taken for questioning. Through extralegal procedures he was judged to have committed the thought crime of "maligning Zhu Xi and the Cheng brothers in annotating the *Great Learning*" and was condemned to death.

At the same time the Guangxi *juren* Lu Shengnan was also condemned to death. He had not only committed an intellectual crime, in his *Notes on the Comprehensive Mirror* (*Tongjian lu*) he had used the method of exposing human motives used by Confucius in the *Spring and Autumn Annals*, and had criticized the emperors Qinshi Huang, Han Wudi, and Sui Yangdi as instituting autocracy out of selfish motives. He had also praised Li Mi's discourses on the system of military settlement (*fubing*) and had criticized Wang Anshi for not acting in accordance with his office. At the same time he had committed the crime of "belonging to the same region." He was from the same province as Xie Qishi, yet there was no known evidence of his ever having been acquainted with him. Therefore Yongzheng personally made the following judgment against him: On the first count he cursed him, saying "his lack of fear and respect had reached such a point that he falsely used the ancients to express his resentment against unequal treatment." The second count was intended to prove that "in his everyday life he must" have had occasion to conspire together with Xie. So both Guangxi men were condemned to death, and disaster befell all officials from the province who were in Beijing, as well as *jinshi, juren,* and *shengyuan* who were seeking candidacy. Each was subjected to individual investigation.

41

News of the above case was rapidly disseminated throughout the country and was enough to cause civil officials and those *jinshi* and *juren* who had completed their qualifying examinations for civil posts to shudder in fear. Yet Yongzheng did not feel this was adequate; he still had to rectify and purify the thinking of the lesser gentry. A chance incident gave him the bright idea that he should use Lü Liuliang, a man who had already been dead for fifty years, as a chief exemplar of criminal behavior to warn the people. Lü Liuliang was well qualified for this purpose. He was a scholar who had devotedly believed in Zhu Xi and avoided all heterodoxy. He was famous for his literary compilations, and nearly all of those who had studied eight-legged essays had read his books of selected writings. After he entered the Qing, he passed the *xiucai* examination yet declared himself part of the remnant loyal to the Ming, so he was typical of someone who really adhered neither to the victorious dynasty nor to the previous dynasty. He and his disciples left behind a huge number of poems and essays in the forms of books and manuscripts that contained bitter criticism of the Qing dynasty and considerable support for the three feudatories, so he could be taken as an ironclad example of the rebel. His son had been an official during the reign of Kangxi and had been drawn into a plot of rebellion, so this was further irrefutable evidence that "rebellion and insubordination were passed down within families." Articles within his prose selections that discussed ideas on defense against barbarians once inspired Zeng Jing, a primary school teacher in Hunan, with a strange idea, which was to write a letter and advise the governor general of Sichuan and Shaanxi, Yue

Zhongqi, to take up arms against the Qing, yet another reason for him to be taken as a good object lesson for intellectual crimes. Finally, he was from Zhejiang province, and from the late Ming this southeastern region was the center of the movement of scholarly societies and was always the point of departure for the Qing government's cultural policies. To take him as a public example was thus to hold an even more important advantage.

Yongzheng took the unprecedented step of personally playing the role of supreme court judge and bringing Zeng Jing to trial while at the same time acting as defense for this primary school teacher from a mountain village, patiently leading him through the part of the one who had been wronged, and having him confess that his intention to rebel had been entirely due to being poisoned by the thoughts of Lü Liuliang, that his words against the emperor had been due to believing mistakenly the rumors spread by the court eunuchs of Aqina and Saisihei as they were being taken into banishment. In this way Yongzheng succeeded in ingeniously linking up rebellious thoughts with the behavior of his political enemies. No wonder he was so pleased with himself.

Besides exhuming Lü Liuliang's body and having the head cut off, he spared no pains in compiling into a book Zeng Jing's statements made under examination, the record of his dialogue with Zeng Jing, and his successive instructions on the case. The book was called the *Record of Resolving Delusion (Dayi juemi lu)*. It was printed in a deluxe edition, distributed throughout the country, and made required reading for teachers and students of all schools, public and private. As for the outcome, there were of course certain unintended consequences. For example, this book made public some of the inner plotting of the court, in strong contradiction to the ancestral principles that family scandals should not be spread abroad. The Chinese were easily aroused to suspicion, and they became more and more suspicious that the abominable actions that the emperor strenuously denied were actually true. One can use this unintended outcome to judge Yongzheng, as Meng Sen did. By the very fact that he tried hard to cover up his own act of killing his father and appropriating the position of heir, it is hard to avoid the conclusion that he had actually done this. In fact, from Yongzheng to Qianlong, there was a continuous process of publicizing the literary inquisition.

It is true that after Qianlong came to power, he ordered that the *Record of Resolving Delusion* be confiscated, but only for the reason that he had noted its unintended effects. He continued the literary inquisition, dealing with the people in the very same style. Every time there was an upsurge of literary terrorism, the first group to be thrown into panic were the gentry, including officials and those who had not yet become officials. The ordinary people thus had a change of attitude, now being more afraid of officials than of the local gentry, which was opposite to the usual situation. More and more, all saw national affairs as matters of the emperor's family and had not the least concern for the fate of the country itself. Was not this the very outcome that Yongzheng and his son Qianlong had sought?

42

Qianlong had an intense desire to become the greatest ruler of all time. He was emperor for sixty years and was supersovereign for four years. He did in fact break historical records on many counts. The first was the record of the length of one period of autocratic rule, which was longer than that of his grandfather Kangxi by several years. A second was the record for squandering the national currency. The estimated cost of his "ten greatest military accomplishments" was over 1.2 billion taels of silver, and this did not include the regular costs of maintaining the army. The third would be his record for eating, drinking, and amusement; during the sixty years of his reign, he went on twenty-four long trips, for fifty summers he went to his resort in Chengde to hunt, and of course on each occasion he took along his harem of wives and concubines as well as many officials. On his six trips to Suzhou and Hangzhou "to make his southern rounds" alone, he spent twenty million taels of silver from the national treasury, and there is no way of knowing how much was spent by the local gentry and officials who received him. The costs of the luxury and ceremony that accompanied the birthday celebrations for his mother and himself were also without parallel in history, and when he laid out the "banquet for a thousand old men" to celebrate the fiftieth anniversary of his ascension to the throne, he actually invited over three thousand guests, who were all over sixty, and with their retinues the total added up to over ten thousand. As for the beautiful women given to the emperor to enjoy, probably even Song Huizong and Ming Wuzong would admit they could not match him on this count.

Fourth was his record for conniving at corruption. In his latter years, among the powerful officials and eunuchs to whom he gave important responsibilities, over a twenty-year period it is estimated that only a quarter were dismissed and had their properties confiscated, and that this alone added up to over 2.2 billion taels of silver. Given this situation, how could one prevent official corruption from being anything but endemic? Fifth was his record for posing as a refined literary type; he was the spitting image of Jia Zheng in the *Dream of the Red Chamber*, nauseatingly shallow and stupid in his thinking, yet he had a liking for composing poetry and prose. He wanted to surpass the Southern Song record for composing ten thousand poems on six journeys, and after coming to the throne he soon published the *Poems Composed by the Emperor (Yu zhi shi)*. Thereafter he composed another forty-two thousand poems, averaging about two a day, certainly an unprecedented record. Unfortunately not one poem, not even one couplet, gained any attention, perhaps because he lacked a ghostwriter who had real poetic talent.

We could continue to recount ways in which he broke historical records. For example, he broke the record for cluttering up places of scenic beauty and historical interest with plaques announcing "We have been here for a visit." He broke the record for boasting and telling barefaced lies. He broke the record for thinking up the most despicable reasons for the emperor to divorce his older wives. No more needs to be said about this. Books of anecdotes with their thousands of strange tales cannot be fully believed, yet neither can they be proven wrong. Much less should we imagine that just because Qianlong left his inscription all over the place, even on broken down walls and dried up wells, this raises his status.

43

Nevertheless, during the rule of Qianlong several important things happened in China that could be said to have broken records, and that give adequate reason for his name to be inscribed on a list of immortals among medieval rulers. The first is that on the military and political fronts he basically completed the process begun by Kangxi of reinforcing control and order in the border regions, so that China achieved a greater political unity than ever before. The second was a continuation of the policy begun by Yongzheng of restricting trade with the outside world and the entry of foreign merchants to China. Trading posts in the north were in the erratic state of being sometimes open, sometimes closed and so were set up only by Russians. In the south only Guangzhou remained as the common liaison point for British traders, as well as those from other European countries. Thus China took on the face of a nation under lock and key, something that had never happened before. The third was his success in consolidating the cultural policies of Kangxi and Yongzheng and in weaving what has been described as a cultural net that combined breadth and tightness. The first two points do not lie within the scope of investigation of this volume, but the third is a subject that must be discussed.

44

In 1736, in the month following Qianlong's grand coronation, he issued an imperial edict saying that his grandfather's and his father's ways of ruling had been good, yet "the officials below had not implemented their policies well," causing malpractices of intolerance and extreme severity. "We dislike the harshness that has brought harm to the people's livelihood" and "We hate the pretense to generosity that has brought harm to national affairs." He sternly rebuked his officials for "little by little misunderstanding our will and tending toward a lazy and negligent attitude." This was the keynote of the "middle way," which he wished to implement.

The descriptions of his behavior given above already demonstrate that his concerns in adopting this approach were certainly not fear of bringing harm to the people or hindering the affairs of the nation. In the *Comprehensive History of the Qing Dynasty* (*Qingdai tongshi*), after giving details on Qianlong's six southern journeys, Xiao Yishan prepared a table to show the years in which the breaking of the dikes on the Yellow River had occurred up to twenty times. He then commented that "Kangxi went on his southern rounds in order to regulate the Yellow River, but in Qianlong's southern journeys there were no problems in the south. Tens of thousands in currency from the treasury were spent for nothing. Was there any benefit in him coming back by Haining to be sure the stone dikes were strong?" What a bookish kind of judgment! No matter how severe the floods of the Yellow River, they only affected the lives of people in two provinces. If the emperor went to Haining for an inspection, and if by chance the dikes were not firm and he slipped and fell into the water, surely this event would not affect the safety and well-being of all under heaven! Clearly this was a matter of autocratic behavior, and one can see that Qianlong was determined to maintain his father's policy of strict control over the thoughts of both officials and people, yet he also admired his grandfather's ability to create an image of generosity. He wanted both the fish and the bear's claws. How was he to manage that? How else but to catch fish and cook them, yet to use the bear's claws for propaganda purposes. But to nurture jealousy and acrimony in the heart and show benevolence and justice on the outside requires finesse, and this son of a dandy, who was by his very nature a lover of extravagance and luxury, had naturally developed habits of incredible corruption when all power was concentrated in his hands.

In the early years of Qianlong, while Ortai and Zhang Tingyu were in power and there was a division between the military and civil governments, the measures taken on both sides complied with the old patterns established by Yongzheng. When Qianlong was still getting used to the job of emperor, the conflicts between Manchu and Han officials had already flared up to a degree that caused him real headaches, as evident in the requirement given in one of his imperial edicts that ''Manchus were to attach themselves to Ortai in their thinking, while Hans were to attach themselves to Zhang Tingyu.'' Nevertheless, he himself had a fairly quiet life during this period. When Ortai died and Zhang Tingyu was forced to retire, however, Qianlong got rid of old officials who were an impediment and went on to conquer the Dajin River and the Dzungar tribes. The officials under him eulogized this great achievement and daily became more and more wanton in their behavior. While he never forgot his own origins, the more familiar he came with Han culture, the more fearful he was that the Manchus would be assimilated to the Han and that he would lose the backing necessary for his autocratic rule. He was therefore extremely neurotic over the Manchu-Han problem.

45

''We will never incriminate people on the basis of the spoken or written word.'' This announcement brought great jubilation, the more so since it appeared in an imperial edict in September of the sixth year of Qianlong's reign (1741). Yet if one imagines it meant that those who spoke out would not be accused of crimes, this would be mistaken. The emperor emphasized that he would not put blame on any person, but he did not promise not to condemn thought. This particular edict ordered the new governor of Huguang, after he took up his post, to make the investigation and elimination of the version of the *Four Books* annotated by Xie Jishi his first priority.

The new emperor, just like his father before him, sincerely believed in the maxim of his grandfather to the effect that ''The most important thing for those who study the Four Books and learn Confucian philosophy is that they practice what they preach, not that they make fine distinctions of language and interpretation.'' One hardly need mention the fact that Kangxi had already raised Zhu Xi to the position of one of the ten Confucian sages in the sacrificial rite and venerated him as a kind of yardstick for all scholars under heaven, and the like of Xie Jishi had dared to create something new and original. Was not this extremely deleterious to techniques for manipulating popular feeling? Thinking is a criminal activity, and to harbor thoughts out of tune with those of the Manchu emperor is an even more serious crime. This is the footnote that should have been added to Qianlong's announcement that he would not incriminate anyone on the basis of the spoken or written word.

Therefore, when the famous scholar Hang Shijun went so far as to say that the emperor gave preference to Manchu over Han in making appointments, he got what he deserved in having to leave his official position and ''be given an imperial assignment to buy and sell junk metal.'' The Jiangxi *shengyuan* Liu Zhenyu went so far as to memorialize a request that less importance be given to the worship of Guan Yu as a ''military sage'' in the custom of the Qing ancestors, so he got what he deserved in being punished by beheading. Furthermore, when the distinguished Hanlin scholar Hu Zhongzao dared to sit down as an equal with Ocang, the nephew of his examiner Ortai, to drink and match poetic couplets together, causing this Manchurian hereditary servant, the Gansu governor Ocang, to write a poem calling the Mongols ''sons of barbarians,'' ''forgetting his class and slandering his own people,'' this was a case not only of thought crime but of an actual crime of the person. It was impossible that he should not be given the death penalty.

From this time on, ''the imperial we'' that spoke for the country would certainly use the spoken and written word to incriminate people. If one wrote a poem with a classical allusion, did not this mean one was quoting the ancients in order to attack the present? If one wrote an essay making use of history, one was certainly painting an image of the past that would reflect unfavorably on the present. If one was writing the record of a journey with descriptions of scenery, of course one was using these to attack one's superiors. If one researched characters for their original meaning, this could well be a kind of rebellion and slander against the ruler. This resulted in error-mongering and nitpicking, the drawing of far fetched analogies and punishment for imagined intentions, constant petty surveillance, a situation where informing against people became a trend and a tendency to be suspicious even of one's own shadow and protect one's official position above all. Going too far was the same as not going far enough, as the cultural net was drawn tighter day by day. It was preferable to be severe and allow no laxity, as the consequence of any slip for one's whole family became more and more serious.

If one considers only the *Documents of the Qing Literary Inquisition (Qingdai wenzi yu dang)*, put in order and compiled by the Documents Section of the original Beiping Museum of the Forbidden City, among the sixty-five or more original documents relating to literary cases, at least sixty-four cases came from the reign of Qianlong. Among these, many were not only laughable but indeed pitiable, for example, the case of Qianlong's son-in-law who wanted to become a Holy Duke (a lineal descendant of Confucius), or those who pleaded with the emperor for an edict that would enable them to marry the women of their choice. This was not just a matter of people being bitten with the bug of romantic novels about gifted scholars and beautiful ladies, some of them were clearly suffering from mental illness. Yet Qianlong felt it was essential to do a thorough investigation into their political intentions. He gave a stern command for such an investigation to be held, and starting from leading figures in his cabinet down to county-level bailiffs, he motivated all to take a hand in this type of petty action, of course at the same time ensuring that important matters of state would be neglected. It goes without saying that this led those of the time who had the slightest tendency toward up-to-date ideas to wonder whether the emperor did not suffer from paranoia.

Everyone knows that the reigns of Yongzheng and Qianlong coincided with those of Louis XV and Louis XVI of France. Yet the circumstances on each side were precisely opposite. Louis XV reigned for a long period and his powers were limited. Louis XVI wanted to get rid of the most extreme malpractices and thereby gave a stimulus to revolution. The Chinese situation was different. Yongzheng was in power for a short period only, yet he was able to confine to prison both obvious and potential political enemies. Qianlong was not equal to Louis XVI, yet after he took over the succession he did not need to fear that the national treasury would be emptied, nor that his political enemies would usurp the empire. For this reason he exaggerated enormously the dangers supposedly facing him, everywhere sweeping up targets of political crime, enforcing punishments that were terrifyingly severe. When it is impossible to explain this in straightforward language, should one not seek out the causes in his cultural psychology and mental attitudes?

46

When you think about it, it is hard to believe that 110 years after the Qing dynasty had been established, the head of the empire would still put such severe restrictions on cultural interaction between members of his own race and members of the Han race, who constituted the majority within the country as a whole. The means used were also incredibly backward, such as not permitting the reading of books, not allowing Manchus to learn Han characters or Han speech, not allowing the study of any knowledge except riding and shooting, and not even allowing Manchus to make friends or have social interaction with Hans. This is unprecedented in any other case of minority rule during China's Middle Ages. What were the effects? There is already considerable historical evidence on this. In the end, the Manchu race finally declined to the point where the term "Eight Banners" was synonymous with parasite at the time of the demise of the empire. Yet there is one point one cannot overlook: throughout the whole Qing dynasty, members of this race were the main body of officials for the imperial government.

According to the organizational patterns of the Qing government, the high officials of each ministry, in the rank of vice-president or above, had to comprise at least half Manchus; the latter were arranged in ranks higher than those of Han officials at the same level. According to Qing tradition, all regional viceroys and high garrison officials, as well as half of the governors of each province, had to be Manchu, a convention that was not set aside until after the Taiping rebellion. At the same time, in the selection of officials at middle and lower levels, Manchus always enjoyed priority treatment. For historical reasons, the cultural level of the Manchus was originally rather low, and they had only begun to develop their own written language, just before they came to power. For this reason, after they had united the whole country under their rule, starting at the highest level, more and more members of the race made positive efforts to study Han culture— in fact, it was a culture that all races had collectively created over one thousand years earlier. Not only was this an indication of a strong desire to reform their own backward culture, it was also extremely beneficial for improving the cultural structure of the government and the military. Yet

Qianlong reprimanded Manchus for studying, with such phrases as "excessive attention to trivia saps the will," "they engage in plagiarizing for ostentation," "their minds are daily more crafty and narrow," and "the farther they get from the old customs, the more arrogance and boasting become a habit." Over and over, orders were given strictly forbidding study, informing men of the Eight Banners that "it was their duty to abide by the honesty and simplicity of the old ways and not to lose their own distinctive customs," that is, "you must take the Manchu language and riding and shooting as your duty."

Naturally he did not stop at reprimands. Not only did he adopt measures to arrest and severely punish high officials such as Ocang and to create a strong antagonism to Han assimilation, he also gave a guarantee to men of the Eight Banners: anyone who abjures study and becomes adept at riding, shooting, and the Manchu language "I will personally employ; priority will not be given on the basis of whether one has knowledge or not; even for a Manchu to become a Hanlin, all that is needed is to learn a few things in preparation for the examinations." He even extended this principle to the appointment of Han officials. He did not take into account their examination results, nor did he consider their ability, nor did he care about their political achievements. All those who came from backward regions or border areas were given priority in selection or promotion, whereas scholar-officials from Jiangsu, Zhejiang, and such regions were suppressed and not allowed to transfer or to be promoted.

In this respect, the whole scholar-official system, which was based on certain standards of culture, continued to exist in name only. Since among the high officials who constituted the nucleus of this regime about half were selected on the counter-cultural principle that the more you study the more stupid you are, and since the other half of the high officials and the majority of middle and lower officials only had to pass examinations in "eight-legged essays" to become qualified for officialdom, and all were promoted on the assumption that culture is of no use, then of what value was the whole system of examinations for scholar-officials that had been continuously refined from Tang to Ming? When knowledge was no longer a kind of force motivating officials to keep forging ahead, then all levels of official would cease their quest for knowledge. Was this not the general situation of the Middle Ages? When cultural attainment was no longer the main standard whereby members of the ruling apparatus judged human behavior, then even what was popularly opposed in the Middle Ages and commonly recognized as being despicable forms of behavior would become widely adopted as legitimate means of grasping after power, wealth, and social position. Was this not a common pattern in the Middle Ages? From the time of Qianlong onward, the corruption and ineffectiveness of the imperial government increased daily, the Eight Banners became daily more backward in both weaponry and techniques for warfare, and by the time Qianlong died they had pretty well lost the ability to enter into combat. Can one say there was no link between this and Qianlong's cultural psychology and cultural policies?

47

Of course, it goes without saying that Qianlong's personal will could not hinder the progress of historical forces. Yet this is true only of the overall trends of history. In the Middle Ages, when the final deciding power for all policies was in the control of the autocrat himself, especially in the case of such rulers as Yongzheng and Qianlong, even the cabinet meetings of high court officials were a matter of empty form; in other words, even that tiny amount of "democracy" at the highest level of the ruling apparatus had been abolished, and in its place the military establishment had been given the task of implementing the emperor's will. In this situation the will of the autocrat has a tremendous impact. At the very least, within a limited period it can change the course of history. In my essay "Traditional Culture and Cultural Tradition,"[20] I pointed out that the distorted cultural attitudes that are commonly associated with cultural tradition actually took shape in the reigns of Yongzheng and Qianlong. In fact, cultural developments suited to historical progress in that period could not avoid being forced into an undercurrent, if they were to survive in the cultural net cast out by the autocratic rulers. What has been called the Han learning of the Qianlong and Jiaqing eras is one of these undercurrents, a point that is discussed in detail in chapter 5 of this volume.

48

What is most interesting about this father and son pair, Yongzheng and Qianlong, is that they claimed to be strong promoters of virtue, and it was a virtue defined by the neo-Confucian philosopher Zhu Xi's school. Yongzheng's invocation of principle (*li*) in killing people was explained by Dai Zhen early in the reign of Qianlong as a Mencian form, in a veiled yet penetrating criticism. This is something that many scholars have noted. Like his father, Qianlong could certainly not be considered a virtuous ruler, yet he loved to talk about and to promote virtue. On the surface he revered Zhu Xi, yet in fact in his dalliance with the neo-Confucian scholar he only selected fragments from Zhu Xi's discourses on virtue that suited his own purposes. "Manchu customs are simple in their respect for the ruler and devotion to superiors, their basis is frugality, sincerity, loyalty, and respect." "The Manchu has never studied books, he simply knows the great principle of respecting the ruler and being devoted to one's superiors. As the Confucian school taught in the *Book of Odes* and *Book of History*, which have been handed down to posterity, it is also of utmost importance to serve the ruler and serve one's father." This was Qianlong's concept of virtue. If one manages to respect the ruler and be devoted to one's superiors, one is virtuous by definition.

According to this standard, Heshen was the most virtuous of all. Probably Qianlong knew that he was manipulating power for personal ends and accepting bribes, yet he doted on him nonetheless. Absolute loyalty to the ruler was the secret of Heshen's success. If one takes this slavish conception of virtue as the standard whereby the behavior of officials is judged, then the problem of rewriting history will inevitably arise. In the early Qing a group of high officials of the Han were denounced as turncoats to the Ming, and Qianlong commanded that they be listed in the *Biographies of Ministers Who Served Both Dynasties* (*Erchen zhuan*). This included such officials as Chen Mingxia, Feng Quan, and Qian Qianyi. Yet there was an inconsistency here, as without the assistance of Chen Mingxia and others, could the Qing state have managed to get firmly onto its feet? So from the perspective of the Qing dynasty, they were at the same time both loyal and subject to blame. The result was just in line with what Rousseau said in his attack on despotism: "After this moment also there would be no morals or virtue, for despotism, in which there is no hope to be derived from an honorable deed admits, wherever it prevails, no other master; and as soon as it speaks, there is neither probity nor duty to consult, and the blindest obedience is the solitary virtue which remains for slaves."[21]

49

This is how it was in the latter part of China's Middle Ages. Those conceptual realities that had been useful for ruling, from standards of value to regulations for conduct, were all profaned and trampled under foot in the eighteenth century. And the greatest blasphemers of all were the very Qing autocrats who declared that these standards and regulations should be preserved. Then what about the crystallization of these theories, the neo-Confucian philosophy of the Cheng brothers and Zhu Xi, which had repeatedly been patched and refurbished as Ming and Qing rulers made reforms in the system: Could it continue to serve as a dike that could hold back the torrents of human thought? There is no need to speak of any others, one needs only to look at Kangxi, who raised Zhu Xi to the position of one of the ten Confucian sages, or Yongzheng, who loved to hold forth on "heavenly principles" (*tianli*) and "conscience" (*liangzhi*), or Qianlong, who professed, in all seriousness, to believe in and observe the "way of the mean." It is clear that not one of them believed in it. Yet they all felt that this teaching could be a dike that would hold back all thought, for the simple reason that they lacked a leader of the sheep who would personally practice the doctrine. Thus they constantly scorned and satirized what they called the false Confucianism, just as if placing the blame for the breaching of the Yellow River's dikes on the inability of the governor of the river.

Was it the case that a person had failed, or was it that neo-Confucianism itself had failed? From the early Ming, when Zhu Yuanzheng laid down the requirement that Zhu Xi's teachings should be respected and believed by all, history repeatedly demonstrated that what has been called Song neo-Confucianism was a stumbling block to China's march out of the Middle Ages. Of course, to estimate just how strong this force was, serious research is needed. Yet from late Ming to late Qing is there any example of a person concerned to cure the evils of the times or to seek social reforms who got inspiration from Zhu Xi's ideas? Not only is there no such example, but just the opposite is the case. None of those who commended neo-Confucianism and revered Zhu Xi ever cast eyes of doubt, reprimand, or antagonism toward the ruling apparatus. The reason is simple enough: neo-Confucianism was a dike restraining all thought. The breaching of this dike became the focal point of cultural conflict as the period superseded itself. This is a point for later explication; I won't enlarge on it here.

50

The transition from the Middle Ages to the early modern period cannot be explained exclusively from the cultural perspective. It was a process in which the whole face of society underwent change. So far I have not discussed changes in social structure, changes in the political apparatus, changes in China's relations with the outside world, the distortions in intellectual and cultural evolution after China sunk into the position of a semicolony, the conflict between old and new culture that followed the rise of political reform movements. Might not the investigation of all of these problems from a cultural perspective lead to some new and different discoveries? If we stitch together these patches of history would it not at least be an expression of hope—hope that in our investigation of the historical transition from the Middle Ages to the early modern period we may examine this process from many perspectives yet at the same time integrate them into a whole, rather than imposing all kinds of boundaries on our scholarship? Hegel expressed this well in his comment that it is just at the point when we are able to stipulate something as a limit that we have overstepped this very limit.

2 | The Drama of "God-Making" 360 Years Ago

From the beginning in fact there was no way out for him, as if this was brought about by god or the devil.[22]

The establishment of temples to worship spirits goes back to a very early period. This was one way of making provision for the dead.

Beginning roughly in the time of primitive society, there has been a belief that every human being has two selves, the physical and the spiritual, with the latter controlling the former. When people die, it is only a matter of the physical frame being dismantled; the soul continues to exist, but it has lost its home. This lonely self is thus a ghost, with the body dispersed and the soul taking flight, yet desires remain and reason remains. Just as during their lifetime, ghosts pay close attention to their children and grandchildren, or their officials and people, as the case may be. They continue to be concerned about how they are treated by all those they loved or hated while alive, as most had some kind of power during their lifetime, at the very least that of the head of a household.

Needless to say, to allow these disembodied spirits to move around freely is dangerous. If their children and grandchildren or officials and people are around, they may well provide housing for them, a good strong coffin and a tombstone to match; they may also do their utmost to provide satisfactory burial items. Yet the ghosts may not still remain in confinement, especially those who have been heads of families, heads of clans, teachers, or officials. They will certainly not be indifferent to the power they held during their lifetime. In the section of the *Book of Changes* (*Yi jing*) attributed to Confucius, there is a warning that "a spirit may take physical shape, and wandering spirits may take on strange forms."

For this reason, those who were sensible among the ancients thought out clever ways of turning these dangers to profitable ends. If they thought certain ghosts would refuse to keep quiet, especially those who had had positions of power and influence, they made temples for them, had them move into these as gods, and provided lavish banquets at fixed times, including pork, lamb, and beef, praying to them to send blessings and ward off disasters.

What is strange about this is that as history proceeded out of the Middle Ages, this system of establishing temples and worshipping ghosts, which had its origin in ancestor worship, expanded to include the worship of living people—what were called shrines for the worship of the living.

According to the textual research done by the Qing scholar Zhou Shouchang, shrines for the living made their first appearance between the reigns of Han Zhaodi and Han Xuandi in the Western Han dynasty with the "Yu Gong shrine."[23] That would be the first century B.C. Personally, however, I think they go back to the latter part of the third century before the Common Era, when the bandit emperor Han Gaozu established the Hei Di shrine. This was the first case of a shrine being set up for a living person, who received sacrifices and offerings like those given to the dead.[24]

In establishing a shrine for a living person, is not one treating that person as half human and half divine? Is not one assuming that the two selves can be separated before death, so the spirit directs the body, regulating eating, drinking, defecating, and all biological functions as well as matters relating to one's reputation and position, and at the same time leaves the body and moves about investigating and judging people's requests?

It is already strange enough to imagine normal human beings having a personality split in this way, with the body in one place and the spirit in another, and people praying to a tablet with their name on it or a statue looking like them in the belief that they can distinguish truth from error, send blessings, and ward off harm. What is even stranger is that a living person would go so far as to affirm that his own soul not only could fly to other places, but could be present everywhere, as if it could be broken into innumerable fragments.

Is there historical evidence of this? People will of course immediately point to Wei Zhongxian.

This leader of the "faction favoring the eunuchs" in the late Ming period has never had anything good said about him up to now; he is one of those examples of absolute evil that is rare in history, where final judgment can be made as soon as the lid is laid on the coffin. He was originally a small-town bandit from Suning in Hebei, who lost too much money in gambling and so, to repudiate his debt, castrated himself and entered the palace as a eunuch. He first curried favor with the head of the eunuchs, Wei Zhao, and subsequently seduced Wei Zhao's lover, Ke Shi. Then, through Wei Zhao, he curried favor with the eunuch master above him, Wang An, and immediately incited Wang An to demote Wei Zhao. When Ming Xizong became emperor, Ke Shi, who had been the emperor's wetnurse, suddenly became valuable to him. He immediately colluded with her to bring about Wang An's death. Although he did not know a single character, he then became the chief eunuch in charge of ceremony for the emperor, which involved authorizing all official documents. From this time forward, he had the court's support in extending his power.

When Ming Xizong came to the throne as the Tianqi emperor, he was only fifteen years old. His mother had died early, and the only person he listened to was his wetnurse. This enabled Wei Zhongxian to use the emperor's name in organizing cliques and pursuing his own interests. He behaved in an absolutely tyrannical manner, doing whatever he liked. In a short time he was in control of the highly secret interrogation quarters (Dongchang), the imperial bodyguard (Jinyiwei), and the highest court of justice (Sanfasi). He believed that none dared to harm him and carried out an extreme purge of the bureaucracy so that all, from prime minister to members of various ministries, had to bow to his orders.

In this situation, was there any reason for Wei Zhongxian not to become a living god? Just five years after he gained power, the governor of Zhejiang, Fan Ruzhen, was the first to request permission to build a shrine to Wei Zhongxian at West Lake in Hangzhou. The Tianqi emperor not only approved of this but personally presented a horizontal tablet with the words "spread his virtue abroad" inscribed on it. From this point on, an absolutely outrageous situation developed. From June 1626 to August 1627, a mere fourteen months, shrines revering Wei Zhongxian appeared all over the country.

The *Veritable Records of the Ming Xizong Reign* (*Ming Xizong shilu*) and the *Ming History* (*Ming shi*) are full of reports such as the following: Kaifeng prefecture tore down over two thousand houses belonging to the people in order to establish a shrine to Wei Zhongxian. The governor general of Ji-Liao (now Hebei and Liaodong) established seven shrines in his constituency, spending hundreds of thousands of taels of silver. The shrine at Yansui had a roof whose tiles were of colored glaze. The Jizhou shrine had a statue made of agolloch eagle-wood. Even around the environs of Beijing, shrines were set up. Outside the East Floral (Donghua) gate, there was a shrine that used space right on the imperial route from the palace to the imperial university (*taixue*). An impertinent fellow in the Ministry of Works who made a complaint about this was immediately dismissed from his position by an order from Wei Zhongxian.

There were two prefectural officials who either did not make a report to the court before setting up a shrine or did not kneel in worship on entering the shrine, and both were imprisoned and condemned to death. Eunuchs were sent out to supervise the building of these shrines. There is one shrine in Jinzhou where a eunuch came and placed a gold crown on the statue, but because the statue's head was too large and could not hold it, the craftsman immediately rushed to make the head smaller. At this the eunuch put his arms around the head and scolded the craftsman with tears.

Every place where a shrine was erected, a ceremony was held to praise the merits of Wei Zhongxian, in an even grander way than the ceremonies for Yao and Shun, with some essays and songs appearing that called him most holy, most divine. There was one local official who entertained the Minister Huang Yuntai and, when receiving the statue of Wei Zhongxian before his living shrine, went so far as to make five bows and three nods of the head, calling out "nine thousand years!"[25]

The most ridiculous event of all happened in May 1627, when a student in the College of the Sons of the Emperor (Guozijian) memorialized the court with the serious request that Wei Zhongxian be admitted to membership in the Confucian temple. The reason he gave was that Confucius had written the *Spring and Autumn Annals* and the "*Chang* official" (that is, Wei Zhongxian of course)[26] had written the *History of the Three Reigns*

(*Sanchao yaodian*), Confucius had punished Shaozhengmao, and Wei Zhongxian had punished the Donglin clique. Therefore they should be given equal respect. Another case relates to the Jiangxi governor Yang Bangxian setting up a shrine for Wei Zhongxian in Nanchang. He wanted to expand the base for the shrine and so destroyed the shrines of Dantai Mieming—that is, the disciple whom Confucius himself had personal regrets about since he had "chosen on appearance and lost Ziyu"[27] (another name of Dantai Mieming)—and of the three worthies, Zhou Dunyi and the Cheng brothers. Thus Wei Zhongxian was raised by members of his clique to a position near to that of Confucius. Not only were Confucius's disciples no longer worthy of mention, but even the revered neo-Confucian philosophers, whom the Ming dynasty had listed among the ancestors to be worshipped, also disappeared from vision.

Unfortunately, Ming Xizong was short-lived, and when Yang Bangxian came to the court in August 1627 to report that he had set up a shrine for Wei Zhongxian, Xizong's fifth brother had already become emperor. This new emperor took the reign name of Ming Chongzhen, his posthumous name being Ming Yizong and his family name Zhu Youjian. When he came to the throne he was also only seventeen years old, but he was able to anticipate fully the actions of Wei Zhongxian and his clique. He dared to raise his head above this person who had been wished "nine thousand years," focusing on the issue of the shrines for the living. In August he took power, and in October he dismissed the minister of war, Cui Chengxiu, who had helped the Wei clique. The next person he dismissed from office was Zhejiang Governor Fan Ruzhen, who had proposed the first shrine to the living. At this point Wei Zhongxian displayed his true slavish temperament. Having lost the protection of the emperor, like a dog that has lost its home, he personally requested that all the shrines to the living be abolished and begged for mercy from the Chongzhen emperor. This only seemed to strengthen the emperor's resolve to wipe out the whole Wei clique. In early November he sent down the order for Wei Zhongxian to be exiled to Fengyang. Wei killed himself on the way, and his followers fled in all directions, either dying or being dismissed. This political upheaval in the court lasted for a mere two months.

And what about the shrines to the living that were spread throughout the country? They were all condemned as "shrines of rebellion" and destroyed, with their remnants sold off for what they were worth. A lively drama that involved raising a living person to a pedestal of divinity thus came to an end. Was this simply the achievement of one person, the Chongzhen emperor? Of course not. History had already begun its move out of the Middle Ages, yet, strange to say, the medieval movements of god-making had not yet exhausted themselves.

3 | The Confucius of History and the History of Confucius

For rightly is truth called the daughter of time, not of authority.[28]

The False Confucius and the True

For some time now, Confucius has been a problem personality. For example, did Confucius represent progress, or did he represent conservatism and perhaps even a reactionary standpoint? This problem was debated from the late Qing up to the May 4th period, and indeed from May 4th to the early 1950s. Right up to the present, that is, for nearly a hundred years, the problem has been basically the same.

Where does the crux of the problem lie? The answer can only be very complex. Many factors play a part, including political, social, psychological, and methodological factors, not to mention factors relating to historical documentation and even to individual human emotions. If one tried to compile a "History of Research on Confucius" this would certainly make very interesting reading.

When it comes to the question of how to do research on Confucius, however, the highly regarded classicist Zhou Yutong put forth a suggestion half a century ago that I feel is still worth taking seriously today. This suggestion can be found mainly in two works: *The New and Old Text Classical School* (*Jing jingu wenxue*) and *Confucius* (*Kongzi*). The point is that we must distinguish between the false Confucius and the true in our research on Confucianism. This is needed because such traditional perspectives as the "transmission of the way" (*daotong*) and the "transmission of learning" (*xuetong*) are misleading. They have resulted in certain subjective depictions of Confucius taking the place of the genuine Confucius of history, a situation that has been common through the vicissitudes of scholarly and intellectual history.[29] Liang Qichao made the point that gradually over time, Confucius became Dong Zhongshu and He Xiu; he then became Ma Rong and Zheng Xuan; next he became Han Yu and Ouyang Xiu; and finally he became Gu Yanwu and Dai Zhen.[30] We might even extend this list to include Kang Youwei, Zhang Binglin, and others.

If we recognize that this phenomenon pointed out by Liang Qichao is true of China's historical process, then we would have to recognize that Zhou Yutong's emphasis on investigating the historical fate of Confucius and his theories from the perspective of historical change is important as a methodology for doing research on Confucius.

For this very reason it is important to ascertain the genuine words and actions of the historical Confucius, and even more important to note what were *not* his words and actions.

Among the Qing dynasty textual critics there was a commonly used term—the so-called bamboo stripping method of studying the classics. It was necessary to strip away layer after layer of the outer covering before one could reach the pure inner content. This was a rather accurate analogy for depicting this particular methodology.

The reason the image of Confucius went through so many vicissitudes was that there were too many of these "outer coverings." At one point he became a prophet, at another point a teacher of magic. Here he was portrayed as the "uncrowned king" (*suwang*) who had the qualities, though not the position, of a king, there as the "first teacher" (*xianshi*), who held firm to his principles undeterred by poverty. Some people saw him as a believer in the suppression of all desires, while others as a hedonist. In some periods he was taken as a supporter of autocracy, in others as one who advocated restraints on autocratic power. His social status went up and down with the times and his character also fluctuated wildly, the titles assigned to him changing many times, as his function changed in different periods.

Let us take the early Tang period as an example. In this period, which has been depicted as one in which "the classical texts were unified,"[31] Yan Shigu's *Definitive Edition of the Five Classics (Wujing dingben)* appeared, as did *The Correct Meaning of the Five Classics (Wujing zhengyi)*, written by Kong Yingda, Jia Gongyan, and others. All of the classical texts that had been credited to Confucius since the Han dynasty were brought together in both text and explanation through the intervention of state authority. Logically one would expect the image of Confucius to become fixed at this point. At least among the ruling group one would expect consistency.

But what happened in actuality? From emperors Gaozu and Taizong to the early period of Gaozong of the Tang, that is, a period of less than half a century, the image of Confucius changed at least three times. In A.D. 619 Tang Gaozu gave an order to erect a temple to the Duke of Zhou and one to Confucius in the College of the Sons of the Emperor (Guozijian), showing reverence to the Duke of Zhou as the "first sage" (*xiansheng*) and to Confucius as the "first teacher" (*xianshi*), so giving Confucius a subordinate position to that of the Duke of Zhou. He was merely recognized as the forefather of all educators, not as having the authority to stand in the most important position and enjoy the highest level of reverence. This provision made by the emperor was changed by his son, however. In 632, while Tang Gaozu was still alive, Tang Taizong gave an order to destroy the temple to the Duke of Zhou and raise Confucius to the position of the "first sage" and make Yan Yuan the "first teacher." This meant having Confucius sit on a throne facing south and enjoy the prerogatives of a primordial savior figure, while giving the honor accorded to the first teacher to his most important disciple.

In A.D. 647, that is, when *The Correct Meaning of the Five Classics* was being revised, Tang Taizong passed another edict for Confucius to be given several more companion figures, all followers of his who had become famous for their explanations of the classics.[32] Who was to guess that his son Tang Gaozong, shortly after coming to power in 655, would make an edict canceling his father's provisions and reviving those of his grandfather, making the Duke of Zhou once again the "first sage" and Confucius the "first teacher," with the only point of progress lying in the fact that Yan Yuan, Zuo Quming, and others were kept in the position of "subordinate figures worthy of reverence"? This reform in the system clearly carried the mark of Wu Zetian, who had just succeeded in gaining the position of empress, and for this reason it met with strong opposition from such elder statesmen as Suan Wuji and others. In 657 they made a joint resolution that the relegating of Confucius to a position subordinate to the Duke of Zhou lowered his dignity, and that of Zuo Quming and others to the position of "subordinate figures worthy of reverence" demoted them in a way that went against "historical truth." The weak Tang Gaozong had no alternative but to toe their line and cancel the edict he had put forward two years earlier.

The attitudes of these emperors of the early Tang toward Confucius might be regarded as practical examples of the negating of negation. The way in which this process repeated itself again and again is another question, but what is evident here is that even though they ordered people to standardize the classical texts, they themselves did not share a common understanding of Confucius. Each of them upheld his own subjective image of Confucius, and each compelled the students of the imperial university to join in the farce of worshipping this image.

Parallel incidents to this one in Chinese history are too numerous to mention. In the late Warring States period Han Feizi made the following mocking comment: "After Confucius and Mo Zi, the Confucian school was divided into eight groups and the Motian one split into three; the reasons for accepting and rejecting each were quite different, yet all felt that the one they chose was the true Confucius or the true Mo Zi. Confucius and Mo Zi could not return to life, so who was to decide what later generations were to learn?"[33] Even though he forgot to make light of the fact that he himself was not a true follower of either Shen Buhai or Lord Shang of Yang (the two founders of Legalism), still with these words he hit the mark by a kind of fluke, giving evidence that, as early as the third century B.C., the true image of Confucius was already being obfuscated by a whole range of pseudosages. If we do not patiently peel away all the layers that have accumulated over more than two thousand years of history, how can we reach the original Confucius?

Pseudo-Confucian Figures
in the Early Modern Period

In discussing the history of research on Confucius, we cannot avoid giving special attention to two pseudo-Confucian figures who made their appearance between the late Qing and the May 4th period. They were first depicted in turn by Kang Youwei and Zhang Binglin. Kang Youwei's *Confucius the Reformer* (*Kongzi gaizhikao*), which was published on the eve of the Hundred Day Reform Movement in 1898, was undoubtedly the most influential of his many writings on Confucius and the classics. In it he departed from the kind of explanation provided through the "transmission of the way" (*daotong*), which had been in vogue for a thousand years, and gave the view that Confucius's "commendation and use of Yao and Shun and his choice of King Wen and King Wu as examples" represented an important principle but had no factual basis. He felt that both before and after Confucius there were other parallels to this—Lao Zi commending and drawing on the Yellow Emperor, Mo Zi on Xiayu, Xuxing on Shennong, all being similar to Confucius's upholding of Yao and Shun, kings Wen and Wu, and the Duke of Zhou. In all cases these figures were passed off as early kings to gain people's confidence, and all in fact belonged to pseudohistory. Kang Youwei felt people always "value what is old and lack respect for the contemporary." Thus anyone who genuinely intends to bring about reform will always come up against the strong opposition of traditionalists. By claiming one's suggestions for reform are drawn from the views put forward by the early sages, however, it is possible to quell opposing voices. If by any chance the reform fails, one also does not have to take the blame! Therefore, in his quest for the ideal of a "peaceful universe," Confucius had to manufacture history in such a way as to create an inverted image of the future.[34]

In Kang Youwei's original conception, he emphasized the way in which Confucius drew upon ancient precedent to bring about reform, how he was able to use the authority and prestige of the original "sacred texts" to attack the authority of feudal classical institutions and philosophy. Far beyond his own expectations and those of his followers, *Confucius the Reformer* challenged the image people had had for centuries of Confucius as a conservative who wished to restore the classics, with a counterimage of Confucius as a reformer of the system and a promoter of renewal.[35]

As the saying goes, "hate the monks and you will also dislike the cassock." After the Hundred Day Reform Movement Kang Youwei changed the central focus of his attack from the Qing ruling apparatus, led by Dowager Empress Cixi, to the democratic revolutionary party led by Sun Yat-sen. This, of course, raised the ire of the more progressive reformers, and, as a result, Kang's image of Confucius the reformer met its demise.

In the early part of the century Zhang Binglin, whose fame as author of "An Argument against Kang Youwei and for Revolution" shook both China and the outside world, published such further articles as "A Revised View of Confucius" ("Ding Kong") and "On the Pre-Qin Schools of Thought" ("Lun Zhuzi xue").[36] In his depiction of Confucius three personas emerged—"the reviser of history," "the educator," and the Confucius who epitomized the "national passion" for wealth and fame. In his view, the Confucius who had written the *Spring and Autumn Annals* and thereby become the master historian, as well as the Confucius who had organized private schools for the masses and so become the first teacher, were past history. All that was left was the Confucius who was bent on climbing to the top and who felt that "in morality and ideals there is no need to seek the truth, but only hope for an expedient way to get things done." It was this Confucius who left a profound and long-lasting influence on succeeding generations.[37]

Zhang Binglin later admitted that this Confucius whom he had depicted was a pseudofigure, established as a counterimage to the one set up by Kang Youwei. Of course, he could not anticipate the fact that once his thoughts took the form of a series of essays and entered the objective categories of certain special conditions, they would no longer change in accord with the subjective thought of their author. Thus it was impossible for him to divert the influence they had already had in the world of the spirit. His early ideas already had wide reverberations, even though he personally regretted that he had "not held his tongue, and that even the fastest horses could not bring back what he had said."[38]

If one takes the perspective of the complementarity of opposites, one can see that Kang Youwei and Zhang Binglin's depictions of Confucius were opposite in form and intention yet similar in that both were pseudofigures. Although so different from each other, both acted from a deep desire to see China make progress, and for this they cannot be censured. The problem lay in the fact that both, more or less consciously, felt that it was only necessary to carry out good intentions, and it did not matter what means were used. History itself was seen as merely a means to achieve certain practical goals. In reality, however, history is not the means to an end, but a past that cannot be changed. It has an objective existence that no subjective intention can do anything about. People can find connections between the past and the present in history, but they cannot find a ready-made medicine to cure present ills in history. If they try to do so, they are bound to mystify the boundary between history and the present and fashion history to suit their own needs. The mistakes made by Kang Youwei and Zhang Binlin on the question of Confucius arose in this same way.

There is no doubt, of course, that it was these very mistakes that created their great popularity. Just because the purpose in establishing these false images was to overcome obstacles to progress in the area of thought, all those who were seeking progress, especially the young, were ready to believe in the illusions they had constructed, despising as a kind of pedantry the explanation of history from a truly historical standpoint. For this reason Kang Youwei and Zhang Binlin's widely divergent views on Confucius each separately attracted a group of young scholars. After a period of debate, there were some who rejected their early points of departure and who once again upheld such images as "the most holy first teacher" and even "the greatest and most sacred king of letters," people such as the disciples of Chen Huanzhang. There were also some who progressed to the Marxist view of Confucius and who tried to make an objective historical analysis of him, including Li Dazhao and others. Nevertheless, in the period before and after May 4th, the works intended to repudiate Confucian ideas through criticism of Confucius inevitably reminded readers at some point of Zhang Binlin or of Kang Youwei.

Many of the editors of and contributors to the famous journal *New Youth*, with its call to "knock down the stall of the Confucian clan," had historical connections with Zhang Binlin, a fact that is well known to everyone. Chen Duxiu, Qian Xuantong, Lu Xun, Zhou Zuoren, and others all maintained relations with Zhang Binlin as friend and teacher, and many of their articles opposing Confucian teachings and traditional morality bore a clear mark of influence from his early writings. As for Hu Shi, he wrote an article on the theory that the pre-Qin schools of thought (*zhuzi xue*) did not have their sources in the imperial bureaucracy of the Zhou dynasty in order to challenge Zhang Binlin, yet his *Outline of Chinese Philosophy* (*Zhongguo zhexue dagang*) had an undeniably close and derivative connection to Zhang Binlin's "On the Pre-Qin Schools of Thought" and other works. Therefore after May 4th, when Liao Zhizheng attacked Hu Shi and others for refuting the traditional theories about Confucius and the classics and claimed that they had been mainly inspired by the early writings of Zhang Binlin, he was not far off the mark.

Nevertheless, the criticism made by Zhang Binlin, at the very time when he was regretful that he himself had written so little, that Hu Shi and his fellows were "directly stealing Kang Youwei's leftover spit"[39] was also true. Nor did this stop at Hu Shi. Although *New Youth* strenuously attacked such crazy ideas as Kang Youwei's supposed intention of making Confucianism the national religion, this was merely its political perspective. A number of its well-known writers had not broken their links with Kang Youwei's intellectual ideas. One only has to look at the arguments in the second half of Yi Baishi's famous essay "A Critique of Confucius" ("Kongzi pingyi") and similar ideas in Kang Youwei's *Confucius the Reformer* to see this connection.

For this very reason, it was not at all strange that after May 4th the early founders of *New Youth*—Hu Shi and Qian Xuantong—soon became the mainstay of the school known as "studies in ancient history" (*gushi bian*). They combined the theories of Kang Youwei and Zhang Binglin to develop a new kind of apologetics.

To put it in a nutshell, this new apology claimed that Confucius was good and his theories were good, but unfortunately his reputation had been spoiled by disciples who did not do him credit. This of course was not the discovery of Hu Shi and Qian Xuantong, as Liang Qichao and Yi Baishi had said the same sort of thing much earlier,[40] yet Hu and Qian seem to have had a somewhat greater actual influence on scholarship.

Let us take Qian Xuantong as an example. This extremely progressive "new young person" of May 4th had been taught by Zhang Binglin in his early years and later had given homage to Kang Youwei and Cui Shi. After May 4th he became the chief sage of the fortress of the "studies in ancient history," even changing his name to Yigu Xuantong, which means "Xuantong who doubts antiquity." So he was a typical case.

This very "doubter of the classics" in his *Studies in Ancient History* (*Gushi bian*) led the way in pointing out that "if we do not separate the six classics from Confucius himself, the Confucian religion cannot easily be overthrown."[41] He doubted that Confucius had compiled or written the six classics, believing that the five classics now in existence were unconnected books that had been put together in the late Warring States period; he even doubted that Confucius had written the *Spring and Autumn Annals*, something that scholars had agreed on unanimously for many centuries. From this type of criticism arose the "theory that Confucius had no connection with the six classics," which objectively denied all ancient and contemporary scholarly theories about the writings of Confucius. This at least got rid of many biases and provided an important stimulus in helping researchers free themselves from traditional prejudices.

Yet this very doubter of the classics, who cast suspicion on all the "ancient teachings" of Confucius's disciples, never had any doubts about the "ancient tradition" surrounding the person of Confucius himself. He strongly denied any connection between Confucius and the six classics; his purpose in this was to develop an apology for Confucius. He himself was prejudiced in that he cast doubt on all the classics yet defended the *Analects* as beyond suspicion, since he believed the *Analects* revealed an image of Confucius as the "great scholar" of ancient times. He flatly denied that the *Spring and Autumn Annals* came from the pen of Confucius since he felt they were a kind of "dynastic report that had spoiled on the shelf" or a "leaking account book." "We have no way of knowing what Confucius's research was like, but knowing his scholarship and talents, they were certainly far above this kind of shabby historical work."[42]

What kind of standard was this? Of all of the literary heritage labeled Confucian, that which he personally felt to be up to the mark was accredited to Confucius, and that which he personally felt to be not up to scratch was blamed on Confucius's followers. There was no objective standard as to what was acceptable or not, because basically it was impossible to know "what Confucius's writings were actually like." According to this logic, the only standard of measurement was an entirely subjective judgment on Confucius's so-called scholarship and talent. Can this be seen as anything but subjectivism? If one used this sort of perspective to assess Confucius, it would be impossible to arrive at the true image of the Confucius of history. What one depicted would be simply another pseudo-Confucius, one even more far-fetched than those that had gone before. If, for example, one says that Confucian scholarship was ruined by his followers, was not this to repeat what Kang Youwei had said in his claims that Confucius was a single scholar, and might one not just as well go back to Zhang Binglin?

"When the False Is Taken as True, the True Is Also False"[43]

In trying to understand historical persons or events, one is inevitably influenced by all kinds of subjective factors, so that when describing or evaluating history it is hard to avoid the imprint of a subjectively imposed standard.

The persons and events of history belong to the past, however. The history of time in some parts of the universe may sometimes turn back on itself, but in the history of the earth this has not happened so far. Thus it is absolutely certain that past events can never be affected by the interference of subjective factors in such a way as to change their nature.

Since this is the case, even though we cannot detach ourselves from reality and make an absolutely objective account of history, we ought to strive constantly for greater objectivity and less subjectivity. We should strive to avoid distorting history either consciously or unconsciously through personal knowledge or emotions, and avoid making what is false appear as true or blurring the truth by a false interpretation. It is often the case that radically opposite subjective intentions produce outcomes of identical value. This is a phenomenon we often see in historical research.

Without doubt, when we come upon this kind of distortion of history, we need to take note of the author's subjective intentions, whether the intention behind a particular distortion was good or bad. Yet the study of history is not the same as the study of law. In law the intentional killing of persons and their accidental killing are judged very differently, for the simple reason that it is the living, not the dead, who make this distinction. In history the issue at stake is not measuring out punishment for the dead, what traditional historians call passing historical judgment. Rather, it is a matter of verifying events that have already taken place, and it is important not to get entangled in any kind of apologetics.

All the pseudoimages of Confucius produced by history might be viewed as the products of a range of particular apologetics. The subjective intention of the various advocates may have been very different, yet they all shared the same lack of respect for history. They were not able to make a clear distinction between objective and subjective history, and they all saw history mainly as what was depicted by those who make the records. For this very reason, when they discovered contradictions among different accounts, they did not make an effort to understand the subjective factors that influenced particular accounts of history and led to these contradictory records, so as to uncover the objectively existing facts behind the records. Rather, just the opposite happened. They took the position that there was no possibility of an objective history, with the result that each person could carve out the subjective account that suited his or her own wishes. Due to the strong tendency toward utilitarianism in its advocates, this kind of childish epistemology reached a point where there was little concern about even the simplest facts of history. One example is the historical work of the classical scholars of the Han dynasty in which Confucius was transformed into a superhuman savior figure.

The new apologetics of Confucius that have been described above were precisely opposite in intention from those of the Han dynasty scholars. They did not try to transform Confucius from a human being into a god, but rather to bring him back from being a god to an ordinary human being. Yet their method of doing this was wrong, as they started not with accurately investigating historical facts but with assuming a certain model of history. They did not collect material with the objective of clarifying historical facts revealed through the various contradictory historical accounts. Rather, they used certain materials to prove their own hypotheses. In using this method it was essential first to establish an argument, then to seek for evidence; actually it was the traditional method of "the six classics all being my footnotes" (liujing jie wo zhujiao).

Therefore, even though the intention was to turn Confucius from a son of God back into a son of man, the prior assumption or hypothesis was that Confucius was the perfect man for all ages. They quoted copiously from many sources, did textual research to expose what was false, and put enormous efforts into ordering historical sources, to prove this hypothesis. In reality, however, human persons cannot rise above their own times in either their thinking or the activities they pursue, nor can they detach themselves from the social and political relations peculiar to their own period of history. So Confucius can only be a historical personage, one whose lifestyle was determined by the living conditions of the Wu and Wei kingdoms during the late *Spring and Autumn Annals* period. The Confucius who is the "perfect man" for all times and all regions never existed as a real person, only as a product of the imagination. Thus the subjective purpose of the new apologists, just like that of the ancient classicists, produced quite opposite effects. They did not succeed in bringing Confucius back from heaven to his actual humanity, but rather simply added one more pseudo-Confucius to the existing collection, a figure whose personality and talents were so far above spatial and temporal limitations as to be a mere illusion.

Are not good intentions worth being affirmed nevertheless? Of course not. We have already discussed the images of Confucius created by Kang Youwei and Zhang Binglin, one intended to attack the authority of the feudal classical establishment, the other intended to enable people to go even farther in destroying their faith in Confucian teachings. Both had liberating effects in different historical periods. Similarly, Qian Xuantong's denial of any linkage between Confucius and the six classics was useful in the 1920s as an attack on the conservatism and traditionalism of scholarly circles. So we fully recognize that their main intentions had historical significance in early modern intellectual history.

What is under consideration here, however, is the scientific value of the various arguments about Confucius. In his discussion of the history of economic theory, Marx pointed out at an early stage that just because a theory has no scientific signficance does not mean it has no historical significance. It goes without saying that none of the historical reasons for the existence of false images of Confucius would stand up to scientific probing. We are scientific researchers, and as such we reject any kind of historical superstition, much less any affirmation or demonstration of contemporary superstitions. The reason we use Marxism and historical materialism to research Confucius and his theories is not, of course, to defend the various images of Confucius that have been formed over the ages, but to make a realistic investigation into the true face of Confucius and his theories.

"When the false is made true, the truth is inevitably false." In the history of research on Confucius, the phenomenon of taking what is false as the truth or obfuscating the truth through false impressions has been only too common. There is no need to mention the intentional distortions and misrepresentations. Even if one takes only those distortions that have arisen from the best of intentions, the actual needs of those who made these pseudoimages of Confucius have already become a part of history. If the false images of Confucius that they created are not subjected to a scientific squaring of accounts, what are likely to be the social consequences? Could it be that through a belief in the good intentions of those who created these false images, the images themselves may be taken as true? There is evidence to show this is a real possibility. People are imperceptibly influenced by what they see and hear. If they become accustomed to seeing what is false as true, once they come across an honest image of Confucius, they are likely to reject it as false, seeing it as either blasphemy or excessive praise. There are many examples of this sort of thing.

A Reliable Account Must Have True Evidence

This brings us to the importance of a scientific approach to research on the history of Confucius. While the necessity for this is evident, the problem is how to do research that accords with science.

I personally feel that we should try a whole range of methodologies as long as they help in reconstructing history. In fact, in the research done on Confucius since 1949, many methods have been used, from traditional textual criticism to modern systems theory. This is probably due to the fact that different people see things differently, but it may turn out finally to open up the way to a genuinely sound type of research. For myself personally, although the application of a number of different approaches has stimulated me, I have followed the research method suggested by Marx: "Inquiry . . . has to appropriate the material in detail, to analyze its different forms of development, to trace out their inner connection. Only after this work is done can the actual movement be adequately described."[44]

There are difficulties, however, in trying to apply this scientific method to research on Confucius. As I see it, the main difficulties lie in clarifying the inevitable obstacles to a history of Confucius, and much effort is needed to achieve this.

First, detailed materials must be collected. In discussing the thought of Confucius, no one can neglect the *Analects* (*Lun yu*). This is correct since generations of scholars have repeatedly made investigations and proven that the *Analects* is an original record preserving the words and actions of Confucius and one of the comparatively reliable sources. Yet if one takes Qian Xuantong's perspective that all research on Confucius should be based solely on the *Analects*, there is a problem with reliability.

The present version of the *Analects* was compiled in the second century A.D., six hundred years after the death of Confucius. Actually it is possible to prove that the original compilation came from the hands of Confucius's disciples, yet it is not clear when the compilation was made or who edited it. It remains a puzzle how it was copied and handed down by each sect, a process resulting in there being three different versions by the first century A.D. All we know is that the present version is the product of two new collections made by Zhang Yu of the Western Han and Zheng Xuan a hundred years later in the Eastern Han, and there were changes in both the list of contents and the text. It is impossible to compare it with the earlier version. This of necessity reduces the reliability of the present version, as there is a strong possibility that the writings of other authors were added in.[45]

Even if the present version of the *Analects* had not been subjected to revisions and additions by later writers, there would be serious drawbacks to taking it as original material for research on Confucius—it is too simple,

too sweeping, and too unidimensional. According to Confucius's self-por-
trait, he "established himself at thirty" and had an active life thereafter for
forty-three years on the stage of history in the late *Spring and Autumn Annals*
period. Yet the present version of the *Analects* has only 17,700 characters,
which averages out at about 300 characters for each these forty-three years.
Most of its contents consist of a record of Confucius's dialogues with his
students and masters, and there is hardly any record at all of the context of
these dialogues, to the extent that very often even the name of the interloc-
utor was not recorded. This makes it difficult to use the *Analects* for a truly
historical investigation of Confucius's thought. My own research indicates
that the material preserved in the present version of the *Analects* was
probably largely a record of Confucius's words and actions after he had
passed the age of fifty, so at best it can only be used to investigate his thinking
in his later years, and there is a need first to do textual research that will
clarify the historical period in which it was compiled. Although there have
been many textual studies done of the *Analects* over the years, very few
scholars, with the possible exception of Cui Shi in the Qing dynasty, have
done the kind of work that was done by European scholars on the Bible in
the nineteenth century, work that involved establishing the time period in
which each book, and even each chapter, was collated and the likely author
of each. It is precisely for this reason that the *Analects* can be used as a
foundation source, but not as a reliable basis for research, and certainly not
as a ready-made source.

In the writings from before the Qin dynasty through the Western
and Eastern Han there is hardly an item that does not mention Confucius, and there are not a few that were edited or collated even earlier
than the *Analects*. While it is true enough that some absurd fables and
popular legends far removed from reality and intentionally made up
are found in these texts, there are also some extremely valuable ancient historical materials here. For example, each recorder of tales
wanted very much to have some material about Confucius's life and
times, something that was hard to find in the *Analects* but could be
tracked down in the Schools of Thought of the Warring States period
and in the historical books and classical commentaries of the Western
and Eastern Han. What is rather strange is that the closer one gets to
the early modern period, the more one sees neglect and even outright
rejection of this kind of material. As scholars tended more and more
to use only the *Analects* in their research on Confucius, thus in effect
turning somersaults in the hands and minds of Zhang Yu and Zheng

Xuan, their image of Confucius naturally became more fuzzy as they wrote.

Needless to say, one has to be extremely careful in using materials other than the *Analects*. But caution is not the same as total repudiation. Even the various books of divination of the Eastern Han, with all of their sorcery, and the evidently fabricated *Sayings of Confucius as Passed Down by His Family* (*Kongzi jiayu*) should not be completely dismissed. I once introduced an essay by Zhou Yutong entitled ''Confucius the sage and his disciples as portrayed in the books of divination,'' giving the view that this essay was a successful example of the use of the books of divination to do research on a false image of Confucius, since it revealed how classical scholars of the Eastern and Western Han transformed Confucius from a human being into a transcendental figure, and ultimately into the true image of the Savior on High.[46] But this is only one aspect of the problem. Another aspect involves the way in which material from the books of divination might be used to aid research on the true Confucius and his real life history.

If one tries carefully to amass material here for this purpose, there is not a great deal, and it is essential to analyze the different developmental formations.

The history of the development of the false Confucius is, in a word, the history of the deification of the true Confucius. Confucius's transformation from a human being to a god, which began just after he died and reached its peak in the early part of the Eastern Han dynasty, took about four hundred years. To this day we have no collection of early materials on the history of Confucius that is comprehensive and accurately ordered chronologically in a way that could support discussion on the process. By a general estimate, over this five-hundred-year period, the image of Confucius went through four transformations. From the time Zi Gong made the tomb figure, Confucius was raised from an ordinary man of virtue to a superhuman worthy. At the initiation of Mencius and with the later approbation of Xun Kuang, he was raised from a worthy to a sage and given a position higher than that of human kings or of sages who had no power in the human realm. Starting with Dong Zhongshu and echoing through the work of the new text doctors of the Western Han, Confucius was transformed from a sage into his third persona—the ''uncrowned king'' who was the bearer of divine inspiration and legislator of the Han system. Finally, with the initial effort of Wang Mang and later support of Liu Ji, Confucius made his fourth transformation from the ''uncrowned king,'' who had been commissioned by heaven to prepare a book of legal codes for the Han dynasty, to the universal savior, who transmitted all of heaven's will.[47]

These four transformations naturally had a whole range of intermediate links, connecting up the different stages of development and enabling one image to change into another. Materials were needed to manufacture these linkages. Since those undertaking this task were mostly focusing on the person of Confucius, this meant they had to collect all kinds of material about Confucius. Since the purpose of these constructions was to make use of Confucius, they were sure to take special note of materials that suited their purpose and use their own viewpoint in judging the materials, in enthusiastically explaining hidden meanings and imagining hidden stories within them, and in deriving far-fetched mystical revelations from them. Thus they preserved some materials and destroyed others. Certain fragments concerning Confucius's life and teachings, whether textual materials or oral traditions, were preserved through this process of selecting certain items, rejecting others, then restoring what had earlier been rejected. Nevertheless, due to the additions, deletions, and embellishments, it is not easy to distinguish the genuine from the false, or to explain the mystical aspects in these original written records and relatively early oral traditions. There can be no doubt that there are many difficulties in using them, yet it is not impossible. One can draw lessons from such examples as the methodology of traditional textual criticism or the way in which Engels explained the mysteries of the Book of Revelation, and can sift out the gold from the dross. What is even more difficult, of course, is explaining the internal linkages among all these formations.

This is not to say that earlier scholars paid no attention to different formations within materials on the life and teaching of Confucius—for example, Zhang Binglin and Liu Shipei showed considerable interest in the historical materials contained in the books of divination and their possible connotations in the late Qing, and later scholars noted how non-Confucian fables had infiltrated and even replaced the stories of Confucius. They never did anything more than make a formal comparison, however, laying out the material to clarify the similarities and differences between each type of image; they paid little attention to the actual historical happenings of the time. For example, what event took place in the early part of the reign of Han Wudi that stimulated the rather timid and cautious Dong Zhongshu to dare to make a public announcement in the court that Confucius was the ''uncrowned king'' of the Han legal system? This is a question that has been given little attention over a long period. Let us take the position that the four successive stages in Confucius's transition from a human being to a god enumerated above accord with history. If one does not research the historical events that brought about these changes, if one does not analyze the practical contradictions that lay behind these changes, how can one clarify the objective process of the history of Confucius's transformation into a god? On the other hand, once we grasp this actual process, we can begin to peel away the various "layers" surrounding the historical materials on Confucius and bring to light the original simple facts of history.

Of course, research must not be limited simply to the ordering of source materials. Yet, in research on the history of Confucius, there is an urgent need to emphasize this aspect of putting the materials in order.

According to a preliminary estimate, in the thirty years between 1949 and 1979 there were five hundred articles on Confucius and his theories published in scholarly journals.[48] There are no accurate figures for the last five years, but a quick calculation suggests there have been another two hundred items. These covered an extremely broad range of topics, including Confucius's views on social history, philosophy, politics, the military, education, and fine arts; also, works on his life. Syntheses are most common, making up about one-third of the total. With the exception of the articles published during the Cultural Revolution, which had the intent of "criticizing Confucius," most of these articles are scholarly pieces. There have been only a handful of specialist books, however, except for collections of essays.

What is strange in all of this is that there has not been a single biography of Confucius worthy of the name, nor has there even been a newly compiled chronology of his life history, even though the range of topics covered has been broad and the quantity of work considerable. For this reason, whenever our discussions of Confucius begin to touch upon his life and achievements, we tend to descend into vague and impressionistic talk. If we want to understand Confucius and his thinking, yet we don't understand his life and times, his personal development and the context in which he spoke, we cannot achieve the proper harmony between logic and history, and we will have great difficulty in writing a reliable history.

Nearly twenty years ago, Zhou Yutong wrote an essay entitled "A Few Suggestions Concerning the Discussion of Confucius." In it he pointed out that if we wanted to talk about Confucius we must first pay attention to the problem of historical materials; second, we must make clear distinctions among the terms Confucian (*Ru*), the Confucian school (*Rujia*), and Confucian teachings (*Rujiao*); third, we must give adequate importance to the influence of Confucius in world cultural history; and finally, we must be sure to master the "basic skills." These were all positive suggestions, and they still merit our attention.[49] At that time Zhou Yutong had already made an appeal about the urgency of the need for a large-scale "Biography of Confucius" and a "History of the Development of Confucian Learning." From the perspective of the present time this task seems even more urgent.

4 | Johann Adam Schall von Bell and Yang Guangxian

In order to progress rather than going backward, we must continuously move beyond ourselves and break new ground, at the very least we must draw material from different regions; if we are hamstrung by all kinds of scruples—to do this would go against our ancestors, to do that would be to ape the foreigners—if all our lives we are as fearful as if skating on thin ice, trembling over whether the time has come yet or not, we'll never get anything done.[50]

1

In the 1660s the Qing court was greatly shaken by the *I Could Not Do Otherwise* (*Bu de yi*) case, in which Yang Guangxian laid accusations against officials of the Bureau of Astronomy.

In the official records of the Qing dynasty, however, it is difficult to find a trace of this matter. The records of the reigns of Shunzhi and Kangxi were revised over and over from Yongzheng to Guangxu, and the record of this particular case became vague and unclear at an early period. If one consults such sources as Jiang Liangqi's *Archival Re-*

cords of the Qing Dynasty (Donghua lu),[51] there is only a brief note on the outcome of the case, a record that not only lacks detail but is clearly prejudiced in favor of Yang Guangxian. Although Ruan Yuan's *Biographies of Mathematical Astronomers (Zhou ren zhuan)* includes biographies of Adam Schall von Bell, Ferdinand Verbiest, and Yang Guangxian, it is an even more brazen apologetic for Yang Guangxian.

In spite of this paucity of information, it is possible to demonstrate, through fragmented records from both official and private sources, that this case had some remarkably "coincidental" linkages to important events in the Shunzhi and Kangxi reigns. For example, why did the Qing government take on this case just at the point when the Shunzhi emperor had died and Kangxi was child emperor under the regency of four high Manchu officials, including Oboi and Suksaha, among others? Why was it that when Kangxi managed to snatch power away from these four officials, he immediately rehabilitated Schall and had Yang Guangxian sent into exile for the crime of "having helped Oboi in ensnaring people by fabricated statements"?

The only way we can make a clear analysis of these various suspicious linkages is by getting hold of more complete historical materials, especially those relating to the person under accusation. Of course, we need to start with some sort of premise: let it be that we should not wear glasses of any color as we seek clarity on this issue.

Early in the twentieth century Lu Xun used the selections in Ruan Yuan's excerpted account of the *I Could Not Do Otherwise* case to demonstrate cogently that Yang Guangxian was wrong from the perspective of science, and that it was the Qing court, then in control of the Han, that recognized the Westerner Schall as being correct in the end. Yet, Lu Xun never took this discussion any further. Helpful material in solving this puzzle is the biography of Schall published by the German scholar Alfons Väth in 1933. The author of this volume used over two thousand items, including both handwritten letters and published books of the missionaries in China in that period, and some of this material is relevant to the question under discussion here. The book as a whole tends to view the author's compatriot, Schall, as a holy martyr worthy of a special accolade, yet one cannot really say it is any more prejudiced than Ruan Yuan's account. The latter was even mistaken about the age of Schall, while Väth was at least knowledgeable enough to subject historical sources to critical testing before believing them.

Surprisingly, although the Chinese version of this book appeared in

1949,[52] only in the last two years have historical materials on the Qing dynasty cited it.

My intention in this essay is to draw upon sources relating to both sides of the case and construct a description of this important early confrontation between Chinese and Western culture.

2

In the history of cultural interaction between China and the West during the seventeenth century, Schall's reputation is nearly as illustrious as that of the great Italian Jesuit Matteo Ricci. In fact, the practical contribution of this German Jesuit to China might be seen as even greater than that of Matteo Ricci.

Matteo Ricci entered China in 1583, reached Beijing in 1601, and died there in 1610, having lived in the imperial capital for just ten years. His work was appreciated by the Wanli emperor, and he had close relations with many high officials. He cooperated with Xu Guangqi in translating the first six books of Clavius's *Elements of Euclid* under the title of *A First Textbook in Geometry* (*Jihe yuanben*) and the *Measures* (*Celiang fayi*) of Clavius, and with Li Zhizao in translating Clavius's *Astrolabe* (*Hun gai gongxian tushuo*) and *Arithmetic* (*Gongwen suanzhi*), among other works. There can be little doubt that his greatest achievement was to enable Christianity to be revived and given a public hearing again, after it had been virtually silenced and left without a trace for two centuries. He also gained the respect and even the envy of the scholar-official class. He died too early, however, and his successors, Longobardo and Diaz, were men of more ordinary talents. Longobardo was so ignorant of Chinese national feeling as to plan revisions to Ricci's legacy, which had given such respect to Chinese cultural tradition. If the great Christian scholar-officials Xu Guangqi, Li Zhizao, Yang Tingjun, and others had not put out tremendous efforts to defend this legacy, the European missionaries might have been expelled from China in 1616.

Just when "the Nanjing Church persecution" was nearly over in 1622, Johann Adam Schall von Bell, a missionary sent out by the Society of Jesus in Portugal, entered Guangzhou through Macao. This German missionary soon demonstrated that he alone had the talent to follow in the footsteps of Matteo Ricci.

On entering China, he chose for himself the name of Tang

Ruowang,[53] and the studio name of Daowei. In the spring of the following year he reached Beijing and took up Chinese studies with Xu Guangqi. When he had mastered just enough Chinese to express what he wanted to say in a simple way, his knowledge of astronomy became known, as he was preparing to measure a lunar eclipse. This left a deep impression on Xu Guangqi. Later, after his chief assistant in calendar reform—the Swiss missionary Terrenz—had died of illness in 1630, Xu immediately made a memorandum to the court asking that Schall be transferred from Xi'an to Beijing, and that Schall and the Italian missionary Jacobus Rho, who had been originally in Shanxi, be given posts in the Calendrical Bureau.

Unfortunately, Xu Guangqi died in 1633, and his successor, Li Tianzong, was weak and ineffective. He was unable to fend off attacks from Wu Wenkui, the head of the Imperial Astronomical Bureau, who was intent on defending the traditional calendar. To make matters worse, Rho also died in 1638, and the whole responsibility for the reform of the calendar fell on the shoulders of Schall. By that time he was already an old China hand, thoroughly familiar with the intrigues of the imperial bureaucracy.

He originally had little knowledge of craftsmanship or technical work, but through self-study and experimentation he succeeded in manufacturing all kinds of ingenious instruments relating to astronomy, optics, and mechanics. These he constantly presented to the Chongzhen emperor. This caused the emperor to view him as a polymath and to request that he cast "red barbarian cannons" in order to hold off the Manchu Eight Banner cavalry troops that were getting near the city gates. Schall could not refuse this request. Without anyone to instruct him, he got enough information from books to guide the workmen in casting powerful cannons. The fact that he succeeded in this project gave him the reputation almost of a magician. When the Manchus, by capturing the craftsmen as prisoners of war, got control of the technology for making cannons, Schall's reputation reached their ears as well. That he was thoroughly versed in astronomy further enhanced the mystique surrounding his name.

In the summer of 1644, when Beijing changed hands three times in less than three months and the whole city was a site of violence and devastation, Schall decided to escape. He expected martyrdom and never imagined that things would turn out just the opposite. Li Zizheng, who was just preparing to take the throne, treated him with great favor. The next government to take over the city also held him in high regard.

In July 1644 by the old calendar,[54] Dorgon rejected the new almanac put forward by the astronomical officials of the Ming dynasty and ordered the Westerner Schall to take the lead in establishing a new calendar for the next year. This shows how, in a close parallel to the situation of other newly established dynasties, the heads of this new dynasty were immediately set on "setting the first day of the year and of each month," which meant using the name of the new imperial ruler to publicize a new calendar. This was intended to let the whole country understand that the new emperor was the only one who could truly represent the will of heaven.

Dorgon selected Schall to undertake this highly prestigious commission, not because he was a Westerner, but because under the Ming dynasty he had already developed an excellent almanac, which had not been issued or implemented. In his view, it did not matter much whether the imperial astronomers among those he had subjugated were Chinese or Westerners, since the Manchus themselves had been regarded as barbarians under the Ming dynasty.

For his part, Schall viewed both the Ming and Qing dynasties in the same light. He was a Western missionary, and the changes in China's secular government were not important to him in themselves. What mattered was which secular rulers would have policies favorable to the work of the missionaries. His only reason for feeling regret at the death of the Chongzhen emperor was that "if he had not died, the deeds he could have done for the Church and the people would certainly have been even greater."

When the Qing army occupied Beijing and the troops threatened the very existence of his church, he immediately presented a petition in person to the new government, requesting that he be treated differently from Han residents. Fan Wencheng immediately ordered that protection be given to Schall's church, the three thousand volumes of Western literature, and the Chongzhen calendar, which was already cut in blocks for printing. Of course, Schall understood the implications of this. Therefore, in July 1644, the first year of Shunzhi, when Dorgon called Schall in and asked him to prepare a new almanac, he immediately presented Dorgon with a set of Western astronomical instruments and "asked that all those who were using new calendrical methods should always rely on calculations made with new Western methods."[55]

Schall's decision to cooperate with the Qing rulers undoubtedly arose from a calculation of the secular advantages and disadvantages. While he himself did not turn to a nonsecular source of help, its power presented itself through a coincidence—the eclipse of the sun on September 1, 1644 (Western calendar). This eclipse was predicted by Han, Mongol, and Western astronomers of all persuasions, but since it happened precisely in the period of dynastic transition from Ming to Qing, it had implications for the accurate announcement of the collapse of the Ming, for the appropriate time and place for the ceremony of prayer to avert disaster, and for demonstrating to the people the level of heaven's concern for the new dynasty. The imperial government led by Dorgon gave a particular importance to this kind of natural occurrence. Yet they were faced with three different predictions, and they had to make a choice, in order to send out a notice to the whole country concerning this ceremony. The practical outcome was a victory for Schall. The prediction he made through Western methods of calculation was completely accurate, whereas the predictions made by the Han and Mongol astronomers were clearly inaccurate.

As a result, the next month the Qing rulers held the ceremony for entering the capital, and even before this Schall was made head of the Imperial Astronomical Bureau. That this position, carrying heavy responsibilities though not much prestige, was given to a European who came from the other side of the great ocean was unprecedented in Chinese history.

Nevertheless, Schall was hesitant about accepting it and going against a personal vow taken when he left his home that he would never seek any secular honor. Finally, under pressure from Dorgon and at the urging of the head of the Society of Jesus in China, Francisco Furtado, he accepted the post somewhat unwillingly, on condition that he should not actually be on duty at the Astronomical Bureau, and that he would not accept a government salary. Furtado ordered him to accept the post based on a calculation of the secular consequences—in other words, fear that if he persisted in refusing the post, this would lead the new dynasty to harbor suspicions about the missionaries.[56]

3

The Shunzhi reign lasted for eighteen years, a period in which much happened. There was continuing internal warfare, and social order remained chaotic, as the new government was feeling its way with both Manchu and Han members. Also, internal power struggles were endemic in court.

As the chief imperial astronomer, Schall could not have avoided facing the political intrigues of the palace. "The Manchus hold the highest respect for astronomical science. So they looked upon Schall, the representative scholar in this field, as an outstanding and excellent person; since he had such a thorough knowledge of heavenly phenomena, he must by definition have a thorough understanding of all that happened on earth."[57] This astrological role, of course, was not an easy one to fulfill, especially when the matters on which he was consulted related to power struggles at the highest levels.

Clearly, Schall did not do a bad job, since he was quickly able to make friends with a group of princes, dukes, and ministers. Among these was the eldest son of Nurhaci, the first of "the four great *beile*,"[58] Prince Li, whose name was Dai Shan.[59] He enabled Schall to learn all about the founding of the Qing dynasty. There was also the "Zhuge Liang" of the early Qing, Fan Wencheng, one of the grand secretaries. He protected Schall from the time he entered Beijing, and overcame all the obstacles thrown up by his opponents, ensuring that Schall was made head of the Imperial Astronomical Bureau. There was also the then king of Korea, who was in Beijing.

But Schall's greatest triumph lay in the fact that he successively gained the confidence of Dorgon and Shunzhi, and also the empress. Dorgon was actually prince regent. He had so much respect for Schall's ability to predict heavenly phenomena and his thorough understanding of physics that when he revived the Ming dynasty plans for large-scale construction of the Forbidden City, no one dared to offer any objections, since Schall said that it was not in accord with heaven's will for this project to be given up half way. Boerjijite, Shunzhi's own mother, who was the daughter of a Mongol aristocrat, through a small stratagem of Schall's in 1651, came to believe that he had cured the serious illness of her niece, who was about to marry Shunzhi and become empress. She was so grateful to him that she treated this Western missionary with the same respect as her own father and his generation.[60]

The decade in which Shunzhi reigned personally might be seen as the most illustrious period of Schall's forty-four years in China. Shunzhi got to know Schall at the age of fourteen, the year he came to the throne. At this time Schall was already a silver-haired old man of sixty. An old man of such rich life experience easily gained the interest of a young man bursting with curiosity, especially since this old man came from Western Europe, where there was a tradition of respect for youth. Even more to the point, this old man well understood the great benefits that could be derived from making friends with a young man who was emperor. Thus Schall quickly gained the trust of the young emperor, and this trust was undoubtedly enhanced through the recommendation Fan Wencheng gave to Schall and the praise accorded to him by the dowager empress. If one judges from the letters and reports sent by Schall and others to Europe,[61] the feeling that Shunzhi had for Schall clearly exceeded the normal category of relations between emperor and official.

The emperor called Schall "mafa," which means "grandfather" in Manchurian, quite likely because the dowager empress always regarded Schall as a kind of "father" figure, and not merely because of the gap in age. The head of the Astronomical Bureau was only an official of the fifth rank, which was eight levels below a grand secretary, so his reports should have gone through an official at the same level in the Board of Rites, then been registered with the Transmission Office before they could be sent up to the emperor. But the emperor had stipulated that "grandfather" should not be constrained by this kind of red tape, and that he could personally present at any time any request he had for the emperor to look over. Not only did the emperor absolve "grandfather" from the requirement of kneeling before him on approach, but even when he was lying in bed he had "grandfather" sit by his bedside and answer all his questions about many things in the world. Also, the emperor disregarded his own position as superior to Schall and often came to Schall's residence in the church at the Xuanmen gate to see "grandfather," either taking a light carriage with a small entourage or slipping past his bodyguard completely. Schall's biographer, Väth, estimated that in the thirteenth and fourteenth years of his reign (1656–57) he made this kind of visit twenty-four times, that is, about once a month.

We should recognize that the circulation of information in the Middle Ages was not as poor as one would imagine, especially information relating to the activities of the emperor, which could be circulated throughout the country in about fifty days through official reports, word of mouth, and private letters. This makes it easy to understand that the special relationship between the emperor and Schall was likely to carry with it dramatic consequences.

The first group to benefit were the Christian missionaries and believers. Any missionary in China who ran into difficulty in any region within reach of the Qing army "only had to claim to belong to the same group as Schall or be one of his relatives, and he could get permission to move freely in the country, also gain the importance and respect accorded to high officials or other levels of official by the people. Furthermore, he could demand the right to proselytize freely."[62] According to the report made by Verbiest to the head of the Society of Jesus, Christianity was known in the early Qing dynasty as "the religion of the great Adam Schall," a polite translation of "old Schall's religion."[63]

Can one say, on the other hand, that the emperor and his representatives gained no benefits from this interchange? By no means. It is true that Shunzhi was underage when he took over the government, yet due to his position and the environment, he seems to have matured very early. Therefore he had only come to trust Schall after a period of doubt. This forced Schall to be especially careful and circumspect, making sure he never stepped beyond the limits of the authority given to him, and never sent letters to the court unless he absolutely had to. This meant, of course, that the messages he sent in relation to important events had even greater force, since "he was a man of few words, but what he did say hit the mark."[64]

Let us take two examples. In 1659 the invading armies of Coxinga had quickly subdued the three large land areas in the lower reaches of the Yangzi River. Nanjing was surrounded, Anqing was conquered, and many people in the Jiangnan area were hastening to proclaim themselves "antigovernment." The twenty-two-year-old Shunzhi was at first frightened out of his wits and was preparing to abandon Beijing and flee back to the Northeast. For this he was severely rebuked by the dowager empress, and in his violent anger he went to the opposite extreme, announcing that he was about to personally lead a punitive expedition. Everyone knew that for him to lead such an expedition personally would be a hopeless act, staking everything on a single venture, and they were even more afraid. Yet no one could control his rage, not even his mother or his stepmother. "In this situation there was only one person who could help, that was Schall. All of the imperial relatives and nobles, all of the heads of ministries, and many court officials formed a long line going to Schall's residence, earnestly begging him to assist. He refused for some time, but finally he gave in and acceded to their request, because if the Manchu regime was thrown into chaos the church would also suffer the consequences. So he resolved 'for the sake of the people's safety, the reputation of the Jesuits, and the future of the church, to place his own life at stake.' "[65] The next day, after prayer and a tearful farewell to the priests staying behind in the church, he went to see the emperor, trembling for his life. Naturally he used the pretext of the will of heaven to bring the emperor around. To his surprise, the emperor accepted his view, since he felt that "grandfather's" proposed strategy of sending out a new army and promising substantial rewards if they pacified the "pirates" would be even more effective than his idea of personally leading an expedition. "For this reason Schall was called a savior of the nation, and many nobles and distinguished people constantly came to his abode and bowed down to the priest in a show of respect to him and his colleagues."[66]

In the early spring of 1661, the emperor became infected with smallpox, one of the most frightening diseases of the time. His favorite concubine, Donger, had died in childbirth with her infant six months earlier, and this had grieved him to the point that he did not want to live. After three days of illness, he suddenly died. These three days were undoubtedly the most disturbed period since the Qing dynasty had come to power. According to the teaching of Nurhaci's ancestors, the Qing emperor did not establish a crown prince in advance, but the heads of the Eight Banners were to recommend a successor for the position of ruler. Although this regulation had been more or less broken by the fact that Huang Taiji, Shunzhi's father, had concentrated power in his own person, nevertheless it was still formally part of the "ancestral regulations." Although Shunzhi was a young man, he already had four sons. Therefore, when he had contracted what everyone knew to be a fatal disease, the problem became urgent: should a successor be established in accordance with the tradition of earlier Chinese dynasties, or in accordance with the traditions of their own Manchu race? Perhaps because he was feeling repentant that he had not paid respect to the ancestral teachings in his own behavior, the twenty-four-year-old Shunzhi suggested that the succession be given to one of his cousins. His mother, Dowager Empress Boerjijite, discussed this matter with the leaders of the Eight Banners and concluded that to make one of his sons successor would be more conducive to maintaining order and stability. The emperor, who was by now critically ill, immediately sent someone to ask "grandfather's" opinion. We do not know Schall's original thoughts on this; we only know that he immediately sent in a memorandum, with a proposal affirming the views of the dowager empress and the leaders of the Eight Banners, also specifically suggesting as successor the third son of the emperor, Xuanye, who was the most outstanding of his sons. The reason he gave was that Xuanye had already had smallpox, so he would be able to fill the post of emperor for a long period without anxiety about his health. This suggestion clearly touched the emperor, who was by this time on the verge of death. He immediately ordered a draft will to be written, saying that Xuanye be made his successor, and then died at once.

In March 1661 Xuanye succeeded to the throne at the tender age of eight, and this year was known as the first year of Kangxi. Just before death, Shunzhi gave the responsibilities of rule while the young emperor was a minor to a group of high officials, in accordance with precedent. There were four of them in all, and the leader was Kangxi's maternal grandfather, Soni. The other three were Suksaha, Ebilun, and Oboi, none of whom was from the imperial household. Possibly Shunzhi's idea was that bannermen who were not from the imperial household would be more easily controlled by the emperor. Who was to know that opposite would be the case? Soni was too old and died shortly after. Ebilun was too stupid, and whatever the situation, he simply held his tongue and kept silent. Suksaha had been an official in Dorgon's family, and although he was in a position close to the ear of the young prince, he lacked any hold on the power of the army. So Oboi came to the fore. He was a military noble from the Bordered Yellow Banner, one of the three most highly ranked banners. It was directly under the emperor, and he should have been loyal to the Kangxi emperor as the leader of these three banners. Who was to guess that he would quickly adopt the stock tricks of a Cao Cao in the *Romance of the Three Kingdoms* and plot to bring the emperor under his power and order the dukes about in his name?

Since he was plotting to control over the emperor, of course he did not want Schall to continue as an adviser to the new emperor. Schall had had such a position of prestige and influence, he probably never imagined that as a result of this reign change he would find himself in prison.

At this point we must turn to Yang Guangxian.

4

In the late Ming period Yang Guangxian had had a great reputation. He was an assistant guard commander (*fu qianhu*) of the Xinanwei, a position very close to that of a vice-regimental leader in the succeeding dynasty. Just like Xi Wenqing, the guard commander depicted in the novel *Golden Lotus* (*Jin ping mei*), this man also used the technique of raking up charges against others as a means of promoting his own interests. He had his eyes fixed on the money pots of wealthy families, and he would fabricate criminal accusations and uncover shameful secrets as a means of blackmail. It is said that he hounded to death over a hundred persons, so one can be sure that the profits he gained for himself by this means were considerable.

Possibly because he was so successful at the local level, he suddenly decided to go to the imperial capital to display his skills to the full. So he handed over his military position to his brother and left Anhui for Beijing in 1637 to ''bow before the palace gates and present a memorandum.''

The first person to come under his attack was Chen Qixin, who was supervising secretary in the Board of Civil Appointments. Yang claimed that Chen's origins were base and that he was practicing favoritism and accepting bribes. To his surprise, this memorial to the throne was rejected by the Transmission Office. After he came up against this stone wall, he simply bought a coffin, had it brought to the entrance to the Forbidden City, and made an accusation against Wen Tiren, the grand secretary. This carrying of a coffin was a rare sight, especially since the one under accusation was prime minister of the ruling dynasty. It naturally caused a sensation in the capital city. Wen Tiren already had a reputation for being an evil prime minister, so Yang Guangxian's behavior was seen as heroic. As they passed by, people wrote poems and threw them into the coffin. But when he went to the gate of the palace with the coffin full of poems and commentaries, he was met by the full blast of the emperor's rage and was first beaten before the court, then sent into exile in Liaoxi. Later Wang Shizheng described this incident, giving his assessment that, while Yang Guangxian got the reputation of someone who dared to speak out, ''he was certainly the epitome of a philistine.''[67]

His period of exile came to an end with the destruction of the Ming. Yet during his years in Liaoxi he had learned some new tactics for embezzling money—practicing astrology and telling fortunes. Later he left the army, returned to the village, and again took up his old tricks of litigation, but evidently now that he no longer had the position of a vice-regimental leader, he got into such a dangerous situation that there were people after his life. So he escaped death by going to Beijing. In Beijing he used his magical techniques to gain familiarity with a certain Manchu prince and as a result managed to pose as an expert in astronomy and move in noble and official circles.

Just at this point his jealousy flared up and he became furiously envious of the reputation Schall had built up as an astronomer among the Manchus.

In 1659, he wrote a book criticizing the Western calendar entitled *On Collecting Errors* (*Zhai miu lun*) and a book attacking Christianity under the title *On Exposing Heterodoxy* (*Bi xie lun*). But it was only at the end of the following year that he finally sent up a memorandum to the Board of Rites entitled *A Call to Rectify the Country* (*Zheng guoti ching*), which laid accusations against the calendar put together by Schall. In this document, he claimed, was found over and over the annotation "in accordance with the new Western calendar." Schall's hidden intentions were unfathomable and included "stealing the authority to define the first month and giving it to the West," and "clearly telling the Great Qing to fall in line with the Western calendar." He also accused Schall of using the Western calendar secretly to perpetrate evil teaching, and of seeking a hold over the nation and people by this teaching.[68]

In a way different from his accusation against Wen Tiren twenty-five years earlier, Yang launched this attack on Schall. From the opportunity used to the reasons given, it was clear that he had carefully selected every point.

The emperor had already begun to develop a strong interest in Buddhism from about 1657, and he had come to like the cleverness of the Chan monks. Thus, while he showed as much respect to Schall as ever, he gradually had less and less contact. Especially after the death of Donger in August 1660, Shunzhi was grieved to the point he did not wish to live. Unwilling to listen to the dissuasions of the dowager empress and "grandfather," he insisted that he wanted to become a monk and had the famous monk Mao Xisen shave his head for him. For a while the court was in chaos, and no one was able to get the emperor to change his mind. Just at this point Yu Luxin, the teacher of Mao Xisen, hurried up from Hangzhou and immediately used the technique of the head of the Chan religion, Peng Ke, ordering the monks to build up a pyre and to burn Mao Xisen to death on it, since he had dared to make the nation lose its ruler. It was only at this point that Shunzhi became "aware" that he should not have given up his duty to "all living things" just because he had lost interest in worldly phenomena. He agreed to find someone to take his place as a monk and to return to secular life and let his hair grow again.

But this tragicomedy had a clear message—that Schall's influence over the emperor was on the wane. It was thus an opportune moment for those who saw religion as linked to secular advantage to get close to the emperor.

Those who felt they had suffered certain losses due to the activities of Schall were a very complex group. There were certain Manchu and Mongolian nobles who secretly clung to old-fashioned ways of life, and from an early period they had noted with displeasure the fact that the emperor and the dowager empress had lost some of their earlier enthusiasm for Buddhism and Lamaism. In 1652, the Dalai Lama had entered the capital, and the emperor did not personally go out to welcome him at a distance. The dowager empress also showed indifference to him, something that clearly showed the effects of Schall's admonishing. In the trade between China and the outside world, the merchants of the western region (Xinjiang and parts of Central Asia), who gained great benefits, particularly enjoyed the advantages of the tradition that Mongol astronomers control the Astronomical Bureau, since the latter could explain the will of heaven along lines that were beneficial to their trade. When Schall and his Christian disciples controlled the Astronomical Bureau, however, this was a serious threat to them. When the Buddhist monks spoke to Shunzhi, there were always eunuchs standing in the background, as ever since the Ming period they had been the representatives of the monk landlords in the palace. While the various forces had conflicts among themselves, they were all united in opposition to the power of the heretical religion that Schall represented.

Thus, even though it had been Buddhist believers who lured Shunzhi to leave his household, and Buddhism and Islam were both foreign religions, Yang Guangxian did not say a word against them when he called for "rectifying the spirit of the nation." Rather, he laid all the blame for the national spirit being "unrectified" on Schall and the Christian Church. From this one can see the traces of some sort of hidden plot.

This petition of Yang Guangxian was not accepted by the Board of Rites. Perhaps this was because the head of the Board of Rites judged that the emperor still doted on Schall. Events proved this to be the case, as within a few days Shunzhi contracted smallpox and died, and the opinion that finally persuaded him to agree to the dowager empress's wish that Kangxi be his successor was none other than Schall's.

The death of Shunzhi and the minority of Kangxi, however, created a situation in which the four high officials jointly ran the government as regents. Yang Guangxian had a supporter among these four officials. According to the letters of the missionaries at this time, it was Suksaha. Later, when Kangxi rehabilitated Schall, it was thought to be Oboi.

At this time Yang was secure in the knowledge that he had strong backing so he continued to push Schall along the road leading to death.

5

Thus Schall found himself in the difficult position of being attacked front and rear. To make things worse, he had already lost several years in fending off attacks from some of his fellow missionaries just before this time.

From the time of Matteo Ricci, the European missionaries in China had normally carried out their activities as "visiting foreigners." They did not take official positions and did not accept salaries. The first recorded instance of one taking an official position in the Chinese government was that of Schall. Not only did he become an official of the Qing court, but the number of his official titles gradually increased and the level of his rank rose. From the beginning he held the position of head of the Astronomical Bureau, but over the twelve years from 1646 to 1658 he was continuously raised to higher positions. The titles conferred upon him included subdirector of the Court of Sacrificial Worship, director of the Court of the Imperial Stud, director of the Court of Sacrificial Worship, commissioner in the Transmission Office, high senator, and high honorable bearer of the imperial banquet. This meant that he was at the level of a bureau head and by imperial favor was treated as a mandarin of the first rank. Furthermore, in 1653 Shunzhi conferred on "grandfather" a special title—"teacher versed in metaphysics" (*tongxuan jiaoshi*)—to recognize him as the greatest expert in astronomy and calendrical studies, one who could not be equaled by anyone, from Luo Xiaheng and Zheng Heng in the Han dynasty to Guo Shoujing in the Yuan dynasty. According to custom, all officials higher than the third rank had a patent, which meant that titles were conferred on their relatives. Schall received this honor twice, with the second patent going back three generations to his grandparents.

Needless to say, no matter what Schall's personal inclinations were, his main activities were in official circles rather than in the church and his home became more like a kind of official residence than a church. He gradually became more and more absorbed in official duties and had a difficult time observing religious rules.[69]

Since this was the case, he was not really a monk in the eyes of Chinese people, and in the eyes of the other European missionaries he was suspected of having turned his back on the pure rules and laws of the Society of Jesus.

The Society of Jesus was originally a conservative body that opposed the Protestant Reformation. The brothers who entered the society had to swear that they would never aspire to or accept positions of honor, unless ordered to do so under obedience. When Schall accepted a high-ranking official position in China, he and his supporters saw this as a sacrifice that had to be made for the sake of doing missionary work. It nevertheless was in accord with the goal that had been laid down for the mission—to use European science and the moral integrity of the missionaries to gain the respect and trust of the Chinese scholar-officials, and then by setting an example for the scholar-officials to gradually preach Christianity. But was his sacrifice a genuine one? Was not his occupation with public duties, official responsibilities, and activities of the court proof that he had been contaminated by secular life? Otherwise, since he was on such intimate terms with the emperor and notables of the court, why did he not persuade them to believe in Christianity? Furthermore, his Chinese housekeeper, Pan Jinxiao, was abrupt and rude in his dealings with the outside, yet Schall went so far as to ask the emperor for a grace-and-favor title for him and adopted his son as his own—at Shunzhi's suggestion. Did this not show that there were many questionable areas in his personal life?

In the secret discussions that went on among the missionaries, suspicions accumulated and were soon translated into public censure and the exposure of supposed misdeeds. The first to censure Schall were the Italian missionary Luigi Buglio and the Portuguese missionary Gabriel de Magalhães.

These two men had originally propagated the faith in Chengdu, and when Zhang Xianzhong established the Great Western Regime, he commissioned them to take responsibility for the Imperial Astronomical Bureau. In 1646 when the emperor's relative Haoge defeated Zhang Xianzhong, he took them as prisoners of war, along with the other officials who had been taken prisoner. When Magalhães was about to be put to death, he cried out in desperation that Schall was his "elder brother." Haoge immediately ordered a stay of execution and had them sent to Beijing. Dorgon confirmed that they were "implicated in rebellion" and ordered that they be made slaves in one of the banners. Even though their masters dared not treat them as slaves, because of their relation to Schall, and actually gave them the courtesy of guests, they still felt their adverse situation was due to Schall's unwillingness to save them. Thus they were extremely angry with him. Their individual prejudices soon developed into sectarian conflicts. From 1649, they joined up with Furtado and Longobardo and made a whole series of accusations against Schall to both the China mission of the Jesuits and the headquarters in Europe, saying that he had behaved incorrectly, that he had violated his oath, that he was corrupt in his manner of living, and that his morals had become decadent. After many years of repeated debates, investigations, countercharges, and so forth, it was proven that Schall's private behavior was beyond reproach, except for the fact that he had a tendency to be quick tempered, and he could also be very sharp tongued.

But a more serious accusation than that against his personal morality was that he had betrayed the teachings of Christianity in taking on the headship of the Imperial Astronomical Bureau and the task of compiling the almanac. The first to express misgivings over this was the Italian missionary Aleni. When he entered China, during the Wanli reign of the late Ming, he had been nicknamed by the scholar-officials "the Confucius of the West," and he was the most senior of all the missionaries in China in the early Qing.[70] The main point of his criticism focused on the issue of whether or not Schall ought to hold his position as head of the Astronomical Bureau. After Schall had been given the chance to respond to the charges laid and had gained the support of Furtado, the whole case quietly subsided. But in 1649 Magalhães brought the matter up again and managed to persuade Furtado to change his original position of support for Schall, getting him to sign the draft of an article opposing Schall's holding the position of head of the Astronomical Bureau and his editing of the almanac. Using Furtado's authority as head of North China Mission, he drafted and sent out an official notice demanding that Schall resign from his post.

This notice listed ten reasons for demanding Schall's resignation.[71] The first charged that the duties of the head of the Astronomical Bureau were not in accord with Christian beliefs, and that the almanac and the predictions of heavenly phenomena given to the emperor included superstitions and practices of divination. Second, Schall was charged with having said things that contravened "the Scripture" and the Church's teaching after he became head of the Astronomical Bureau. The document contained threats that Schall's words and behavior were already seriously enough at fault for a case to be made to the Vatican court, and if he insisted on remaining in the post, he would have to be excommunicated.

Naturally, Schall raised a counterplea to this notice. He presented his famous appeal, the *Document of Refutation* (*Bianbo shu*) to the Society of Jesus on March 7, 1652 (Western calendar). (Unfortunately, this document has not so far been translated into Chinese.) Standing on his side were the Italian missionaries Brancati and Gravina, also the Dutch missionary Jacobus Motel. Later the Portuguese missionary Diaz, who was head of the China Mission of the Society of Jesus and who had originally had an attitude of suspicion, also took his side, as did the Italian missionary Martino Martini.

Schall and his associates focused on the first point of accusation in their refutation of the charges. They did their utmost to prove that the Astronomical Bureau was not a superstitious organization and that the almanac was not primarily a book emphasizing divination. They took examples from the Christian saints to show that the relation between heavenly phenomena and human life had always been recognized by the Church, and that astronomical phenomena directly affected both the fate and the personalities of people on earth. They pointed out that the lucky and unlucky times stipulated by the Chinese almanac were no different than the prophecies and predictions made by European almanacs. They particularly emphasized that in the period since Schall had been heading the Astronomical Bureau, he could not take responsibility for the whole almanac, since there was evidence to show that the parts which he had edited were all clearly marked as "according to the new calendar." Those parts not annotated in this way had been edited by Chinese officials of the Astronomical Bureau who followed traditional means of calculation. Schall did not interfere with their work out of respect for Chinese culture, but he could not be held responsible for it.

It was easy to see that if the first point was successfully refuted, then the other nine points could be turned back without any question. For this reason the controversy among the missionaries in China, which went on over a long time, mainly centered on this point.

Finally the conflict reached the point of disturbing the Jesuit Curia itself. In 1655, the head of the Society of Jesus in Rome commissioned five professors to organize a "committee to investigate the problem of the Chinese almanac." It made its first adjudication and the content was supportive of Schall, yet in the matter of whether the Chinese almanac was superstitious or not, the wording was ambiguous. Therefore, after the document reached China in 1659, it once again aroused the counter-charges of Magalhães and Buglio and their supporters. And the Belgian missionary who had come to China most recently, Schall's assistant Ferdinand Verbiest, wrote a very long memorandum in defense of Schall. The Society of Jesus in Rome again commissioned four professors to reexamine the problem of the Chinese almanac, and they made a second adjudication in April 1664 (Western calendar), stating that Schall could continue in the position of head of the Astronomical Bureau as before, "since this work had such a strong connection with the propagation and defense of Christianity in China, also it upheld the dignity of the Church."[72]

No one knows when this document reached China and whether or not Schall ever saw it. But everyone knows clearly that the Chinese government was interested solely in Schall's ability as an individual in giving him an official position in the beginning. The purpose was to hire an astronomer and not to reward or support a European missionary. Even when Shunzhi came to have such respect for and trust in Schall, this distinction was still rigorously made.[73] In the period in which he led the Astronomical Bureau, of course Schall could carry out his own purposes, putting all his efforts into both scientific and religious concerns, but this could only be limited to his individual knowledge and faith. The missionaries might well censure him for his individual morality as a missionary, but for them to claim that in his post of official responsibility, or in the content of his work, he departed from the Scriptures and betrayed the faith was already a matter of using religion to interfere in the process of government in the foreign country where they resided as guests. And since the head of the Society of Jesus went so far as to organize a committee to investigate whether or not the Chinese almanac went against the teachings of the Church, no matter how the judgment on this benefited Schall as an individual, it could still only be seen as a clumsy act of interference in China's internal government.

This kind of clumsy act did not help Schall in any way but rather forced him to put forth enormous efforts to defend himself. It was even less helpful for the cause of "disseminating and defending" Christianity in China, as it actually prevented Schall from enhancing his influence as a missionary at the same time as he carried out his public duties. Especially in that transition period between two rulers, Schall had to devote his main energy into ending internal strife, and he could not give his attention to seeking a means to deal with the attack of Yang Guangxian. In the end he was overthrown by a Chinese who was a past master at litigation, and the missionaries in China were more or less knocked out in force by this happening. If one said that the attack launched against Schall by Magalhães and Buglio and joined by Longobardo, Furtado, and other leaders in the Society of Jesus was enough to give a real boost to Yang Guangxian and the other medieval-style Chinese politicians, would not this be close to the truth?

6

Nevertheless, the contest between Schall and Yang Guangxian went on for more than three years. The reason for this was related to the fact that there were natural adjustments in power during the transition period, that the four high officials of the regency government were seeking to keep a check on one another, and that the mother of Shunzhi and grandmother of Kangxi, who had already become grand dowager empress, had not yet lost her position as arbitrator for the four regents. In this situation Suksaha and Oboi showed courtesy to Schall on the surface at least.

Meanwhile, Yang Guangxian was seeking a good excuse to bring about the demise of Schall and his associates. It was Schall himself who finally provided the excuse, and those who brought this disaster upon him were Magalhães and Buglio.

After the first ruling of the Roman Church concerning the Chinese almanac was made in 1651 and brought to China by Simon de Cunha,[74] Magalhães and Buglio did not accept it at the beginning. Yet it was just at this time that Yang Guangxian began to publish, one after another, his *I Could Not Do Otherwise*, *A Call to Rectify the Country*, and other works that demanded that Christianity be strictly forbidden. Probably because they felt a common threat, they gradually changed their position to one of support for Schall in opposition to Yang Guangxian.

In 1664 Li Zubai, the vice-head of the Astronomical Bureau, published his famous *Survey of the Propagation of the Teaching of Heaven* (*Tianxue chuangai*).[75] The book directly refuted Yang Guangxian's *On Exposing Heterodoxy*. The actual authors are said to have been Magalhães and Buglio, but it had been polished by Li Zubai, had been given a preface by the Hanlin academician Xu Zhijian, and those responsible for publishing it were Pan Jinxiao and the eunuch Xu Baolu.[76] The latter four Chinese were all Christians, Li Zubai and Pan Jinxiao being respectively Schall's student and his housekeeper.

Schall himself, however, was not clear about this development. In the late spring of that year he had had a stroke that left his limbs paralyzed so that he could neither move the lower half of his body nor speak. He was only able to carry out his duties with the help of Verbiest.

The absurdity of the arguments devised by Magalhães and Buglio in the book paralleled that of Yang Guangxian's writings. According to Väth's account, they asserted that Christianity was the oldest and most complete religion and that it had been followed by China's earliest peoples. Since Fuxi originally had been the descendant of Adam and had moved from the land of the Jews to China to become the founder of the Chinese race, "Chinese philosophy is like the light of a firefly, if compared with the illustrious light of Christianity."[77]

Was not this a ridiculous thing to say? Xu Zhijian's preface took this argument further, adding insult to injury. Apparently the Christians thought that since the Manchurian aristocrats who had just taken over China were regarded as barbarians by the Han, they might appreciate this kind of argument, which showed how barbarian culture had changed China. Who was to know that it would be seen in just the opposite way—as an attack on one of their important taboos. After the Manchus took up rule, even though they were actually forcing the Han to adopt Manchu customs, their propaganda emphasized that they maintained continuity with the Ming rulers. Schall was deeply aware of this subtlety. And so the clumsy argument of Magalhães and Buglio was probably the result of his having lost control of the situation due to illness.

This mistake was immediately snatched up by Yang Guangxian, who pointed to Schall as the chief force behind it. Schall was extremely ill and could not use his personal influence to protect himself adequately, providing a God-given opportunity for Yang Guangxian. Is there anything more pleasing than the chance to attack an opponent who has no way of retaliating?

He first made the fullest possible use of the foolish statements that appeared in the *Survey of the Propagation of the Teachings of Heaven*, quoting points that he then criticized and refuted in published articles. It has been estimated that about five thousand copies of such articles were distributed in Beijing alone that year. All of his points of refutation can be found in his book *I Could Not Do Otherwise*. Even though his arguments here were equally absurd, they were effective in stirring up antiforeign feelings. Subsequently, in September of the same year (1664) by the Western calendar, he formally submitted a petition to the Board of Rites, making an accusation against Schall and eight others[78] under the title of "A Complaint Requesting Punishment for the Evil Religion" ("Qing zhu xiejiao zhuang"). This was immediately accepted by the Board of Rites and on the same day submitted to the Deliberative Council of the regency. Such efficient treatment gives a clear indication that Yang Guangxian had reached a private agreement or gained a secret promise in advance from Suksaha, Oboi, and the others.

There was another high Manchu aristocrat supporting Yang Guangxian from behind, that is, Anggede, the minister of the Board of Rites. This man had been condemned to death in 1660, because he had privately changed the day chosen by the Astronomical Bureau for the funeral of the child of Shunzhi and Donger, so he was made responsible for the death of Donger, which took place shortly afterward. Yet because Schall made an appeal on his behalf, he was sent into exile rather than being put to death. Because of this old case he still hated Schall and wanted to bring disaster upon him. He therefore positively supported Yang Guangxian and played a key role in the process of overthrowing Schall.

Thus in only ten days, according to the instructions given by the four regents, Schall and the other eight became the first persons sacrificed to Yang Guangxian's accusations. The whole trial lasted for seven months, from September 1664 to April 1665. It was a typical medieval-style trial, even though in appearance correct legal procedures were followed. First Schall was treated as a court official and given a joint hearing by the Board of Rites and the Board of Civil Appointments. Then he was treated as an official removed from office and handed over to the Board of Punishments for interrogation and to the highest court for reexamination. Finally he was brought to judgment before the Deliberative Council, comprised of the princes, regents, grand secretaries, and heads of the six boards and nine bureaus and the Eight Banners. The decision, however, lay not with the law but with power and money.

The detailed sequence of events will not be recounted here.

Väth's biography of Schall, drawing upon the letters and reports of the missionaries of the time and all kinds of documents relating to the trial, provides the most thorough textual research that has been done so far on the subject. So readers who are interested may look at it. Here I only give a few highlights.

In his initial charge, Yang Guangxian accused Schall of three crimes: plotting rebellion, propagating a heretical religion, and disseminating erroneous theories of astronomy. What was the evidence? Some seemed to be given, but in fact there was none. Therefore, in the first stage of the trial process, that is, in the hearing before the Board of Rites and the Board of Civil Appointments, they were refuted one after another by Verbiest. The seventy-two-year-old Schall, because he had had a stroke and could not speak clearly, had instructed Verbiest to speak for him in the investigation.

Take, for example, the charge of plotting rebellion. Yang Guangxian made the accusation that Schall and his associates already had made preparations for an invasion and gave as evidence the fact that the Westerners in Macao had thirty thousand soldiers hidden and waiting for the opportunity to seize control of China. Verbiest claimed in defense that the population of Macao was only two thousand, and that the Chinese living there were under the administration of the authorities in Guangdong. Would it therefore be possible for thirty thousand soldiers to be billeted in Macao without the Chinese knowing about it? The Qing court should send people to Macao to investigate, if there was any truth to the accusation.

Take, for example, the calendar. Yang Guangxian charged that Schall's new calendar was entirely contrary to reason and erroneous. There were altogether ten points of error, and in calculating solar and lunar eclipses it was completely unsuited to the actual movement of heavenly phenomena. As evidence, he stated that the calendar of that year had made an incorrect prediction of the solar eclipse that was expected on the first day of December. Verbiest's defense claimed that Schall's new calendar was different from the old one, that there were forty-two main points of difference, and these could be seen in the *Treatise on Mathematics (and Astronomy) According to the New Methods (Xinfa suanshu)*, which he edited. There was evidence for how it had been used for twenty years in the Qing court, and all of the errors which Yang Guangxian had pointed out had been proven by this book to be actually from the old calendar. As for the coming solar eclipse, the regents and the court should watch this carefully as a test case.

The most difficult charges to respond to were those concerning propagating a heretical religion. The Manchu and Han officials of the Council knew nothing about the tenets of Christianity. But Verbiest made every effort to explain that the reason the missionaries did not marry and crossed the ocean to China to preach their religion was not out of disrespect for the principles of morality held by the Chinese. Rather, they were sacrificing themselves to save mankind. Still, the Christian notion of original sin was difficult for a group of rulers who followed neo-Confucianism to accept. Furthermore, Yang Guangxian provided evidence of the views of Magalhães and other missionaries that all nations, including China, were the descendants of Adam, and this was even more likely to arouse antagonism from the Chinese. Thus, Verbiest's defense of these points was the most difficult for the Manchu aristocrats and officials to understand.

The real problem lay in the fact that the outcome of this lawsuit had actually already been determined at the very beginning. Since the regents had given the order for the interrogation, this meant that the persons under accusation must certainly be in the wrong. Would the council of four regents, who were acting on behalf of the emperor, give a command to interrogate someone who had committed no crime?

No matter how reasonable the defense provided by Schall, Verbiest, and others, it was inevitable that they would be condemned. Yang Guangxian was an old hand at litigation, and of course he knew that if he wished to succeed with the lawsuit and make sense out of something senseless, he needed some secret help from Mammon in addition to openly framing up charges. According to the record of the French missionary who was in China at that time, Adrianus Creston, "in the whole process of the lawsuit, 400,000 taels of silver were spent and there were eighteen precious jewels given to Yang Guangxian by the Muslim believers."[79] Apart from the rich merchants of the western district, who were Islamic believers, there were also Buddhist believers, Lamaist monk groups, and Buddhist eunuchs who provided the wherewithal for Yang Guangxian to bribe the main investigating officials.

Thus, in face of the great and interlinked forces of power, wealth, and tradition, were not Schall and his fellows destined to inevitable failure? Their situation now went from bad to worse. In November 1664 (Western calendar), without waiting for the investigation of the Board of Rites and the Board of Civil Appointments to be completed, the regents used the pretext of the "divine will" to have all eight men thrown into prison. In January 1665 the regents granted the request for Schall to be officially moved to the prison under the Board of Punishments. In only ten days the Board of Punishments made the judgment that Schall should be hung and that Verbiest, Magalhães, Buglio, Li Zubai, and the rest should be given a hundred lashes and expelled from the government. Then they should be reexamined by the highest court.

Just at the time of this reexamination, on the first day of December in 1664 (January 16, 1665, by the Western calendar) the eclipse of the sun took place. To demonstrate that they "enforced the law strictly," and at the request of the four regents, the inner cabinet sent people to observe. They ordered the Western, Han, and Muslim officials of the Astronomical Bureau to calculate the exact time when the eclipse would take place. Verbiest had done the calculations on behalf of Schall, who had already been removed from office, while in the Muslim section the one who did the calculation was an Arabic astronomer who had been nominated by Yang Guangxian. When the actual test came with the first appearance of the eclipse, the group that turned out to be most seriously mistaken was none other than that around Yang Guangxian. Its prediction was half an hour too early. The prediction made according to calculations of the traditional Han calendar was fifteen minutes too early, and the one that turned out to be exactly right was based on the calculations made by Verbiest.[80]

Facts had won a victory over eloquence of argumentation. If there had truly been a will to act according to the law, then this happening alone was enough to show that Yang Guangxian had committed the dual crime of framing someone and of duplicity. He should have been put to death. In the Middle Ages, however, would power bend to the law in this way? Would not the will of the powerholders prevail over the regulations of the law? Eighteen hundred years earlier, that epitome of the rapacious underling, Du Zhou, had expressed the situation in this way: "Where do the law books come from? What earlier rulers thought was correct and wrote down was called law. What later rulers thought was correct became the interpretation of the law. Whatever is said by the rulers of the time is always correct, so what does ancient law mean anyways?"[81]

In this kind of period, under this kind of law, naturally the one to receive severe punishment could only be Schall. Yet this situation actually gave Suksaha, Oboi, and their fellows a problem. They had to take into account that the present dowager empress was a kind of god-daughter to Schall, and that the emperor himself had been selected only after Schall had given his views. Kangxi had been brought up by his grandmother from the time he was very young. Once he was grown up, would he use the pretext that the regents had ignored the facts and punish them? Yet to shrink now from what they had done would be difficult. To admit that Schall's almanac was correct meant, without doubt, to admit that they had ratified Yang Guangxian's error in framing someone. This would not only cause them a "loss of face" before the whole nation, it could well lead to a counterattack by the forces supporting Schall. After one month of secret consultation, they finally thought out a strategy. They decided to call a meeting of the Deliberative Council in the name of the emperor and to hold a formal trial for Schall before this council.

In the new year this imperial assembly was held, that is, between

March and May 1665 by the Western calendar. There were nearly two hundred princes, aristocrats, and eunuchs, including twenty Manchu and Mongol princes, fourteen Manchu and Han grand secretaries, the twelve Manchu and Han heads of the six ministries, the heads of the Eight Banners, and all the members of the cabinet and heads of the various bureaus.[82] This assembly of princes and officials met altogether twelve times. In mid-August they reached their decision: Schall should be put to death by gradual dismemberment, and Verbiest and the other seven should be beheaded. Also, the other six officials of the Astronomical Bureau who had been implicated should be put to death. But this decision had to await approval by the grand dowager empress.

Just at this point the heavens apparently felt there had been a miscarriage of justice and so used a disaster to issue a warning to the son of heaven. Just before the judgment was reached, a comet appeared in the sky. Just after the judgment, Beijing suffered an earthquake that went on for four days. The superstitious princes and officials were frightened to death, and they quickly promised certain blessings to avert catastrophe, on the fourth day of the earthquake announcing an "imperial decree" that pardoned Verbiest, Magalhães, Buglio, and Xu Baoli and had Schall's punishment changed to beheading.

Even though the earthquake ceased, however, other disasters continued to shake the palace, forcing the emperor and his grandmother to sleep out in the open. Since the heavens gave such a series of warnings, the grand dowager empress spoke out. She issued an edict to the regents severely castigating them for having gone against the will of the former emperor in persecuting the high official whom he had specially favored to the point that heaven had to act by sending down disasters. Oboi and his associates had no recourse; the only thing they could do was pardon Schall and his housekeeper, Pan Jinxiao.

But the unfortunate ones were Li Zubai and the other five officials in the Astronomical Bureau, as they were sacrificed by Oboi and the other regents as a means of saving face. They were beheaded in May of that year.

After going through the long drawn-out pressures of prison and trial, Schall became even more severely ill, and not long after he was released from prison he signed his famous *Declaration of Penitence* (*Huigai shu*)[83] in the church, confessing that all the disasters he had brought upon the missionaries and the believers were the result of the fact that he had profaned his sacred mission. Then he calmly pointed out all the outrages Yang Guangxian had perpetrated in his official residence and awaited the homecall of his God.

On August 15, 1666 (Western calendar),[84] in precisely the forty-fifth year since he had entered China, Schall died in Beijing. In accordance with his will, he was buried beside the tomb of Matteo Ricci.

7

And what about Yang Guangxian? Even though events proved that he had made a false accusation and had calculated incorrectly the eclipse of the sun that had just taken place, he was nevertheless commissioned by Oboi and the other regents to be the vice-head of the Astronomical Bureau, taking the place of Li Zubai, who had been put to death. Who was to know that he would not be satisfied with this position and between April and July 1665 would run to the palace five times to tender his resignation? At one point he claimed that he only had theoretical ideas on the almanac, but no practical experience. At another point he said he was getting old and his faculties were not as clear as they had once been. A third story was that he feared reprisals from Schall's supporters in the bureau, since Xu Zhijian was still in Beijing and those working in the bureau were colluding with the followers of the evil religion.

After a period of this kind of whimpering and whining behavior, Oboi and the other regents decided in August of that year to appoint him head of the Astronomical Bureau. In this situation he no longer kept "knocking at the palace gate with threats of resignation" but immediately took over Schall's residence, insisting that it was the official residence of the head of the Astronomical Bureau and not Schall's private home. He led a group of henchmen into the residence to tear down all the religious decor, destroying it completely. He put up his own picture in the place where the picture of Jesus had been, ordering people to place their offerings there morning and evening. He got rid of all the officials in the Astronomical Bureau who taught the Western calendar and promoted the younger brother of Wu Mingxuan, an official who had already been removed from his position in the Imperial Astronomical Bureau. This younger brother, Wu Mingxuan,[85] was of Arabic origin and was made vice-head of the bureau. He used the Muslim calendar, which had already been proved erroneous, to replace the Western calendar. All of this shows clearly that Yang's earlier attempts to resign had been nothing but a kind of pose. In fact he felt he had great merit and his salary was very low, so his offer to resign had been a ploy to gain advancement. All that really mattered to him was to have the position Schall had enjoyed.

Still, he seemed to be aware that he was no more than a snarling dog in the hands of Oboi and the other regents, and the astronomical report of the Imperial Astronomical Bureau had to contain proof of empirical testing for its predictions. To avoid being eliminated, now that his usefulness to the regents was over, and to strive for further official advancement, he used two different ploys.

The first was to publish his *I Could Not Do Otherwise.* This was a collection of twenty-eight essays in which he attacked the Western calendar and Western religion. In it the essay "Requesting the Emperor to Allow My Resignation" ("Kouhun cixu") and, most strikingly, "The Investigation of Heavenly Phenomena in the Solar Eclipse" ("Rishi tianxiangjian") make the meaning of his title clear. This second article was intended on the surface to distinguish clearly the strengths and weaknesses of the new and old calendar, based on the eclipse of the sun that had taken place in 1664. In reality it completely contradicted the results of this test case, saying that Schall's prediction "had been entirely out of accord with the heavenly phenomena," and the traditional Han calendar had been 80 percent correct. What calculation was entirely in accord with the heavenly phenomena? Needless to say, it had been his calculation based on the Muslim calendar. How dared he lie so shamelessly, as if by raising a hand he could close the eyes and ears of all under heaven? Clearly it was only possible because Oboi and the other regents had not dared to announce publicly the results of that test. But did Yang Guangxian do this simply to cover up their mistakes for them? By no means.

"The missionaries' calculation of the calendar was not correct—yet even if it had been, could the bedroom of the Great Qing be opened up to Westerners who are given to plotting to steal nations away from others?" "Guangxian's stupidity is such that he would rather see China without a good calendar than see China having Westerners staying within her borders. Not having a good calendar would only mean not knowing the correct first day of the month and having solar eclipses more frequently on overcast days, such as was the situation in the Han dynasty. Yet did not the Han still enjoy four hundred years of rule? However, I fear the way Westerners living in China throw money about in order to capture the hearts of all our people, like a fire lurking under a pile of dry kindling. The disasters that result will be unlimited. In any case their calculations of solar eclipses are completely false!'' With these words he both attacked the Westerners and threatened the Manchus. He also begged sympathy in advance for the fact that he would not be able to prepare a good calendar. You must excuse the old dog; after all, at least he was absolutely loyal to the Qing court. He repeatedly emphasized that in this recent test it was the Westerners who had calculated erroneously, and there were underlying layers of meaning here. ''You regents must conceal my errors. If you sacrifice me in the future, then I may well strike back with a counter accusation.'' He announced that he could not help becoming a dog and he further hinted that if he was a disloyal dog, this would also be because he could not do otherwise. This was the self vindication of Yang Guangxian, the author of *I Could Not Do Otherwise.*

His second ploy was to advertise the fact that he was reviving the traditional calendar. After he took up the headship of the Astronomical Bureau, Yang and Wu Mingxuan together used the Arabic calendar, which had been proven riddled with errors, that is, the Datong calendar, to replace the new calendar, which Schall had developed. The Datong calendar had been first used in the Yuan dynasty, and it was also a foreign calendar that negated the traditional Han calendar. In plotting to conceal what was actually a parallel case of ''using what is barbarian to reform Han customs,'' Yang Guangxian thought out an idea—that of requesting the Qing court for permission to revive the ancient calendar of Hou Qi in the Northern Qi dynasty. The calendar established by Hou Qi had actually been used in both the Western and Eastern Han dynasties. As for his preference for emulating the Northern Qi dynasty, Yang Guangxian could only give one explanation, which was that the Northern Qi was under the government of the Xianbei Han people, and the Qing rulers traced back their ancestry to this Xianbei group.

Thus the implications behind the revival of the ancient calendar of the Northern Qi was that it was a revival of a Chinese calendar that the ancestors of the Manchus had also accepted. Naturally, Oboi and the other regents gave their approval. So Yang Guangxian requested that the Board of Rites provide the material for him to manufacture meteorological instruments. After this request was tossed back and forth for some time, finally the bamboo pipes that were specially produced on Jinmei Mountain in Yiyang county, the square-shaped millet that was the special product of Shangdang county in the Yangtu mountain in Shangdong, and the young reed shoots specially produced in Henei prefecture were all collected and brought to him. But how was he to manufacture the meteorological pipes? Though there was a record in the calendrical section of *The Records of the Historian* (*Shiji, lishu*), unfortunately it did not have a detailed description of the method of construction. The ignorant and incompetent Yang Guangxian probably did not realize that *The History of the Han Dynasty* (*Han shu, luli zhi*) and many other such books all had records on meteorological technology. Or possibly he was aware but could not understand these volumes. As a result, he was stymied and "there was a wait of two years without any outcome."[86] All he could do was continue to use the Arabic calendar for calculation.

In the tensions of the situation, this bogus astronomer, who had been given the highest imperial position, followed in the footsteps of Schall and had a stroke. Responsibility for establishing the new almanac had to be taken over by his assistant Wu Mingxuan. Who could guess that this fellow was not even up to the level of his brother? Though he was of Arabic descent, still he didn't know how specialist work on the Arabic calendar proceeded. He too was a fake. After many difficulties, this fellow set the almanac for 1669 and offered it to the imperial government in the late autumn of 1668 (October 1668 by the Western calendar), asking that it be promulgated throughout the empire in the emperor's name, and never thinking that it would have serious flaws.

It turned out that the calendar that had been set by Yang and Wu Mingxuan had two vernal equinoxes and two autumnal equinoxes, and it also had an intercalary month that was one year ahead of time. This was a mistake of a magnitude such as had never happened before with Chinese, Arabic, or Western calendars.

If the almanac had been like the writings of the famous neo-Confucian scholars—that is, if it was never subjected to practical testing and investigation—and if the responsibility of the head of the Astronomical Bureau had not been to assist the emperor in using the calendar to guide agricultural production throughout the country, as well as in religious life, and indeed, if Yang Guangxian's supporters, the four regents, had still been in power, this mistake might well have been overlooked or at least remedied in some way.

Unfortunately for him, however, the most important condition was already lost. The four regents of the interim government had already become embroiled in internal conflict. In December 1666, Oboi had first falsely issued a divine edict attacking Suksaha, and in July of the next year he had forced Kangxi to agree to Suksaha being beheaded.

The young emperor, who had been humiliated by this, made up his mind, with the support of his grandmother, the grand dowager empress, to take reprisals against Oboi. Thus Yang Guangxian and Wu Mingxuan got the reversal they deserved.

By this time Schall had already died, but his young and competent assistant, Ferdinand Verbiest, had kept his eye all along on Schall's work and the way it had been destroyed by these two pagans. When Yang Guangxian took possession of Schall's residence, his surveillance of what was going on on the other side of the wall was even more convenient.

After the Kangxi emperor himself took over the government, he commissioned Verbiest to take part in ordering the calendar. How could Verbiest let these gross errors in the almanac pass? In October 1668 he exposed all the mistakes in the almanac that Wu Mingxuan and Yang Guangxian had set for 1669 and accused them of "using the old calendar to alter the change of seasons, forcing the heavens to conform to human will, and using instruments in the opposite way to that intended, so that there was no harmony between heaven and the way."[87] After an investigation by the imperial council "Verbiest was vindicated, and Wu Mingxuan was shown to be completely in error."[88] So the emperor issued an edict correcting the error of the intercalary month and ordered that, starting from 1669, the almanac should be arranged by Verbiest.

Yang Guangxian was terrified and hastily submitted a petition to the emperor that he be allowed to prepare a report of his own mistakes, but he did not get the opportunity to make up more lies. The reason for this was that in May 1669 the young emperor staged the prologue to his majestic reign—he orchestrated a group of his playmates to arrest Oboi, who had by now concentrated all power in his hands, and had the whole gang of Oboi's relatives and supporters rounded up in one fell swoop. Thus, the following report of that August was not at all surprising: "Prince Kang (Jieshu) and the others responded after deliberation: As for the accusation against Verbiest and others, Yang Guangxian, in collusion with Oboi, made up charges and framed them, saying that the *Five Elements in the Grand Scheme (Hongfan wuxing)*, which had been used over the ages, was a 'scripture to destroy barbarians,' and causing Li Zubai and all the other officials to be punished; he then arranged to have Wu Mingxuan brought in and given an imperial appointment under false pretenses; he falsely accused Schall of plotting rebellion; his crime was a very serious one and he should be beheaded. Tang Ruowang should have restored to him the title of 'teacher versed in metaphysics.' "[89]

Yang Guangxian was already seventy-five years old, and because he had had a stroke his vision and speech were distorted. The young emperor showed magnanimity, giving a decree that took into account Yang's old age. He was removed from office, but rather than being handed over to the Board of Punishments, he was sent back to his home region where he was to be given into the custody of local officials.

Before this, in March 1669, Verbiest had been appointed vice-head of the Astronomical Bureau and had already set himself to rebuild it. Just as Yang Guangxian was being sent back to his home region, the government gave its approval for Verbiest to redevelop the plan for the bureau's astronomical instruments. As a near neighbor, Yang Guangxian must have heard the news of this. No one knows what he was thinking at that time, or whether he felt even the slightest twinge of guilt over his own inglorious career. What we do know is that while going back to his home region, just as he reached the border of Shandong province, he suddenly died.

Not long after Yang Guangxian's death on November 6, 1669 (December 8 by the Western calendar), the emperor sent people to make sacrifices at Schall's tomb, and an imperial document of memorial was prepared that entirely affirmed the value of Schall's contribution in introducing the Western calendar and editing the Chinese almanac and also offered to restore the title that had been given him of "teacher versed in metaphysics."[90] Four years later, in 1673, the new set of imperial astronomical instruments was completed and Verbiest was officially appointed head of the Astronomical Bureau.

From that time up to the reign of the Jiaqing emperor in the early nineteenth century, the position of head of the Astronomical Bureau was held jointly by a European missionary and a Manchu astronomer.

5 | Han Learning and Western Learning in the Eighteenth Century

All who are accustomed to listening to those of the past are inevitably blinded by their words without realizing it.[91]

The Questions Raised by the Notion of a "Blank Space"

From the late Ming to the late Qing, that is, from the end of the sixteenth century, when Matteo Ricci and other missionaries gained permission to enter China, to the latter part of the nineteenth century, just before China began to send large numbers of students to study "abroad," a period of three hundred years, the major intermediary between Chinese and Western culture was that provided by the Christian missionaries.

If one took the level of activity and practical influence of the missionaries in China as a measure of the extent of Chinese-Western cultural interaction over these three hundred years, then one would discover that within that period there appeared what might be called a "blank space." This "blank space" began in the late years of the

Kangxi reign when imperial orders strictly forbidding the preaching of Catholicism in each province were again and again reaffirmed,[92] up to the early nineteenth century when Protestant missionaries replaced Catholic ones as the major actors in China, a period that encompasses most of the eighteenth century.

In Chinese history, the eighteenth century just happens to be the very period of the height of Qing prosperity. With the exception of the last four years when Qianlong was continuing to control imperial politics as super-sovereign (*taishan huang*) and extensive and large-scale peasant revolts broke out in various places, the ruling order was generally stable over this period. The sense of social harmony that resulted was something that was not known in either the century preceding or that to follow.

In accordance with historical tradition, a dynasty either united or partially united always made the expression of tolerance toward the culture of regions outside of China and other races a measure essential to demonstrating its own prosperity. The wide-open atmosphere of the Han and Tang periods was noted approvingly by Lu Xun, as we all know. The interest shown in the Yuan dynasty in all "foreign cultures" (*semu wenhua*) went far beyond the way they used Han culture, a situation that is worth further discussion elsewhere. As for the Ming, although it was condemned by Wang Fuzhi as "vulgar Song" and derided by Zhang Taiyan as "a totally decadent dynasty," with the exception of a group of teachers of the fake classics who only knew how to chatter interminably about abstruse concepts of neo-Confucianism, the ruling group did not see the rejection of foreign culture as desirable. During the late Ming, when the dynastic crisis was getting worse day by day, "Western learning," as interpreted in the early modern period, was just being introduced primarily because the government allowed foreign missionary activity on certain conditions. The one and only exception to this pattern seems to have been the Qing dynasty. After it had come to power, the more established it became, the more fierce an antiforeignism it exhibited, until finally, in the period of its greatest prosperity, the eighteenth century, the "blank space" noted above appeared. How are we to explain this?

The problem has another aspect to it. Precisely during the eighteenth century, in Qing dynasty scholarly circles a movement for the revival of antiquity (*fugu*) was rearing its head more and more insistently. Ancient texts of the Zhou and Qin dynasties which had been sealed away on back shelves, forgotten commentaries of the Han, ancient philological texts, and wood-printed or hand-copied texts of the Song and Yuan dynasties all became the objects of scholarly debate and investigation. This type of scholarly research had been remarkably well developed by the mid-eighteenth century and was called Han learning (*Hanxue*), because scholars of this school fixed their eyes on the Han dynasty classics, and also because they held an attitude of scorn toward the explanations of the classics given by those connected with the Cheng brothers and Zhu Xi—in other words, Song neo-Confucianism. As Han learning became more and more dominant, Western learning (*xixue*), which had been on the rise in the Ming-Qing transition period, nearly disappeared from the scene, and only in mathematical and astronomical circles were there still some traces of it. From Shen Que's *Essays of an Official in the Southern Capital* (*Nangong shutu*) in the late Ming to Yang Guangxian's *I Could Not Do Otherwise* (*Bu de yi*) in the early Qing, those hoping to use the stale formula of the "transmission of the Way" (*daotong*) to encourage "attacking and repudiating heresy" had their hopes realized precisely in the period when the antithesis of Song neo-Confucianism—Han learning—had made its appearance. No wonder there are some scholars who feel that Han Learning cannot easily evade responsibility for the "break in interaction" between Chinese and European culture that occurred in the eighteenth century. What, then, was the relationship between these two phenomena?

Difficulties in Solving the Puzzle

It is not easy to answer the questions raised above. First, in the Middle Ages, the "real interference of politics in the historical process"[93] was more and more evident as the period advanced. Especially in the reigns of Kangxi, Yongzheng, and Qianlong, this kind of intervention had already made its appearance in the form of the autocratic ruler exhausting all efforts to make scholarship obedient to his will. For this reason the probability of random developments in cultural history greatly increased, making it even more difficult for researchers to clarify the historical necessity in this transition.

Second, because the intermediary between Chinese and Western culture was still the European missionaries, and each of the mission societies in China was strictly controlled by the Holy See in Rome, the rise and decline of Western studies was linked to the strengthening of interference from the Holy See over the traditional customs of Chinese believers, which in turn aroused a counterinterference from the Qing court, all of these being closely interlinked. Nevertheless, these historical events have never been fully explored through the careful identification and ordering of the contradictions implicit in them.[94]

Third, while the progress of scholarly development can certainly never be entirely free from the fetters of political constraints, Marxism never denies the relative independence of any intellectual point of view.[95] If one then claims that the flourishing of the Han learning in the eighteenth century was simply a negative reflection of the Qing dynasty's cultural autocracy, or even a kind of whitewash for the Qing autocratic rule, this could only be described as a misinterpretation.

Fourth, whether one turns to the Wu school of Han learning styled after Hui Dong or the Wan school styled after Dai Zhen, both developed in the lower reaches of the Yangzi River, that is, the Jiangnan region. From the early Qing this was the center of disaffection and resistance for all regions and was targeted for attack by the Qing government, as evidenced by the *Kechang* case (1657), the *Zouxiao* case (1661), and the *Mingshi* case (1663).[96] "If your family is wise, all your efforts will go into explaining the classics and in this way you'll be able to avoid death''[97] was one depiction of the environment in which followers of the Han learning lived. If Han scholars either opposed Song neo-Confucianism or expressed approval of Western learning, one could hardly expect them to be frank about their views, especially those whose sense of unjust treatment aroused in them a particular defiance.[98]

Fifth, undoubtedly there is still the difficulty of getting an overall grasp of the historical data. If one leaves aside the work of the eighteenth-century Han scholars covering the philosophical schools and history from the Qin dynasty and the Western and Eastern Han and only considers the works of textual criticism on the Confucian classical texts, those listed in the *Explanations of the Classics by Qing Scholars (Huang Qing jingjie)* alone add up to 2,700 chapters and include the writings of 157 scholars.[99] If one sought a systematic understanding by reading through one chapter a day, it would take seven years plus one and a half months to read through the whole. Besides, there are still the writings not included in the *Explanations of the Classics* and those recorded in the sequel to it or in such compilations as the *Essays on Statecraft of the Qing Dynasty (Huang chao jingshi wenbian)*. This colossal classical heritage has never been systematically put in order.

As for those of its contents that could be used in debating the relation between Han learning and Western learning, at present there is an even more serious lack of comparative research, either quantitative or qualitative.

Of course, we cannot wait until all these practical difficulties have been solved before attempting to address the problems posed above. Yet any attempt at addressing them will undoubtedly have to take these difficulties into account or it will be hard to avoid a prejudicial view of the whole picture.

The Reversional Development
of Ancient Intellectual History

The Qing dynasty Han learning was by no means a resurrection of the scholarly tradition of the Western and Eastern Han dynasties, as suggested by the Han scholars themselves in the Qianlong period. Zhang Taiyan was the first to point this out in his writing on the Qing Confucians done during the late Qing period. Later, Liu Shipei and Liang Qichao gave concrete evidence of this.[100] Zhou Yutong, in summing up these views, gave the opinion that "the Han learning of the Qing dynasty had its own source and evolution and it was merely the revival of a descendant from the scholarship of the Western and Eastern Han dynasties, by no means the resurrection of the original body of Han scholarship."[101] From the perspective of the historical process of the scholarly cultures that dominated successive periods, I feel this is a correct assessment.

At a rough estimate, from the second century B.C. when the Western Han dynasty implemented the policy of suppressing the hundred schools and upholding Confucian scholarship onward,[102] the theoretical schools that held intellectual sway in this process were as follows: first, the New Text school (*jingjin wenxue*) of the Western Han, then the Old Text school (*jinggu wenxue*) from the Eastern Han to the Tang, then the neo-Confucianism of the Cheng brothers and Zhu Xi, which arose in the Northern and Southern Song, and finally the neo-Confucianism of Lu Jiuyuan and Wang Yangming, which began to flourish in the mid-Ming period.

Starting from the Ming-Qing transition period, however, up to the late Qing, a period of 250 years, the evolution of scholarly culture that had developed over 2,000 years went into a reverse direction. The stages of this reverse evolution were as follows: (1) Scholars of the late Ming and early Qing, seeking to research the secrets of the Ming decline and the rise of the Qing, were almost unanimous in censuring the later stage of Ming neo-Confucianism for empty arguments that harmed the nation. This made the repudiation of Ming neo-Confucianism a popular trend. (2) Gu Yanwu's arguments for "upholding classical studies and downgrading neo-Confucianism" practically negated the Song neo-Confucian philosophy of Zhu Xi, which had held a dominant position in the Song and early Ming dynasties, and went back to a revival of the Old Text studies of the Han and Tang period. (3) From Liu Fenglu up to Gong Zizhen, Wei Yuan to Dai Wang and Liao Ping, the New Text school was revived and became the dominant scholarly trend of the late Qing, leading to a gradual suppression of the Old Text literature. (4) Kang Youwei repudiated the theory of the transmission of the Way (*daotong*), and Zhang Taiyan fiercely attacked the New Text school, bringing both the Old and New Text schools to their demise, or at the very least leaving them empty shells of what they had been. (5) By the late Qing, due to the popularity of theories of evolution, of natural rights, and of bourgeois republicanism, Kang Youwei's discussion of Dong Zhongshu's interpretation of the *Spring and Autumn Annals* and Zhang Taiyan's theory about Liu Xin being the true successor of Confucius had become like discarded paper models left in the dirt after temple ceremonies are over. From the 1911 Revolution to May 4th, Marxism gained the victory over Chinese traditional scholarly theories, and bourgeois liberal theories from the outside gradually became the main currents of scholarly life.[103]

The backward stages of this historical reversion coincided at the beginning with the introduction of Western learning in the late Ming and at its culmination with the revival of Western learning in the late Qing. Could this be merely an accident of history?

Ming Neo-Confucianism and Western Learning

Hegel once said that random events, precisely because they are random, have a certain type of basis, and precisely because they are random, they have no basis; random events are determined, determinism itself defines its own randomness, and from another perspective this randomness might better be called an absolute determinism.[104] I feel that if the technique of the dialectic, as it relates to randomness and determinism, were used in a flexible way in our arguments, we would see that the scholarly culture of the Ming-Qing transition period had reached a position where it had to change, an example of the Hegelian principle.

Already in the early sixteenth century, before the Jesuit missionaries had entered China, the fortress of the ruling intellectual orthodoxy had produced its own heterodoxy, that is, the neo-Confucianism of Wang Shouren. This school of thought, gathered under the flag of Wang Shouren's "attaining innate knowledge," was a random development, yet the various topics that its adherents put forward, although not fresh, were developments on a range of heterodox ideas that had arisen from the Warring States period up to the Southern Song.[105] While Ming neo-Confucianism had many faults, as I have pointed out before, its followers refused to be slaves to chapter and verse of the Four Books, opposed being mere parrots of the ancient sages, and were even known to declare that "the streets are full of sages" in a denial of the view that only the few neo-Confucian philosophers who eulogized the Cheng brothers and Zhu Xi could be viewed as sages. There is no doubt that this presented a serious challenge to orthodox Song neo-Confucian philosophy.[106] According to the logic of Ming neo-Confucianism, it was necessary to cast off the intellectual trammels of the Confucian ethical obligations,[107] including the so-called great barrier between barbarians and Han.

In the late sixteenth century, when Longobardo, Matteo Ricci, and others came to China, it was just when Ming neo-Confucianism was at its height. Among the scholar officials who first showed an interest in the scholarship and doctrines introduced by Matteo Ricci and were even prepared to recognize and adopt the worship of Catholicism, not a few were followers of Ming neo-Confucianism, for example, Li Zhi and Xu Guangqi. On the other hand, in the late Ming collection of materials repudiating heresies, edited by Xu Changzhi and entitled *Refutation of Heresy in the Present Dynasty* (*Shengchao poxie ji*), the chapters that attack the Western scholars and Western doctrine are mainly written by later followers of Song neo-Confucianism, who were trying to defend the orthodox teachers of the Way.

It is worth thinking over what this contrast reveals. If one says it was a matter of chance that Western learning was introduced at the very period when Ming neo-Confucianism was flourishing, then this random happening fortuitously took place in the late Ming. This also shows, however, that the same necessity of moving out of the Middle Ages was pressing upon China as upon Europe of that period. Similarly, if one recognizes that the believers in Ming neo-Confucianism, who were heterodox in terms of the ruling philosophy of the Middle Ages, were certain to have been more open to receiving the foreign culture with its new ideas, then the fact that this school was fiercely criticized and fully repudiated in the Ming-Qing transition period shows that the reason lay not in the logical developments of scholarship itself, but in a certain randomness of history.

If, then, one takes the perspective of Chinese-Western cultural interaction, the neo-Confucianism of the Ming-Qing transition period was not merely a superficial phenomenon, as Wang Fuzhi, Gu Yanwu, and others claimed in censuring it.

In fact, the Fujian scholar Chen Di, who is regarded as one of the pioneers of the Qing dynasty's Han learning because he wrote the *Studies on the Phonology of the Book of Odes* (*Maoshi guyin kao*) in the Wanli period of the late Ming era, was even stronger in his criticism of Song than Ming neo-Confucianism, especially criticizing the way in which the Song philosophers isolated propriety (*yi*) from profit (*li*). He emphasized the utilitarian view that "righteousness can be found in what is beneficial, and principle can be found in what is profitable."[108] This was similar to the view of Dai Zhen two hundred years later. For this reason, scholars pointed out the similarities between Chen Di's theory and Wang Shouren's ideas at an early period.[109] In the early Qing, although Huang Zongxi hated the later Ming neo-Confucian scholars' penchant for empty talk, he did not deny the value of this school in itself. Interestingly, he was also the only one of the great scholars of the early Qing who openly discussed the strengths and weaknesses of Catholic doctrine.[110] As far as we know, *A Plan for the Prince* (*Mingyi daifang lu*), with its vague demands for a democracy approaching the present meaning of the word, was the only such scholarly book of the time. Yan Yuan, the northern scholar of the same period, had a much greater dislike for the Cheng brothers and Zhu Xi than his dissatisfaction with Ming neo-Confucianism, even going so far as to say that the disciples of the Cheng brothers and Zhu Xi were actually the greatest enemies of the sages.[111]

While Wang Fuzhi and Gu Yanwu repudiated Ming neo-Confucianism, they certainly showed no appreciation for Song neo-Confucianism either. Wang Fuzhi insisted that Zhang Zai was the only Song philosopher who should be affirmed, clearly intending to deny that the Cheng brothers and Zhu Xi were qualified to represent the tradition. Gu Yanwu apparently did not openly refute Song neo-Confucianism, yet he strongly promoted what he called "establishing classical studies and repudiating the study of principle," which gives more than a hint that he was demanding that the Song neo-Confucians should give up their empty argumentation and preaching in return for tolerance of this school as the dominant philosophy in form at least.

We can see that from the late Ming to the early Qing, opposition to Ming neo-Confucianism was based only on the point that it fostered empty discourse harmful to the nation, and its followers ended up in the same position as the Song neo-Confucians. Yet no one will deny that the Ming neo-Confucians were open to a foreign culture and were converted to a Western religion. By showing contempt for the ceremonies and traditions that had developed since the Song, in certain objective conditions, the Ming neo-Confucians created a cultural atmosphere that made it possible for Western learning with its new ideas to find a foothold in China. In matters of epistemology, scholars of the Ming neo-Confucian system had especially egalitarian views. Thus, Wang Shouren's notion that "innate knowledge and innate ability put the foolish man and woman in the same position as the sage" persisted in hidden form in the Qing dynasty and actually had an influence on scholars of the Han learning. This may appear a perverse argument, but it is the case.

The Mystery of the Suppression of Ming Neo-Confucianism and the Revival of the Song School

In contrast to the tolerance of Wang Yangming's school in the Ming, the Qing dynasty purposely propped up the Song school and suppressed that of the Ming. The way in which these tactics took shape seems to have been closely connected to the special contradiction that existed between the imperial government of the early Qing and the scholar gentry of the Southeast.

All of the southeastern area, including Zhejiang, Jiangsu, Anhui, Guangdong, and Fujian, was the common source of origin for both the Ming and the Song schools. Yet starting from the mid-Qing, the Ming school, which had arisen later, had overtaken the Song school and become the current of thought favored by all of the scholar gentry. This region, especially Jiangnan, had the most developed economy and the most progressive culture and was at the forefront of the country. The Ming dynasty system of selecting scholar-officials by examination had given scholar-officials of this region the most opportunities for participation in government, with the result that they also enjoyed the greatest political rights and privileges. It is not hard to understand why the scholarly atmosphere in this region during the Ming dynasty was far more lively than in any other area, and why Ming neo-Confucianism, which had fewer traditional restrictions than the Song school, should take this region as the center from which it radiated.

Nevertheless, these conditions were destroyed through the military subjugation imposed by the Manchu aristocracy. The Qing dynasty established by the Manchus had a form of rule characterized by a strong atmosphere of popular repression, and the Jiangnan scholar gentry, who had originally enjoyed the greatest political rights and privileges, now experienced the most severe attacks and humiliations. The broad gate for those entering into the imperial bureaucracy through the civil service examination system was now narrowed, and the proportion of their rents and other income that they had to remit in taxes to the imperial aristocracy increased. At the same time they were forced to abandon their own traditional robes and hats for those of the Manchus. These attacks and humiliations stirred up intense resentment and opposition, which broke out into open rebellion whenever there was an opportunity.

The *juren* who rioted at the examination hall because they failed to gain an official position through the examinations and the gentry and merchants who gave their loyalty to Coxinga after his military invasion and victory caused great consternation among the Manchu ruling group in the late Shunzhi period.[112] Although Shunzhi had actually continually increased the pressure on the Jiangnan gentry during his lifetime, when he was near death he sent out an imperial edict criticizing himself for having gradually adopted Han customs and emulated the Ming system, and for having given preference to civil officials and appointed some Han to official positions. He confessed all this had been a great mistake on his part.[113] The result was that when Kangxi came to power, such high Manchu officials as the Oboi group and others made use of the traitor Zhu Guozhi to concoct the "ten Jiangnan cases," implicating a wide range of people and causing the Jiangnan scholar-officials all to feel endangered. Needless to say, the cultural atmosphere that had been so lively in the late Ming now became subdued and quiet.

In these conditions, it was not at all surprising that the Qing rulers suppressed and cold-shouldered Ming neo-Confucianism, which was regarded as responsible for the atmosphere of scholarship in the late Ming. There were still a few scholars of Ming neo-Confucianism in the early Qing, such as Sun Qifeng, Li Yong, Huang Zongxi, and others. None of them cooperated with the Qing dynasty in the political sphere, but in their scholarly work they all took the approach of harmonizing elements of Ming and Song neo-Confucianism and emphasizing what they called "putting theory into practice." This meant a compromise with the Song school that was rewarded by the Qing rulers. As a result, Ming neo-Confucianism soon lacked followers to pass it on. Sun Qifeng even went so far as to train a group of so-called famous Song neo-Confucian officials (*lixue mingchen*) for the Qing dynasty.[114]

After Kangxi came to power, he clearly upheld the Song school and repressed the Ming school. The "famous neo-Confucian official" Xiong Cili, who was a clever opportunist, specially wrote a book called *Transmission of the Way (Daotong)*, which claimed loudly that only the Cheng brothers and Zhu Xi were the "true transmitters of the Confucian and Mencian way" and that Lu Jiuyuan and Wang Yangming were "impure transmitters" (*zatong*). Even Kangxi felt this claim went too far[115] and publicly rebuked him in an imperial edict. Nevertheless, there was only one famous scholar left by the eighteenth century who could be called a Ming neo-Confucian—Li Fa. After this time Ming neo-Confucianism became a fading echo, until right up to the end of the next century, when it was suddenly resurrected in a miraculous way in the Hundred Day Reform Movement, becoming the most revered theoretical school of both the reformers and the revolutionaries. That is a matter for later discussion.[116]

Kangxi, Yongzheng, and Qianlong, grandfather, father, and son, made respect for Song neo-Confucianism a consistent policy, and one cannot deny the effects of this. Kangxi raised Zhu Xi to a position even higher than that of Confucius, leading the famous Song neo-Confucian philosopher of the late seventeenth century, Lu Longqi, to dare to announce that only Zhu Xi could understand the sacred way of Confucius and Mencius, and that in doing scholarship one only had to read Zhu Xi's books to reach perfection.[117] By the eighteenth century, from the emperor's daily counselors down to the teachers of tiny village schools, the textbooks that were printed by imperial order were Zhu Xi's *Collected Annotations on the Four Books (Sishu zhangju jizhu)* and such books as *The Essential Meaning of Nature and Principle (Xingli jingyi)* and *Notes on the Four Books (Sishu wen)*. All those officials who were cited as models by the emperor were called "famous Song neo-Confucian officials" (*lixue mingchen*) or known as "pure officials" (*qingguan*), such people as Tang Bin, Li Guangdi, Zhang

Boxing, and Yu Chenglong. It is undeniable that this type of book and this type of person had an enormous influence on ordinary people, as a glance at Zhou Jin, Fan Jin, Ma Chunshang, Kuang Chaoren, and other such types described in *The Scholars* (*Rulin waishi*) shows. Nevertheless, although it was common enough for mediocre types to gain a high position and for power politics to dominate in China's historical experience, it still never happened that these types succeeded in hindering the ultimate trends of social development. This was as true in the eighteenth century as it had been earlier.

How was this? Those Qing emperors who promoted Song neo-Confucianism actually believed it least. There is no need to prove this in the case of Kangxi, since in his secret edicts he heaped scorn on the very "famous neo-Confucian officials" whom he himself had honored, men such as Tang Bin, Li Guangdi, and Xiong Cili, as can be seen repeatedly in the *Veritable Records* (*Shilu*) and the *Archival Records of the Qing Dynasty* (*Donghua lu*). Yongzheng most loved to prate on about "heavenly principles and conscience," yet Dai Zhen's *Textual Criticism on the Meaning of the Mencius* (*Mengzi ziyi shuzheng*) has already revealed that he "used principle to kill people."[118] *The Record of Resolving Delusion* (*Dayi juemi lu*), which he personally promulgated, was supposed to be a refutation of Lü Liuliang's theory, and yet Lü Liuliang just happened to be one of the Song neo-Confucian gentlemen who devoutly believed in Zhu Xi's views about putting theory into practice. For the sake of carrying out Zhu Xi's teaching about making a distinction between Han and barbarian, he had even had no compunction about breaking off the relationship with his best friend Huang Zongxi.[119]

Qianlong was even more shameless, on the one hand commending neo-Confucianism and on the other heaping scorn upon it. During his reign he held literary inquisitions several times, and the cases that interested him most were those that exposed the "false Confucianism."[120] The massive bibliographic project, *The Complete Library of the Four Treasuries* (*Siku quanshu*), which he had compiled for the main purpose of being able to ban books, had many of the neo-Confucian writings from the Song to the Yuan dynasty listed in the "index of banned or destroyed books." Ji Yun, whom he entrusted to be the chief editor of the comprehensive index to the *Complete Library* (*Siku quanshu zongmu*), loved most to take as an object of his satire the muddleheaded teachers of Confucianism when he used foxes and ghosts to mock contemporary events in his *Notes from the Yuewei Studio* (*Yuewei caotang biji*). Given that this was the situation among the rulers, how could one expect the ordinary people to believe that they ought to follow strictly the neo-Confucian teachings as the only pure and true pathway?

From the time of Zhu Xi onward, neo-Confucian philosophers liked to talk about "the way of inner holiness and outward rule" (*neisheng waiwang*). It may not be easy for ordinary mortals to judge how far they succeeded with inner holiness, yet in a situation of conflict between races, their idea of outward rule was clear. The first point was to "use the barbarians to control the barbarians," and the second was to "regard the barbarians as Han once they had gained power over the Han." This latter policy allowed those who called themselves defenders of the Way to offer their service to a new dynasty, something that was already clear in the Jin and Yuan dynasties. In the Qing dynasty in the reigns of Kangxi, Yongzheng, and Qianlong, the neo-Confucians had been quick to shave their heads and change their clothing. From Yang Guangxian in the early Kangxi period to Yao Nai in the late Qianlong period, all made noise about "distinctions between barbarian and Han." Their distinction, however, was along the lines of how the Manchus "who had first reached high civilization" and were more progressive than all of the Han should despise and reject the Westerners, who had come to high civilization even later. The real trick in all of this was the transformation of a policy of "using the barbarian to control the barbarian" into one of "using the Han to control the Han."

The Reaction of the Han Scholars of the South

A contradictory phenomenon that has up to now been difficult to explain purely from the perspective of intellectual history can be explained more satisfactorily in this way.

The founders of Han learning in the Qing dynasty were mostly scholars of the Jiangnan region,[121] just as that region had been the source and mainstay of Western learning in the late Ming.[122] Han learning reached its highest point of development in the reigns of Qianlong and Jiaqing, and so it has been described as Qian-Jia scholarship. Archaism and an unadorned naturalism are the special characteristics of the Qian-Jia style of scholarship.

It is well known that the main object of research for the Qing dynasty Han scholars was to pass down the classical texts that had been ordered and taught by Confucius, and that the primary purpose of classical research was to revive the notes and interpretations of the Eastern Han Old Text scholars, which were regarded as the most trustworthy, as well as the commentaries of such great teachers as Jia Kuei, Ma Rong, Xu Zhen, and Zheng Xuan. The Wu group, created by Hui Dong, was so rigid in its view of the ancient commentaries of the Eastern Han as to preach that "the ancient teachings cannot be revised" and one can only "maintain conformity to the family statutes of the Hans." Liang Qichao was certainly justified in his criticism of them for holding that "all that is ancient must be true and all that is Han must be so." The Wan group, initiated by Dai Zhen, was not quite so inflexible as the Wu group, yet it also "took the study of the classics as its main purpose, and did not advocate reading any books after the Han period."[123] In their attitude toward the revival of antiquity, both schools were in agreement.

As for unadorned style, the two schools were even closer on this point. Dai Zhen summed up the common method of doing classical research as "study characters first, then understand phrases, finally proceed to understanding meaning."[124] This was the basic method commonly followed by Han scholars. Thus they started with characters and their sounds, went on to investigate their meaning, then made distinctions among different concepts, which finally enabled them to give systematic depictions of the ancient system. They dredged traditional commentaries and notes, making it their goal to ensure that there was not one character or one event that was not historically accurate. This became the basic task of all Han scholars, and it resulted in an unwillingness to depart from the interpretation of ancient texts in order to engage in argumentation. They all took a cautious approach to any discussion about "the Way." Dai Zhen once put it this way: "My generation does not study in order to compete in establishing theories, like the later Confucians, but simply to calmly appreciate the classical texts. If there is one character wrongly explained, that is, if there is a gap between word and meaning, then the Way is lost at this point."[125] Yet Dai Zhen was one of the Han scholars who most enjoyed argumentation.

Even though Han scholars of the Qing called themselves the true successors of the classicists of the Eastern and Western Han, objective facts still demonstrate that their style of scholarship might be better seen as a resurrection of the formal traditions of Song neo-Confucianism than a revival of the traditions of the Old Text school in the Han dynasty.

Although Han classical scholarship was divided into the Old and New

Text schools, both made the "Five Classics" the totality of religious teaching, and both used belief in place of reason and emphasized "technique" over "scholarship." That is, they researched the classics not in the search for truth, or to recover the true historical character of the Confucian texts, but to use them. They gained assistance from the authority of the canons to promote their own techniques of rule. The neo-Confucianism of the Song dynasty was the product of the renewal of classical studies in the period between the Tang and the Song. The basic attitude of Zhu Xi and his predecessors to the classical texts, recognized by all dynasties from the second century B.C. to the seventh century A.D. as containing the "transmission of the Way" of the Duke of Zhou and Confucius, was precisely not one of simple belief but one of doubt. They did not defend the authority of the classical texts but criticized them, even to the point of denying the historicity of the transmission of the classics. This caused the teachings of the Duke of Zhou and Confucius or of Confucius and Yan Hui to lose some of the luster that had formerly surrounded them. One famous example of "doubting the classics" among the Song neo-Confucians is the fact that Zhu Xi was seen as a successor to Wu Yu, Zheng Qiao, and such people. They went from doubting the false biography of Confucius to doubting the false *Old Text Book of History*, from doubting the preface to the *Book of Odes* to doubting Confucius's own explanation of the *Book of Odes*.[126]

On the surface, the Han scholars of the Qing boasted that they were reviving antiquity, and they appeared to be opposite in style and approach to the Song dynasty neo-Confucians who doubted the classics. In fact, however, these different roads actually led to the same destination.

The devout belief that the sages were infallible and that the sacred texts came by divine revelation was the fundamental reason why the classical scholarship of the Western and Eastern Han dynasties became the foundation of religious and even theological thought. But the Han scholars of the Qing dynasty were not involved in this way. Their point of departure was not a revival of the authority of the beliefs of the ancient saints and sages, rather it was to uncover the original features of the ancient classical tradition. The Han scholars of the Qing emphasized "seeking truth from facts" (*shishi qiushi*). Of course, this did not imply the kind of connection between theory and practice that we mean by this today, but it meant simply reconstructing the true features of the ancient documents and rediscovering their original meaning. They affirmed, however, that there must be proof for every statement, and that the explanation of every event, every meaning, even every word and phrase had to be in accord with historical reality. This scholarly style was the antithesis to superstition and blind faith, and their supposed "restoration of antiquity" (*fugu*) was in reality a "doubting of antiquity" (*yigu*).

"Use the original ideas of Confucius and Mencius in writing the Six Classics to interpret the six classics, use the original ideas of the Cheng brothers and Zhu Xi to interpret their works, use the original ideas of Lu Jiuyuan, Wang Yangming, and the Buddhist teachers to interpret their works, so that Lu and Wang are not interpreted according to the ideas of the Cheng brothers and Zhu Xi, and the latter are not interpreted according to the ideas of Confucius and Mencius."[127] This was the method commonly adopted by the Han scholars, the so-called bamboo-stripping method of approaching the classics. If the classical scholars from generation to generation stripped away all the accumulated layers of superstition surrounding them, then the classical texts would be seen as simply historical documents left behind by ordinary people who lived, acted, and thought in a particular environment in the ancient period. For the most part they could not even be called the writings of any individual, so how could they have any divine quality? Zhu Xi and his predecessors may well have doubted the classics in order to overturn traditional authority and establish a new authority. Nevertheless, they had no superstitious attachment to the ancient saints and sages, and they thus differed very little in reality from the Han scholars of the Qing dynasty.

In spite of this, the Han scholars of the Qing had an intense dislike for the neo-Confucianism of the Song. In the late seventeenth and early eighteenth centuries, the so-called pioneers of the Qian-Jia textual criticism, scholars such as Yan Ruoju, Hu Wei, Gu Donggao, Jiang Yong, and Shen Tong, did not yet openly repudiate Song neo-Confucianism but even wrote books that pandered to it. Yan Ruoju's *Detailed Records of Qianyou* (*Qianyou zhaji*) is full of the putrid flavor of this sort of compromise with neo-Confucianism. Yet after Hui Dong and Dai Zhen made their appearance, all scholars who called themselves Han scholars, without exception, "criticized Song neo-Confucianism." By the end of the eighteenth century neo-Confucian works could not be found for sale on the public bookstalls.[128]

Such is the nature of scholarship that when schools of thought become incompatible, the reason does not lie within the spirit of scholarship itself. For example, even though Ming neo-Confucianism and the Han learning of the Qing seemed to be absolutely at odds in their approach to scholarship— the Han learning being objective, firmly grounded, and dense, while Ming neo-Confucianism was subjective, vapid, and simplistic—still the Han scholars did not take Ming neo-Confucianism as their main target of attack. This is something extremely difficult to understand.

I believe the reason for it lies in the cultural policy of the Qing rulers, a policy of "using the Han to control the Han," which became more and more developed and intense from Kangxi to Qianlong. They spared no efforts in promoting Zhu Xi's system of neo-Confucianism, yet this set of theories had already at an early period in the Ming-Qing transition lost its last bit of vitality. Even if they had been true believers in the neo-Confucian teachings, this behavior might objectively be described as a kind of "restoration of antiquity," a revival of the determination to follow the outdated traditions of the Middle Ages to their final expiry. In fact, however, they were not at all sincere in their motives. They were forcing the people to believe in ideas that they themselves did not believe in. What could be expected of this kind of restoration of antiquity, except the arousal of even greater popular dislike for Song neo-Confucianism and a reaction against it?

The Qing rulers' policy of "using the Han to control the Han" had as its primary target the suppression of the southern culture which was centered in Jiangsu and Zhejiang and found expression in the neo-Confucianism of Wang Shouren of the late Ming. They used a number of methods: a literary inquisition to give warning; the teachings of Zhu Xi to guide; the examinations for mature officials (*boxue hongci*) to enforce scholarly conformity; and the confiscation, expurgation; and banning of books to destroy the historical memory of the scholars. Naturally, they were quite successful. The tendency of the scholar-officials to form societies and organize their own activities was stamped out, as was their will to "reform society in accordance with the principles of the early kings." This resulted in a situation where none dared to talk about national affairs, and more and more scholars passed their lives in practicing eight-legged essays for the examinations. At the basic level, however, they failed. When the cultural net was tightest, that is, in the reigns of Yongzheng and Qianlong, precisely in the region that had been the birthplace of Ming neo-Confucianism, cultural trends not only refused to follow the dead-end road back to Song neo-Confucianism that the Manchu emperors hoped for, but actually progressed beyond the level of Ming neo-Confucianism, as scholars rejected the position that "Zhu Xi in his later years was really the same as Wang Yangming." They showed their fists and lifted their gowns in contempt, taking the repudiation of Zhu Xi as an urgent task and fearlessly criticizing Song neo-Confucianism. This was the reaction of the southern Han scholars to the cultural dictatorship of the Qing court.[129] It was a negative reaction, yet it was also positive in an indirect way.

The Interrelation between Han Scholarship and Western Learning

The success of Ming neo-Confucianism was beneficial to the spread of Western learning in the late Ming, as has been noted earlier. Given this situation, it is no surprise that Catholic belief had greatest popular influence and European scholarship had widest acceptance with the scholar-official class in the Southeast, where Ming neo-Confucianism enjoyed widest recognition. Xu Guangqi, Li Zhizao, and Yang Tingyun, who were called the three pillars of the "sacred religion" in the late Ming, were all well-known scholars of Jiangsu and Zhejiang, clearly no accident of history. As for the famous incidents of the late Ming and early Qing in which Western religion and the Western learning came under attack, such as the Nanjing persecution of Catholics and the *I Could Not Do Otherwise* case, if they did not take place in this region, they were initiated by scholars who wanted to preserve the "national essence." This was also no accident of history.

Every culture has its own internal space-time continuum. The southern culture, which radiated from its center in the Jiangnan region, took the form of Han scholarship in the eighteenth century. That means that Han scholarship and Western learning appeared in succession in the same region. Was there, therefore, some sort of practical connecting link, as has been shown between Han scholarship and Ming neo-Confucianism?

Earlier scholars, such as Liang Qichao, Hu Shi, Liao Zhizheng, and others, all noted this interconnection, but unfortunately, none went beyond seeing the phenomenon as a kind of analogy. They did not explore it in further detail. Later scholars were even more interested in differences than similarities, with the result that they depicted the rise of Han scholarship as having no connection at all with the progressive Western learning. In my view this explanation is even farther from the facts of history than that of Liang Qichao and Hu Shi.

If one takes the perspective of a cultural space-time continuum in looking at the interconnections between eighteenth-century Han scholarship and Western learning, a number of aspects are worth probing.

The Qualitative Connection

If we set aside the controversy over whether or not Matteo Ricci and others used Western learning to proselytize, the Western scholarship that they introduced after entering China was clearly associated with early modern culture in Europe. What we call "early modern culture" might be defined as a kind of negation of medieval culture. This negation, whether in Europe or in China, was not aimed at the whole of traditional culture, rather at those aspects of cultural tradition that held a dominant position at the time and represented medievalism.[130] In their religious views, the Jesuits who entered China in the sixteenth and seventeenth centuries undoubtedly leaned toward a Catholic theology that was obviously outdated in Europe. Nevertheless, one cannot say they were representatives of medieval culture, since this religious society was itself a product of forces for reform within the Catholic church. The broad learning and cultivation of the early Jesuits is well known. Those Jesuits who were well known to Chinese scholars—men such as Matteo Ricci, Sabbathinus de Ursis, Joannes Terrenz, Julius Aleni, Adam Schall von Bell, and Ferdinand Verbiest—all had considerable attainments in both science and technology. The "Western learning" which they introduced to China cannot be simplistically dismissed as outdated European goods, including Tycho Brahe's astronomical system introduced by Matteo Ricci. Ricci has been criticized because Brahe rejected Copernicus's view of a sun-centered universe, yet the fact is that Brahe's system was something new in the practical circles of European astronomy at the time.

In contrast to the Western scholars, the Han scholars of eighteenth-century China had a totally different focus of research. Nevertheless, under the auspices of a revival of antiquity, they repudiated the existing medieval tradition, including the very neo-Confucian tradition that was being raised to the position of official ideology in the Qing dynasty. In this the Han scholarship of the Qing period was in no way inferior to the Western learning influenced by Ricci,[131] and one might even say, from this perspective, that it was a form of early modern culture. Up till now, intellectual history and the history of scholarship have relegated it to a form of feudal culture of the late medieval period, which seems to me mistaken.

Structural Relations

If one takes it as a cultural formation, the internal structure of Han scholarship in the Qing seems to lack any connection with Western learning. One only needs to consider the way in which all scholarship was divided into four categories. First classical studies had to be mastered, then what energy was left went to history and philosophy, and finally to collected essays. This pattern was widely divergent from the European categorization of disciplines.

These differences in form did not necessarily mean, however, that there were no affinities in content. In fact, at an early period after Indian culture was introduced to China, the internal structure of Chinese culture was already experiencing changes in this direction, changes that made it increasingly difficult to use the formal division of knowledge into these four categories. The cataloguers of the Southern dynasties (A.D. 420–589) engaged in an argument that went on for nearly two centuries over whether the works of Buddhism and Daoism could be included in the framework of the four categories.[132] For technical reasons as well as those of precedence, the traditional framework of cultural structure was preserved through the years, even though the content began to change at an early period.

The Han scholars of the Qing mainly worked under the auspices of classical studies. This included ordering and doing research into ancient texts, a field that was divided into phonology, philology, textual criticism, and the exposure of forged texts. It also included the discovery and restoration of documents of ancient scientific culture, what was called the systematic explanation of concepts. All of this was work that had either never been done in earlier periods or had been very rare. It had, however, resonances with the Western learning that had been introduced to China in the early modern period. In mathematics, astronomy, geography, and the technology of weapons manufacture, the work of Han scholars was clearly influenced by Western learning, something that is well known. Even phonology, which Han scholars of the Qing themselves considered to be a secret they alone possessed, something that could not be passed on to others, may have been inspired to some extent by comparison with European linguistics. The results of Liu Xianting's comparative research into East-West linguistics have not survived, yet it is possible to discover the level of understanding that scholars of the early Qing had of Western linguistics from his *Scattered Notes on Broad Experiences* (*Guangyang zaji*).

As for the degree to which the broad interest of the Kangxi emperor in European languages, science, and astronomical instruments affected the direction and progress of Han scholarship, this is a question that has so far lacked specialist investigation. All we do know is that the mathematical and calendar-related astronomical studies of the seventeenth and eighteenth centuries were closely linked to Kangxi's interests, and that he had a special fascination with the European knowledge introduced by the missionaries.[133] If we took the perspective of the structure of culture and compared Han learning and Western learning in the eighteenth century, what is known as Qing intellectual history might take on a different face.

Methodological Connections

From early in this century when Liang Qichao and Hu Shi successively pointed out the methodological problems in the approach to scholarly research of the Qing dynasty Han scholars, sustained attention has been given to research on the similarities and links in method between Han scholarship and Western learning. Of course, the expositions made by Liang and Hu were biased in certain ways. Hu Shi's characterization of the Han scholars as pioneers of the method of "bold hypothesizing followed by careful investigation," for example, seems to me a somewhat subjective assertion. Nevertheless, to deny the reasonableness of these questions just because of their tendency toward bias and arbitrariness would certainly not be an attitude consonant with seeking truth from facts. By the late Middle Ages the Song neo-Confucian ideas of "investigating things and attaining knowledge" (*gewu zhizhi*) or "examining things and exhausting principle" (*jiwu qiongli*) had already become empty terminology, while Wang Shouren's method of "achieving innate knowledge" (*zhi liangzhi*) had never really extricated itself from the subjectivity of Lu Jiuyuan's "using the six classics to express oneself." Even if the scope of research was limited to historical documents, these two methods would still certainly lead people into the same blind alley. Already in the thirteenth century, however, when Chinese scholarly circles were seeking a breakthrough in research method, a type of scholarly work that had the flavor of textual criticism made its first appearance in Wang Yinglun's *Notes on Scholarly Problems* (*Kunxue jiwen*). This was a portent of things to come.

Nevertheless, a breakthrough in scholarly method can never be brought about entirely by the inner logic of the development of scholarship. There must also be certain supportive conditions in the external environment. For water to harden into ice, there needs to be a change in the air temperature at the water's surface, in addition to the water temperature itself going down below zero. The introduction of Western learning in the late Ming and the way in which Matteo Ricci used European nominalism to criticize the Song neo-Confucian theory of human nature (*xingming*) led to a stirring up of the scholarly atmosphere. This inspired scholars with new ideas in methodology. They said good-bye to the empty verbiage of neo-Confucian method and began to develop in the direction of "testing against evidence." With reference to Gu Yanwu's *Five Books on Phonology* (*Yinxue wushu*) and Yan Ruoju's *Explanation of the Old Text Book of History* (*Guwen shangshu shuzheng*), Hu Shi commented that "this type of scholarly method, in its entire approach, was influenced by Matteo Ricci's coming to China."[134] This may not be entirely accurate, but it is certainly worth researching. There was an increasing orientation toward emphasizing observation and experience in the sixteenth and seventeenth centuries. Yet the influence of the methodology of Francis Bacon and René Descartes on the missionaries who came to China after Matteo Ricci is at the very least a subject that has lacked detailed research attention on our part. It is clear, nevertheless, that the later missionaries were close to these thinkers in their ideas on methodology.

The eighteenth-century Han scholars regarded themselves as the successors of Gu and Yan. Nevertheless, in the case of Gu, his political views during his lifetime were never echoed publicly among Han scholars, even though his methodology for researching the classics was accorded extraordinary respect. Does this indicate that Gu Yanwu was a kind of intermediary in terms of scholarly methodology? Were Han scholars influenced by Western scholarly methods in some overall way, beyond the fields of mathematics and astronomy? I feel there is a need for renewed exploration of this question.

Connections in Mentality

In recent years Chinese scholars have begun to emphasize research into cultural mentality, and this is greatly needed. The founders of Marxism never neglected problems of cultural mentality. All one needs to do is have a look at Marx and Engels's descriptions of how they were stimulated by the theories of Feuerbach and Darwin and one can see their importance. Lu Xun also put special importance on dissecting the mental disposition of all types of people in history and in the contemporary period. Historical materialism takes the position that the necessity of history can only be demonstrated through history's randomness. And if one does not investigate this randomness in connection with the mentality of individuals, how can one make any clear conclusions?

If one says, for example, that the eighteenth-century Han scholars nearly all opposed "using historical arguments to establish rules on what is forbidden" and "using the historical appraisal of individuals as a basis for approval or disapproval,"[135] this is of course a kind of mental attitude. Yet this kind of attitude had no foundation in orthodox historical scholarship. Due to the expression "using one character to make an appraisal" (*yizi baobian*) in the *Spring and Autumn Annals*, from Sima Qian and Ban Gu onward, all historians regarded this kind of judgment as central to their craft. How, then, are we to explain how Qian Daxin and Wang Mingsheng got such a different kind of attitude?

Take, for example, the way in which Qing dynasty scholars researched the so-called Confucian classical heritage. Nearly all of them emphasized starting from the most basic work, distinguishing genuine from false texts, ascertaining the original textual content, clarifying terms and pronunciation, and fully explaining all words in the text, to the point even of claiming that "if there is one wrong explanation of a character, then the whole interpretation will be distorted and the meaning itself be lost."[136] This, of course, is also a kind of attitude, one which at that time was interpreted as a psychology of opposition. Since Kangxi, Yongzheng, and Qianlong, and the group of famous neo-Confucians under them, all emphasized the fact that textual problems with the classics had already been entirely resolved by Zhu Xi and others of his time, and the only problems left were questions of how to put these into practice, how were the attitudes of Dai Zhen and his fellows produced?

Take, for example, the fact that none of the eighteenth-century Han scholars failed to uphold the project of restoring antiquity, yet the famous textual critic Zhao Yi wrote the following line in one of his poems: "In every generation China has produced talented people, over many centuries leaders of literary excellence have emerged."[137] His intention in these words of course was to use a commentary on the poets Li Bo and Du Fu to express a feeling common to himself and his colleagues. Can one insist, therefore, that this support for a restoration of antiquity was evidence of a set of antimodern attitudes? This leads back to some reflections on Xu Guangqi. Among the early adherents of

Western learning, no one disputes the fact that Xu was a sincere believer. Nevertheless, he made a whole new set of notes on the *Book of Odes* (*Mao shi*) and *The Artificer's Record* (*Kaogong ji*), which could be seen as a reviving of antiquity. Was not the attitude of the Han scholars of the Qing period similar to that of Xu Guangqi? I think there is definitely a connection.

In the Chinese materials available there is no evidence so far that the missionaries introduced the theories of Bacon and Descartes, yet there are some indirect indications. Bacon opposed the repetition of what others had said and put forward the view that only what one has personally observed can be regarded as truth. Descartes opposed relying on the authority of ancient texts and emphasized that only the reliance on practical investigation could be regarded as science. The disseminators of Western learning in the seventeenth century, whether European missionaries such as Ricci or Chinese scholars such as Xu Guangqi, all insisted that the Chinese classics should be read in their original form and a rigid adherence to the explanations of either the Cheng brothers and Zhu Xi or Lu Jiuyuan and Wang Yangming should be avoided. The *First Collection of Heavenly Studies* (*Tianxue chuhan*), edited by Li Zhizao, brought together representative writings elucidating this sort of attitude. It provides some basis for the view that the mental disposition of Han scholars of the Qing was similar to that of the earlier promoters of Western learning.

All of these questions need research. Just because the Han scholars themselves denied being connected in any way with the proponents of Western learning—an attitude that itself needs to be researched—one cannot deny that there was a connecting link between them. Otherwise history would be somehow too simple.

The Peculiar Character of the Last Rays of Medievalism

At this point one cannot avoid the issue of the individual role of the Qing emperors in history. In China the autocratic system, which embodied the special characteristics of medievalism, reached its most extreme form in the Ming and Qing dynasties. This is a point commonly agreed on by most Chinese historians. Zhang Taiyan's "theory that only slaves could be prime ministers under autocracy"[138] may not have been a fully accurate reflection of the Han, Tang, Song, and Yuan dynasties, but it was an entirely correct depiction of the Qing. Since the Manchu people originally made a clear distinction between lord and slave, all who were members of the various banner groups, whether Manchu or Han, always called themselves "slaves" in the presence of the emperor. After the Qing dynasty became established, the treatment of Han officials who were not members of the banner groups was superficially that of ruler to official, showing them some respect, yet in reality the Han officials were treated as even lower than the banner slaves. Therefore, a prime minister who was not a banner member was in the eyes of the emperor nothing more than a slave leader of a subjugated people. He was not allowed to have any personal views or opinions apart from absolute obedience to the ruler. Chen Mingxia, Qian Qianyi, and others who went over to the service of the Qing put forth great efforts to stabilize Qing rule, yet in the end they were put to death. After they had died, they were called "twice-serving officials." This kind of treatment was the secret of Qing rule.

By contrast, the Qing rulers' favors to the European missionaries seem particularly remarkable. Adam Schall von Bell had served the Ming dynasty. In addition to revising the *Almanac of the Chongzhen Reign (Chongzhen lishu)*, he had introduced the design and manufacture of Western cannons and passed on secrets of a trade that actually caused the Manchus great losses in the Ming-Qing dynastic struggles. Nevertheless, after he moved over to the Qing side, Schall was greatly respected by the Manchu rulers. He was not only appointed the head of the Imperial Astronomical Bureau, a position that had considerable prestige and authority attached to it in the medieval period, but was even taken on as a political adviser by the Shunzhi emperor, who called him "mafa" (grandfather).[139] In the early Kangxi period, with the *I Could Not Do Otherwise* case, Yang Guangxian seemed, on the surface, to be using a problem related to the calendar to launch an attack on the Westerners. In reality, it was a matter of the Oboi group of officials using this as a pretext to purge the Shunzhi emperor's tendencies to assimilate to the Han. Schall's demise was therefore simply due to the fact that he was so close to Shunzhi (see chapter 4). This case was rectified through the intervention of Kangxi's grandmother, not long after Kangxi succeeded in staging the arrest of Oboi with the help of his child companions. Schall's successor Ferdinand Verbiest then gained the very same level of trust with the new emperor as Schall had enjoyed with Shunzhi.

The intense personal interest that Kangxi himself had in all aspects of Western learning has already been demonstrated through a great deal of historical evidence both in China and abroad. He made a point of educating himself in Western science and philosophy, which led him to have such an attitude of tolerance and sympathy toward the religious activities of the European missionaries that the missionaries hoped he would be "China's Constantine."[140] His attainments in Western learning, like his knowledge of Han scholarship, were probably not as outstanding as the Jesuits' *China Letters* or Bouvet's *Biography of the Kangxi Emperor* (*Kangxi dizhuan*) would have us believe, but they were certainly superior to those of his high Manchu and Han officials. In his interest in European sciences, he focused on such areas as mathematics, astronomy, botany, and medicine, and he enjoyed being personally involved in measurement and experimentation. He also paid attention to linguistic comparisons and to music. Given that he was an autocratic ruler, Kangxi's scholarly interests and hobbies were sure to have an influence on his officials and people. We can see that the research of the eighteenth-century Han scholars was largely oriented toward the areas of Kangxi's interests.

Nevertheless, Kangxi's interest in Western learning was always limited to his own personal environment, and he never considered extending this personal commitment to a wider scholarly community. On the contrary, he would not even allow the Han scholar-officials to do research on the Southern Ming, so there was no question of his encouraging them to extend their scholarly interests to a wider world. At the same time, though he always gave the impression of intending to extend East-West relations, once even sending the French missionary Joachim Bouvet back to France to ask Louis XIV to send some missionaries to cooperate in developing science and technology, this sort of interest gradually faded as the years passed.

The reason for this retreat has not so far been carefully researched. Yet one can get an impressionistic understanding through setting forth the various contradictions of the time. It could be related to the "weariness" of his old age, or to the internal and external contradictions he was facing. At a very early period he had made his second son Yinreng the crown prince. This crown prince was even more interested in Western learning than his father, which meant his mental disposition was even more open. Naturally he became the person whom the missionaries vied to have contact with. Unfortunately, however, this crown prince felt the waiting period to succeed his father was too long, and his impatience resulted in conflicts between father and son. He lost his position as heir and was put under restraint, then reinstated, then removed once again. These happenings brought considerable grief to Kangxi in his old age and undoubtedly aroused in him some suspicion toward the missionaries.

It was also at this time that the Jesuits in China became entangled in the so-called Chinese rites controversy, that is, the question of whether or not to allow Chinese Christian believers to worship heaven and revere their ancestors. The real essence of the conflict seems to have been a matter of a struggle for control over the activities of the missionaries in China. The Holy See supported the views of the populist tradition of the Dominicans and opposed Chinese believers continuing to worship heaven and revere their ancestors. Twice it sent envoys to China, who naturally met with a rebuff from Kangxi. The group supported by Kangxi was the French missionary society who later took leadership among the Jesuits. He felt that they were the only ones to show respect for Chinese rites and customs in a way that was consonant with the tradition of Matteo Ricci. Yet many of this group had died in the period between the two visits of the envoys from the Holy See, a fact that naturally made Kangxi feel even more distant from the missionaries in China and led to even greater indignation at the Holy See's designs to interfere with the traditional rites and customs of Chinese believers. The fact that in his last years Kangxi put renewed restrictions on religion was undoubtedly connected to these contradictions.[141]

There is no evidence so far to indicate that Yongzheng was in any way influenced by his father's interests or hobbies. On the other hand, there are materials that show that the two half-brothers whom he regarded as his main political opponents—Yinyi and Yintang[142]—probably had close links with Western religion and Western science.[143] Whether or not the missionaries participated in any way in the power struggle among Kangxi's potential successors, this situation was certainly not beneficial to them. Yongzheng strictly forbade the dissemination of Catholicism, and his successor Qianlong continued the same policies of religious repression. The practical result of this was quite another matter, since the more fierce the autocracy, the more intense were the centrifugal tendencies in the Middle Ages. Engels noted this point at an early period, and the Qing dynasty was no exception to it. For example, Yongzheng and Qianlong repressed religion over a period of eighty years, yet there were still over 100,000 Catholics in the early nineteenth century, an even greater number than a century earlier. This seems to be the inevitable result of the use of force in the repression of thought in history.

Was there then no outcome at all? Of course not. In the eighteenth century, Han scholars who had considerable attainments in Western learning, such as Jiang Yong and Jiao Xun, were as unwilling to admit that they had been inspired in any way by Western learning as they were adamant against becoming officials throughout their lives. This is a tragedy, the kind of tragedy that could only occur in the waning years of the Middle Ages.

A Disposition toward Estrangement

I have no intention of exaggerating the similarities between eighteenth-century Han scholarship and Western learning. In this century there has been an extremely positive feeling toward Chinese culture in Western scholarly circles, and discussions on the letters sent back from China by the Jesuits have become fashionable. Yet from the perspective of Chinese scholarship, the period between the late Ming and the late Qing is seen as one in which there was the greatest estrangement from European culture.

This estrangement, in the final analysis, was created by the cultural policy of the Qing dynasty. Still, one cannot deny the role of the mentality of individual scholars in the situation. The centrifugal tendencies that were exaggerated by the autocratic system created difficulties in the circles of scholarly culture that were even more serious than in other milieus. The so-called oppositional mentality led to a situation where whatever was suggested or supported by the Qing rulers, whether or not the facts behind it were accurate, whether or not it was a correct policy, always came up against blatant or indirect attitudes of opposition, a kind of evidence of this oppositional mentality.

Take, for example, the dispute over the calendar in the early Kangxi period. The person clearly in error was Yang Guangxian, while those who suffered as a consequence were Schall and the Chinese officials in the Astronomical Bureau who supported the new calendar. Many were imprisoned, killed, or sent into exile. Later, when they were released from prison and rehabilitated, the chief culprit, Yang Guangxian, was first condemned to exile, then forgiven and allowed to return to his home region. On the way he took ill and died. Yet in the eighteenth century, when Qian Daxin reopened this case, he chose to believe in rumors that Yang Guangxian had been poisoned to death by the missionaries. Qian Daxin was considered one of the grand old men of Han scholarship, and he had a thorough knowledge of the ins and outs of the calendrical issue. He clearly understood that the Arabic calendar, which Yang Guangxian used to replace the Western calendar, had nothing to do with "national essence." Nevertheless, he paid no attention to the facts of the situation, and all of his sympathies were for the heretical Yang Guangxian. It is difficult to explain this, except by suggesting that it reveals the antagonism of the Han scholars toward the emperor's trust in Western scholars and the Western calendar.

One can have some sympathy and understanding toward this kind of attitude, yet one cannot commend it. These emotional tendencies are a kind of "inflexible formalism" when translated into a methodology, what might be called raising those one favors to heaven and bringing down those one hates. The harm this has brought to scholarly research has been even greater than in other areas. The Han scholars of the Qing all hated neo-Confucian philosophy, and their opposition to the empty argumentation, to the tendency to focus on only the application of theory, to the establishment of theories on a single piece of evidence were all correct. Nevertheless, they themselves tended to extremism, with a kind of textual criticism that focused on tiny, insignificant issues, a superstitious belief in ancient teachings, and an investigation into detail that missed the overall picture. This led to their developing a philosophy that was loaded down with tedious formalities and renowned for its tendency toward a lack of realism. Because the Qing emperors respected Western missionaries at one point and suspected them at another, they either disliked and avoided Western learning, or gave it only the most superficial attention, with results that could only hinder the internal dynamic of the development of scholarship.

The Han learning of the Qing dynasty made an enormous contribution to Chinese cultural history, and anyone who wishes to research the heritage of Chinese classical culture cannot avoid using its research achievements. Nevertheless, it never really extricated itself from the category of medieval scholarship in the forms it followed, even though it should be regarded as an early modern culture. The result was that its content was suffocated by its form, and after less than a century of prosperous development it became rigid and dried up. In the early nineteenth century an opposing force arose within Han scholarship, waving the flag of a "true revival of antiquity"—the so-called New Text school. It used ideas from the classics to criticize the government of the time under the auspices of a revival of the tradition of the Western Han. Externally there was the Tongcheng group, which had from an early period taken the position of reviving the view of the Tang-Song transition period that "literature should have a meaning and purpose." In addition, with the Taiping Rebellion, the geographical home of Han scholarship was turned into a battleground where two armies killed each other. With such internal and external pressures on both the cultural and military fronts, could Han scholarship stay alive? Even though there were such great scholars as Yu Yue and Sun Yirang in the late Qing, the very term "Han scholarship" came to an end. Yet anyone who seriously investigated their ideas and thoughts would not have hoped for this kind of ending.

6 | Yangming Scholarship in Early Modern China

Jerome . . . said, "I thought I was in the spirit before the Judge of the universe." "Who art thou?" asked a voice. "I am a Christian." "Thou liest," thundered back the Great Judge, "thou are not but a Ciceronian."[144]

1

Chinese classical scholarship was the ruling doctrine of the Chinese Middle Ages. If one traces its history from the second century B.C. up to the eve of China's entry into the early modern period, it lasted about two thousand years.

Over a period of two thousand years, the formation of classical scholarship underwent continuous change. The general view is that one can distinguish Han scholarship from Song scholarship, and that within Han scholarship there are the New Text and Old Text schools, while within Song scholarship there is a distinction between Song neo-Confucianism (*lixue*) and Ming neo-Confucianism (*xinxue*).[145]

Ming neo-Confucianism, which is epitomized by the names of Lu

Jiuyuan and Wang Shouren (the original name of Wang Yangming), is without doubt the last of all the formations of Chinese classical scholarship. While its theoretical system had its origins in the work of Lu Jiuyuan in the Southern Song, or in the even earlier work of the Cheng brothers and Zhu Xi, it matured to its final form much later in the period between Chen Xianzhang of the early Ming and Wang Shouren of the mid-Ming. Later scholars called it Wang scholarship (*Wangxue*), but early modern scholars followed the Japanese habit of calling it Yangming scholarship (*Yangming xue*), and probably both are suitable terms for Ming neo-Confucianism.

This scholarship has been subjected to detailed analysis since the late Qing period, analysis that has depended on the abundant materials provided by Huang Zongxi's *The Records of Ming Scholars* (*Ming Ru xue'an*). Nevertheless, opposing views have coexisted for a long time over the evaluation of the historical function of Ming neo-Confucianism. In the recent half-century I think it is fair to say that those who repudiated it have been in the majority, while those who affirmed it have been few. The reason for this repudiation, in general terms, lies in the fact that it is infused with an atmosphere of subjective idealism. Thus the refutations have been conceived largely from the perspective of logic and have very little to do with a historical appraisal. My personal investigation has led me to believe that greater attention to the objective social effects of Ming neo-Confucianism would lead to a different evaluation.[146]

2

At this point I do not intend to repeat earlier discussions of my point of view on this matter, but simply to raise a question.

Who could fail to be surprised if a certain theory, which appears to have already "died" as far as history is concerned, in other words has been completely forgotten by most scholars, suddenly becomes the subject of heated scholarly debate once again? Who could resist trying to uncover the secret of such a "resurrection"?

In recent Western history neo-Kantianism, neo-Hegelianism, and neo-Freudianism are all old theories that have reappeared in new forms and have aroused lively discussion among many scholars. Yangming scholarship had a similar revival in early modern China. The situation is not that simple, however.

In the late nineteenth century, Chinese scholars had not yet used the term Yangming scholarship for Ming neo-Confucianism. As was the custom with all other schools of scholarship, they used a key term (in this case, *xinxue*, which could be translated philosophy of the mind) rather than either the surname or the given name of a scholar to denote a particular school. Nevertheless, in the last years of the nineteenth century, Chinese intellectual circles adopted the Japanese practice and gave the name Yangming scholarship to the school of Ming neo-Confucianism associated with Lu Jiuyuan and Wang Yangming. In the same vein, the Song neo-Confucianism of Zhu Xi and the Cheng brothers was now called Zhu Xi scholarship. This phenomenon in itself hinted at the coming "resurrection" of Ming neo-Confucianism, a resurrection that was rather clearly connected with a certain stimulus provided by early modern Japan.

3

What kind of a connection was this? To put it simply, after 1840, successive military defeats by foreign invaders left the Qing empire in a situation of both internal and external crisis. It could no longer maintain its rule through the system inherited from its ancestors. Thus a new tide of ideas for reforming the embattled government began to rise. China's traditional approach, to "use of barbarians to control barbarians," was now changed to a new approach, that of "learning the barbarians' skills in order to control the barbarian." To be unashamed of learning from one's enemies was originally not a bad attitude. The problem was which enemies one should learn from.

War broke out between China and Japan in 1894, and the result was a tremendous stir among progressive Chinese scholars, a sense of crisis even more intense than that brought on by the Sino-British Opium Wars. The Westernization group (*yangwu pai*) of the Qing government, which for some years had followed the principle of "learning the barbarians' skills in order to control the barbarian," had always fixed their sights on the great Western powers and had apparently given hardly any attention to their Eastern neighbor, Japan. According to the principles epitomized in Wei Yuan's *Blueprint for Maritime Countries* (*Haiguo tuzhi*) and a policy parallel to the Chinese one of learning the barbarians' skills, the Japanese secretly spied out China. The result was that, in a single sea battle, the North China fleet, which China had equipped and trained through learning from the West, was defeated by a Japanese fleet, which had similarly been equipped and trained on Western lines. It was a total defeat, and the Qing government was forced to sign the Treaty of Shimonoseki (Maguan treaty) with the attendant national disgrace and loss of power.

This one stroke not only destroyed the remnants of the so-called restoration that had resulted from the strained efforts made to defeat the Taiping Rebellion, but also dispelled the illusion surrounding the new approach of developing a strong and rich nation through "learning the barbarians' skills." If they wanted to save the nation from subjugation and ensure its survival, it was essential to reform the government. There was a rising clamor for this kind of change, which made itself known through the revolutionary activities of scholars who had been exposed to Western democratic education and by the first efforts made under Sun Yat-sen's leadership to overthrow the Qing dynasty.

Thus it happened that those persons calling for governmental reform began to turn their eyes toward their Eastern neighbor. They hoped to find out what kind of strength had enabled Japan to learn the barbarians' skills and be so much more successful at it than China had been.

The result of their search was quite unexpected. A considerable number of the well-known progressive scholars of the time made the surprising conclusion that this strength came from Yangming scholarship.

4

The Wang scholarship that emerged in the early sixteenth century was a new force within neo-Confucianism that opposed the theories of Zhu Xi. For a little over one hundred years it held a central place in Chinese intellectual and cultural circles.

Furthermore, in the most economically developed part of the country— the southeast region—Wang scholarship more or less completely ousted Zhu Xi scholarship from the intellectual life of the times. One only has to glance at the index to *The Records of Ming Scholars* to get a strong impression of this point.

Nevertheless, from the mid-seventeenth century, criticism and even refutation of Wang scholarship had become the principle current in scholarly circles. For example, such scholars as Gu Yanwu, Wang Fuzhi, Lü Liuliang, and Yan Yuan not only condemned Wang Yangming but believed that his followers had to take responsibility for the collapse of the Ming dynasty.

This is not the place for a discussion of the rise and subsequent demise of Wang scholarship. I have already given my general views on this in earlier articles.[147] Here I will simply point out that, in the early Qing, Wang scholarship managed to survive with some difficulty for a time, but its last group of great teachers had already lost the hope of any vigorous new developments. Huang Zongxi's compilation of *The Records of Ming Scholars* was thus a kind of elegy to this school.

In Sun Qifeng's discussion of Wang scholarship, he was really just using the ideas in Wang Shouren's *Conclusions on the Later Years of the Master Zhu (Zhuzi wannian dinglun)* to cover up his own return to Song neo-Confucianism. That his disciple Tang Bin became the first "famous official of Song neo-Confucianism" (*lixue mingchen*) of the Qing to have his tablet hung in the Confucian temple enables us to detect this.

After the last scholar of the Wang school, Li Fa, was disbarred from office and driven to his death, the voice of this school was no longer heard.

5

But there is no need to wait until these last years of the Qianlong emperor. While the Kangxi, Yongzheng, and Qianlong emperors could not be called believers in Confucius and Zhu Xi, they had all raised Zhu Xi to the frightening heights of being the official successor to the orthodoxy of Confucius and Mencius, in line with their policy of "using the Han to control the Han." In a medieval situation where the emperor was also the religious leader, the emperors consistently used their authority as rulers to discriminate against all other theories as heterodox, not to mention the fact that Wang Shouren was already on record from an early period for opposing the ideas of Zhu Xi.

Thus the few scattered followers of Wang scholarship in that century were soon silenced, and the school itself was destined to become extinct.

By the early part of the last century, in the cultural net that the Yongzheng and Qianlong emperors drew ever tighter, large holes had already appeared. It was no longer so dangerous to censure Song neo-Confucianism. Yet, even though the scholars of Han learning were so inflexible in their dislike of Song neo-Confucianism, they also disliked the careless flow of Wang scholarship. The Old and New Text schools of the Qing dynasty, which succeeded Han scholarship, brought about a "restoration of antiquity" (*fugu*), which raised the flag of restoring the Gongyang scholarship of the Western Han and repudiating the Han scholarship that had been fashionable for a time. They emphasized the positive role of subjective consciousness and insisted that they could not become slavish annotators of the classical canons, an approach similar in spirit to that of Wang scholarship. Nevertheless, they still put importance on their own annotations, which had to be in accord with the "sublime words and deep meaning" of Confucius himself in his writing of the five classics, and they used these annotations of the classics as a means of disseminating their views. They could not really understand Wang scholarship.

Thus Wang scholarship continued to be largely forgotten. *The Records of Ming Scholars*, which might be termed the "History of the Wang Scholars," was still printed and distributed, but after 1821, when the woodblock version cut by Mo Jin in Kuaiji (now Shaoxing) came out, it ceased being published for a period of sixty years. It is not hard to guess how few people there were who sought it out.

6

Of course, Wang scholarship did not entirely die out. A few Song neo-Confucian scholars, who were attempting to mediate the disputes between the Han and Song scholarship, had first to deal with the internal disputes between the so-called Cheng-Zhu and Lu-Wang sects of Song scholarship. Naturally they wanted to draw some inspiration from Wang scholarship in this, and thus it continued to be studied, albeit by its opponents.

In the late Qing a Song neo-Confucian named Zhu Ciqi emerged from the very home village of the pioneer of Wang scholarship in the Ming period, Chen Xianzhang. In his teaching he denied that there was a dividing line between Han and Song scholarship, saying that Zheng Xuan and Zhu Xi were both students of Confucian theories, and that the gap between Zhu Xi and Wang Shouren was even smaller. Thus he proposed using Wang scholarship to complement Zhu scholarship.

Zhu Ciqi taught a large number of students in Guangdong. One of them, a student of his old age, developed and revised his teacher's views and took the position that Lu Jiuyuan and Wang Shouren were of greater importance than Zhu Xi, and their theories were "direct, clear, and genuine, also flexible and useful for analyzing the contemporary period.'' This was already going too far. Even more shockingly, this brash young disciple dared to criticize the *Primer for Teaching the Way* (*Daoshu qianbo*) of Han Yu, who was so revered by his master and who was of course the one who had established the ''transmission of the Way,'' the very foundation of Song neo-Confucianism. The old master became furious, and his disciple had no choice but to roll up his bedding and return home. As far as I know, he was the first person in early modern China to get the idea of ''resurrecting'' Yangming scholarship. This young man was none other than the illustrious leader of the reform movement of the late Qing, Kang Youwei.

7

To grasp a principle thoroughly, indulge in no hesitation, confidently and even superciliously seek ways to implement it, behave in an absolutely stubborn and pig-headed way, and allow one's aspirations for leadership to swell to the point of feeling that ''If Anshi is not willing to come out and organize the government, how will the people manage?''[148]—this is the personality type of those who have challenged tradition in both Chinese and Western history.

Long before he had become well known, when he was still an ordinary person, Kang Youwei had given all of his loyalty to Wang scholarship. I think there is a good explanation for this.

When Wang Shouren's views were first put forward in the mid-Ming period, they attracted a large number of seekers after knowledge. From the worthies of the imperial cabinet right down to the craftspeople among the peasants, there were followers at every level of society. Why was this?

The most economic response to this question is to simply dismiss the reactionary and deceptive nature of their subjective idealism, and of course there is a formula ready at hand for this task.

However, the idealist philosophy of the past, seeing things, reality, and sensual knowledge as a kind of practice to be understood, was actually superior to historical materialism, even that of Feuerbach, in developing the subjective aspect of human ability. Is not this very point part of the heritage of Marxism?

All of Wang Shouren's theories give evidence of this point. Zhu Xi's emphasis on ''exhausting principle and respecting the classics''—

which no one up to now has called historical materialism—was seen by Wang Yangming as rigid and tedious. Therefore, he energetically revived Lu Jiuyuan's precept that "one's own mind is principle" (*xin ji li*), he elaborated the Chan proposition that "the Buddha is one's own mind" (*ji xin ji fo*), and he developed Mencius's view that "all things in the world can be found in my thought" (*wanwu jie bei yu wo*) into a theory of "attaining innate knowledge" (*zhi liangzhi*). No one can deny that all human persons have innate knowledge, thus any person one might meet on the street has the potential to become a sage such as the great Yu. This kind of theory makes the human mind the measure to judge truth from falsehood, though, needless to say, it does rather stink of subjective idealism. Still, Wang Shouren and later Wang scholars opposed a slavish adherence to the "Four Books" and the parroting of ancient sages and worthies. Was this not a welcome message to those who were coming out of the Middle Ages?

To praise the subjective consciousness and appreciate individual liberation are not only not incompatible with one another, they are in fact two sides of the same coin. This explains why, from Kang Youwei and Liang Qichao to Zhang Taiyan and Sun Yat-sen, no matter what their self-proclaimed beliefs and doctrines, all displayed an even more vehement emphasis on the subjective consciousness than Wang Shouren himself, and herein lies the secret of his influence.

8

Kang Youwei's worship of Wang scholarship was not publicly known until November 1899, that is, a year after the failure of the 1898 Hundred Day Reform movement. Liang Qichao had fled to Japan, and he let it out in the form of a biography of his teacher. This is the first indication we have that the first efforts made in China to repudiate medievalism and reform the political system were led by someone who believed that all human persons have the potential to become sages, not by someone who believed in some gobbledegook about three historical periods and three kinds of unification. It was also someone who had a pure conscience and understood the simple doctrine that there is no fundamental conflict between heavenly principles and human desires. No wonder the reform movement, which was started up by a small number of young intellectuals, within a brief two or three years touched a deep chord in the hearts of knowledgeable people of all classes and levels, no matter what their political tendencies. From this perspective I think one could develop a very persuasive explanation.

9

In the final analysis, however, Kang Youwei's courage did not reach beyond the limits set by the cultural tradition of the time. He adored Wang Shouren, but he only dared to reveal this to such favorite disciples as Chen Qianqin and Liang Qichao, when he was teaching in his academy, the Wanmu Caotang. He greatly admired the German Reformation and had a deep desire to become the Martin Luther of China, but his daring only went far enough to develop formula opposite to Luther's efforts at bringing Christ down from a god to being a human person. Following the logic of the Qing rulers, he raised Confucius from being a wholly wise and able person of talent to the position of a universal savior. This led his friends, who were oriented toward democracy and freedom, to become perplexed and lose hope. Sun Baoxin's *Diary from the Mountain Cottage* (*Wang shanlu riji*) provides the most direct and telling evidence of this.

10

In 1898 the Dowager Empress Cixi engineered a violent coup to strangle a peaceful reform movement that was already underway, and thereafter it was clear that the ruling apparatus of the Qing would not allow any genuine political structure reform. Among the "six gentlemen" (*liu junzi*) who were killed, only Tan Sitong could be called a martyr. In his posthumous book, a volume called *A Study of Benevolence* (*Renxue*), which was a somewhat jumbled collection of thoughts, there was just one point that gave a stimulus to radical youth, his call to "burst through the trammels." He declared that all the various traditions that had played a role in Chinese society—official ranks and perquisites, the eight-legged essay style of composition, the worship of heaven and of ancestors, the autocratic system of government, the feudal ethical code of the three cardinal goods and the five constant virtues—constituted the trammels, and that they all had to be smashed, with the exception of the Confucian religion. Even the Confucian religion had to be reformed by purging itself of Xun Kuang's ideas and restoring the Mencian emphasis on democracy and Zhuang Zi's views on opposing autocracy.

Tan Sitong drew Zhuang Zi from the side of Lao Zi to that of Confucius, which was already strange enough, but he also declared that Zhuang Zi's legacy was to be found within the theories of Lu Jiuyuan and Wang Shouren, and that Huang Zongxi's *A Plan for the Prince* (*Mingyi dai fang lu*) came close to a true transmission of this legacy.

Whether or not Zhuang Zi was ever influenced by Confucian thought is quite another question. Yet to say that Wang Shouren hinted at opposition to autocracy is simply a logical inference, that is, it is drawn from Wang Shouren's thoughts on developing the words of Lu Jiuyuan concerning "using the six classics as a means of self-expression" and that "all persons have the potential to become a sage like Yu." From this he inferred that Wang Shouren was hinting that all persons are equal before the "self" and denying that the ruler's "self" was any greater than the "self" of ordinary people. Even though Wang Shouren never had such an idea, from Tan Sitong's inference one gets some understanding of early modern China and the points in Wang Shouren's thought that struck particularly strong chords in Kang Youwei, Liang Qichao, and Tan Sitong.

11

One direct outcome of the failure of the peaceful reform of the late nineteenth century was the high tide of violent revolution that immersed the early twentieth century. The revolutionaries carried the banner of "getting rid of the Manchus" and called for a "glorious restoration of the old times," naively imagining that once the Qing dynasty was overthrown, all would be well. From a scattered group of small organizations they came together in the Revolutionary League (Tongmenghui) led by Sun Yat-sen, all of this taking place in Japan. For this reason, the Japanese experience of restoring the emperor and overthrowing the shogunate in that year naturally became a matter the young revolutionaries wanted to explore.

The outcome of this investigation was somewhat unexpected. On the eve of the establishment of the Revolutionary League in August 1905, at a meeting where the Chinese students in Japan collectively welcomed Sun Yat-sen, a Japanese visitor made a speech in which he said that the reason for Japan's strength was not the fact that Japan had studied Western law but that it had mastered Han scholarship, and particularly Wang learning. "The scholars who engineered the restoration of the emperor and the overthrow of the shogunate were all deeply versed in Yangming scholarship, and were not necessarily familiar with Western law at all.''

Naturally this was a common view among Japanese intellectuals at the time. But it left a strong impression on the revolutionary Chinese students in Japan, as can be seen in the history of Chen Tianhua, who had taken responsibility for recording the minutes of the meeting on that day. Chen was the main person responsible for soliciting articles for the Revolutionary League's publication, the *Min bao*. Not long after this he committed suicide, as he was depressed by the split among Chinese students in Japan over attitudes toward "getting rid of the Manchus." The obituary written by his friend said "he had knowledge and he acted, he respected his teacher Yangming." The capable organizer of the Revolutionary League, Song Jiaoren, had a similar conviction that "the spirit is all powerful" in the task of reforming China, indicating the degree to which he too had been influenced by Yangming scholarship.

12

After the failure of the Hundred Day Reform in 1898, Kang Youwei and Liang Qichao became leaders of the monarchist group in exile abroad, upholding the call for a constitutional monarchy around the Guangxu emperor, who was imprisoned in the palace. They refused to cooperate with Sun Yat-sen and openly opposed the use of violence to overthrow the Qing dynasty.

For this reason, when we are discussing the differences between the reformist and the revolutionary groups in the early part of the century, we always tend to deal with them in an inflexible way—"if they are not this, they must be that"—and we confuse differences over tactics with differences over strategy, differences over politics with differences over philosophy, making what were matters of expediency, adopted to attack their enemies, appear to be a doctrinal conflict between two different lines of thought. This can hardly be seen as a balanced approach or one that accords with historical reality.

Surely in the struggles between the revolutionary army and that of the constitutional monarchists it was a matter of physical survival. The main reason for this did not lie in the realm of thought but elsewhere. To be frank, it lay with the question of personal interest, the conflict between vested interests and future interests. If this were not the case, it would be very difficult to understand how it was that both sides seriously considered proposals for a "ceasefire" during their struggle, and how, after the 1911 Revolution, they would shake hands and make peace, then fall out and become enemies again.

13

At this point I must say something about Zhang Taiyan. In an article entitled "Zhang Taiyan and Wang Yangming" I have already pointed out how Zhang gradually became more and more oriented toward Yangming scholarship after he became editor of *Min bao*, even though he was obliged to take an opposite stand to that of Kang Youwei in order to protect his views on revolutionary politics. For this reason he repeatedly expressed public repudiation of Wang Shouren.

My article has been criticized by scholars in China and abroad,[149] but I have given serious consideration to both oral and written criticisms of my point and feel it has not so far been refuted.

The reason for this is that these criticisms have been based on a certain hypothesis, namely, that there is no connection between theory and political views, and thus if one wants to explore philosophical thought it is not necessary to take the author's political views into account. I completely agree with the point that one should not confuse theory with political views, but it is essential to specify the context in which this is appropriate. It must be in a context in which the person being studied is a pure scholar. The persons we are studying were not pure scholars, however. Thus if you wish to investigate the ideas and philosophy of Kang Youwei, Liang Qichao, Tan Sitong, Zhang Taiyan, and Sun Yat-sen, you cannot omit an investigation of the role of their political careers in influencing the evolution of their thinking. In this matter I believe in the view of Marx and Engels that in doing research on the history of thought, culture, and religion, we must pay attention to "the real interference of politics in the historical process."

14

I affirm that "Zhang Taiyan did not like Wang Yangming," precisely to point out an attitude he adopted for political reasons. If we were to take hold of two or three articles in Zhang Taiyan's latter years as representing a "consistent" view of Wang Shouren held by Zhang all his life, then there is nothing more to be said. "In the end, the only way we can find out the truth is by asking Taiyan himself down below!"[150]

In reality, if we recognize the fact that the social changes of early modern China were extremely violent, and that in making a critical assessment of a particular thinker we cannot take his own view of himself as reliable evidence, then even if a miracle occurred and the dead came back to life, surely we wouldn't have to ask for their opinion in developing a critique of their thinking?

I still believe that the history of thought can only be explained by history itself. To repudiate historical evolution, and to use the opinion a thinker had in his final days to represent all earlier views, is like claiming that just because a person did not maintain his integrity to the end, he had been a "reactionary" from the moment he made the first cry outside his mother's womb. If this is the situation, then who looks more ridiculous?

15

Even though Zhang Taiyan did not like Wang Yangming, Yangming's specter haunted his thoughts. If you read all of his works you will find his estimate of Yangming scholarship was sometimes high, sometimes low, and his attitude was sometimes harsh and sometimes appreciative. This contradiction was not a result of his gazing at the ceiling beams in abstract thought; rather, it was a tendency arising from his political activities.

Zhang Taiyan was undoubtedly a great scholar, but he was not a pure scholar. Before he withdrew from the revolutionary currents, his first concern had been the destiny of the democratic revolution. His first undertaking was to use both his pen and his tongue to refute all ideas and propaganda that were not beneficial to this destiny. Any teachings he felt would lead China in the wrong direction he would refute and expose, in a few cases even purposely using some very extreme language. This meant that his thoughts and opinions were always affected by strategic needs. This certainly had a historical value, even thought it could not be said to have a scientific value.

Zhang Taiyan was clearly drawn to Wang Shouren, yet he constantly criticized Wang Shouren. An adequate explanation for this can only be found by looking at his arguments and actions against his enemies. Kang Youwei advocated respect for Confucius and the protection of the emperor, while Liang Qichao supported enlightened despotism. Later

Liang Qichao, together with Jiang Zhiyuan, Ma Liang, and others, organized the Zhengwen she and promoted constitutional monarchy. All of these opposed the revolutionaries who wished to overthrow the Qing, and all used Wang Shouren's notion of "innate knowledge" (*liangzhi*) to decorate their prose.

In his criticism of Wang Shouren, Zhang Taiyan concentrated his attack on his "technique of action," feeling that he supported outrageous rulers, and that those who suffered at their hands were either the people, who were forced to rebel, or the more honorable of the imperial clansmen. Zhang felt Wang Shouren used the notion of "innate knowledge" to conceal faults and gloss over wrongs. This criticism was actually aimed at Kang and Liang's group. This is not just a guess on my part, but something I have seen in Zhang Taiyan's writing, for example, his "Thesis Refuting Innate Knowledge and Constitutional Government" ("Bo shenwo xianzheng shuo").

16

Ma Liang or Ma Xiangbo also used Wang Shouren's theories to dress up his political views in the late Qing period. This was a fascinating situation.

This famous educator of early modern China, a Catholic who at one time had been a priest, knew a number of European languages and was familiar with various schools of Western philosophy. But in his old age he became the general director of the Zhengwen she, a constitutional monarchist society. This was similar to being president of a political party. In Japan he submitted a report to the head of the Qing government's advisory Political Bureau suggesting that the imperial government order a national congress to be held within two years to establish a constitution. What motivated this behavior? Surely it was the happiness that came from following the dictates of his inner spirit and obeying the orders of his conscience.

This volume of Ma Liang's, which became well known in China and abroad, was actually drafted in cooperation with the real leader behind the scenes of the Zhengwen she, Liang Qichao. Since the Catholic theory of the soul (*shenwo*) was closely related to Wang Shouren's theory of innate knowledge, these two theories became the parents of the illusion of creating a constitutional monarchy in China, a strange twist in the history of political thought. No wonder Zhang Taiyan felt he had to heap scorn on this development in *Min bao*.

Nevertheless, does not this kind of incident go to show the extent to which Wang Shouren's theories played a role in the debates of early modern China?

17

History really does play jokes on people. In a short time the tables were turned, and the very one who had heaped scorn on others himself became the object of scorn. Here I refer to Zhang Taiyan.

Zhang Taiyan was silent at the time of May 4th, perhaps because the outstanding performers on the *New Youth* journal had largely been his comrades in arms or students, perhaps because just at the time he was cooperating with Sun Yat-sen in the movement to "protect the laws," or possibly because the Menieres symptoms he suffered from had recurred. Of course, many other factors may also have contributed to his silence.

But when he finally did reveal his attitude it was already 1924, that is, five years after May 4th. The criticism he offered so late was particularly severe. "Since the late Qing, persons without citizenship have started talking about new politics. Not long after they began to talk about a new morality and new culture. They simply gave their own opinions as truth, in order to repudiate the people's traditional customs."

The indictment he pronounced was also astonishing: "New politics have been tried for over twenty years, like cutting the feet to fit the shoes, but the people have not found any advantage and the government has become daily more chaotic. The promoters of new morality and new culture are again simply encouraging people to be excessively indulgent and turn their backs on traditional morality. It is taking Zhu Xi's theory of renovating the people to its extreme."

"Persons without citizenship" refers to the reformers who had gone into exile, and the "new politics" refers to Kang and Liang's proposed reforms. The reference to "over twenty years" clearly starts at the fake reforms of the Qing government after the invasion of the eight armies in 1900. For Zhang Taiyan to place all the responsibility for the increasing corruption of the government after the 1911 Revolution on the shoulders of the monarchists was unfair, yet it pleased people. But his suggestion that the opponents of traditional morality and culture in May 4th had been influenced by the modernizers of the late nineteenth century, that the outcome of their movement had been extremely deleterious and in no way different from that of the original new parties, all

being poisoned by the neo-Confucianism of Zhu Xi, not only was unfair, but might be seen as intentionally framing them.

Furthermore, Zhang Taiyan used this occasion to praise Wang
Shouren, saying that Wang and his disciples might not be comparable
to Confucius and Yan Hui, but they could be seen as successors of the
Master's teaching. In addition, the theory of innate knowledge and the
theory of the unity of knowledge and action were "an advancement on
the political techniques of Confucius's famous disciple, Zilu." This
great teacher of Chinese scholarship had apparently already forgotten
how he had once excused the Cheng brothers and Zhu Xi and had
excoriated Wang learning. He was now completely contradicting himself. What was even more preposterous, the old fellow dared to suggest
that scourges had broken out between 1898 and May 4th due to the fact
that Zhu Xi had been "taken and used as a handle by certain presumptuous people." Wang Shouren had opposed Zhu Xi's theory of renovating the people and that of investigating things and exhausting principle,
proving that he had tremendous foresight. Wang Shouren's opposition
to Zhu Xi "was demonstrated not in the Ming dynasty but in the present century—if you read his books, take warning!"

This kind of analysis, which is something like fortune telling, can be
found in his preface and afterword for the *Complete Collection of Duke
Wang Wenchang's Writings (Wang Wencheng Gong quanshu)*.[151] Some
scholars have censured me for neglecting these two articles and say it
indicates I am not aware of the respectful attitude Zhang Taiyan had
had toward Wang Shouren all along. I can accept the first half of this
criticism, since in my "Zhang Taiyan yu Wang Yangming" my investigation was limited to the period before May 4th, and it is true that I
did not discuss these two articles. But I beg to disagree with the second
half of the criticism. If I admitted to it not only would this not be in
accord with reality, but I could be suspected of trying to defend the
scales and lacerations on the head of Ah Q.

18

Liang Shuming, the person who succeeded the later Zhang Taiyan, was
also an admirer of Yangming scholarship. He expounded the culture
and philosophy of East and West, giving Wang Shouren a position he
had never had before. He claimed that Chinese culture was a rational
culture. The actual expression of this was in "clarity and harmony"

(*qingming anhe*), while its philosophical expression was in a "non-oppositional stance" (*wudui*). By this he meant there were no contradictions. In his view, the only persons qualified to represent that kind of culture, with the exception of Confucius and Mencius, were Dong Zhongshu of the Han and Wang Shouren of the Ming.

A society of clarity and harmony and a world without contradictions were of course a pleasant ideal. Let us leave aside for the moment the question of whether or not this ideal existed only in the minds of philosophers. If we say that Confucius, Mencius, Dong Zhongshu, and Wang Shouren all held this kind of ideal, we would certainly be ignoring the facts. For example, in Wang Shouren's famous phrase, "it is easy to get rid of the thieves in the hills, but much harder to overcome the thieves in people's hearts," there was a recognition that thieves existed in both society and the mind, a self-proclaimed refutation of the theory of there being no contradictions and a self-admission that his view of the world was not one of "clarity and harmony." Perhaps the ideal belonged to the future. But when Liang Shuming was speaking, there was already a gap of several hundred years since Wang Shouren. According to Mencius's prophecy that "a king would arise every five hundred years," the contradiction should have been on the verge of resolution. Why, then, was it still necessary to mourn a "present day" in which there was no new "Wang Shouren"?

I must apologize for implicating Liang Shuming in this discussion. But to describe Chinese cultural history as a process entirely determined by subjective consciousness can only be called a history that is fabricated by the human mind. History will not change simply because it is fabricated, since it belongs to a past that no subjective consciousness can refute.

19

Those who first promoted political and social reform in early modern China, including Kang Youwei and Liang Qichao of the Hundred Day Reform of 1898, looked both to the West and to China's tradition in seeking spiritual strength for their struggle.

The progressive persons of that period fitted Mao Zedong's description exactly: "They would read any books, as long as they contained new ideas from the West." "Since the Japanese had been effective in learning from the West, the Chinese wanted to learn from the Japanese."

History demonstrates that the kind of learning from the West that went on was actually "secondhand." Many of the new ideas from the West were not introduced directly from Europe and North America, but rather through Japanese translations of Western works. Likewise, in seeking to learn from Japan, the Chinese were not so much interested in how the Japanese had adopted Western methods to their own situation as in what the Japanese had absorbed from Chinese traditions.

In carrying out the Meiji restoration, the Japanese were apparently inspired by Wei Yuan's *Blueprint for Maritime Countries.* Therefore, as Liang Qichao pointed out, everyone in the original new parties associated with the Hundred Day Reform of 1898 had already gone through a phase of being crazy about Wei Yuan. Japanese success in carrying out the "restoration of the emperor and overthrow of the shogunate" has been said to be the crux of the success of the Meiji Restoration, and the Japanese reformers who supported it gained their inspiration from Yangming scholarship. Thus all the new parties, from the reformers to the revolutionaries, studied Wang Yangming.

Even Sun Yat-sen, who had received a Western scientific and democratic education from his earliest years, emphasized in his *Scheme for Developing China (Jianguo fanglue)* that knowledge was difficult while action was easy. This inevitably makes one think of Wang Yangming's view of knowing first and acting later in his theory of the "unity of knowledge and action." That is in spite of the fact that Sun Yat-sen never openly admitted to admiring Wang Yangming.

As for Zhang Taiyan, who is widely acknowledged as the chief revolutionary theorist of the 1911 revolutionary group, he moved from detesting Yangming scholarship to sympathy with it, then from sympathy to praise, and finally in his last years to an affirmation of Wang Yangming as the prophet of republican theory. There were similarities in this view to the idea of the Han Confucians that Confucius had established the great principles for Han dynasty rule three hundred years previously. This is more evidence that a latent influence of Yangming scholarship in the intellectual circles of early modern China cannot be neglected.

20

The fascination that Yangming scholarship exerted over progressive persons in early modern China cannot be dismissed by a simplistic rebuke, nor can it be satisfactorily explained in terms of the attraction of the new Confucianism.

We cannot underestimate traditional forces. Yet the theories of Wang Yangming not only belonged to a heterodox tradition that stood in opposition to Song neo-Confucianism's doctrine of the transmission of the Way, they themselves had been dead for two hundred years by the last century. Thus, in the last part of the nineteenth century they could only be seen as a dead tradition of past generations. Yet this dead tradition turned out to have greater force than the living traditions of the late Qing.

In the normal way of things, when the dead gain a hold over the living, it is thought to be a great misfortune. But in the case of Yangming scholarship in early modern China, just the opposite was true. It was welcomed by a group of people who were struggling to pull away from the traditions of the Middle Ages.

There can only be one explanation why this dead tradition received a greater welcome than the living ideas that dominated thought in scholarly circles of the time. That is that its political and intellectual standpoint was more suited to the needs of another group of living persons.

It is quite true that the thought system of Yangming scholarship was strongly infused with an atmosphere of subjective idealism, yet if one compares it with the formations of other medieval theoretical traditions, can one claim it was more idealist? Let us compare the essence of Zhu Xi's theories, what was called the six-character formula for "cherishing heavenly principles and suppressing human desires," with Wang Yangming's daring assertion of the simple belief that "people are the same as their minds, and their minds are the same as principle," so "everyone has the potential to become a sage such as Yao and Shun." Was not the Song neo-Confucian school even more idealist than that of Wang Yangming?

Even though Wang Yangming and his disciples never reached the level of a conscious demand for "individual liberation" and were even farther from promoting a "spirit of equality," they were still harbingers of certain portents that indicated the coming dissolution of medieval scholarship.

Otherwise, how can we account for the fact that it was the theories of Yangming scholarship, not those of Confucius, Mencius, Dong Zhongshu, Zheng Xuan, the Cheng brothers, Zhu Xi, or Lu Jiuyuan, that had such strong reverberations among those who supported reform in early modern China?

21

"All mysteries which mislead theory to mysticism find their rational solution in human practice and in the comprehension of this practice."[152] Marx expressed this view in his *Outline on Feuerbach*, and it is clearly an insight of the greatest value for research into the interrelation between medieval and early modern thought.

In this essay I have barely covered the subject in outline form. While the role played by Yangming scholarship in the process of continuous conflict between Chinese and Western, old and new ideas may not have been as obvious as that of the Old and New Text schools, the theory of evolution, the theories of natural rights, and parliamentary democracy, there can be no doubt about the reality of its practical role in intellectual and cultural history. Therefore, it is essential for both the history of Chinese classical scholarship and Chinese intellectual and cultural history to break down the boundaries between the Middle Ages and the early modern period.

7 | A Historical Investigation into the Early Formation of the Historical Materialist Viewpoint in China

History is nothing but the activity of man pursuing his aims.[153]

1

The Chinese people came to know about Marx in the latter part of the 1890s, about sixteen years after Marx's death. It was even later before the Chinese people became aware of the Marxist historical materialist viewpoint. So far no translated materials have been found before 1902 that give an accurate picture of this theory. That means there was a gap of at least half a century after the time Marx discovered this pattern of human historical development.

Nevertheless, from the time Marxist historical materialism was introduced to China, it first stirred up reverberations among a small number of progressive intellectuals before the 1911 Revolution, then it gained a greater and greater allegiance from revolutionary youth before and after the May 4th Movement. In a brief ten years it gained a remarkable victory over all the other new ideologies that had been disseminated throughout China from the time of the 1898 Reform Movement and became the weapon of thought that was to save China.

What was the reason for this? Mao Zedong expressed it well: "The reason why Marxism-Leninism has played such a great role in China since its introduction is that China's social conditions call for it, that it has been linked with the actual practice of the Chinese people's revolution, and that the Chinese people have grasped it. Any ideology—even the very best, Marxism-Leninism itself—is ineffective unless it is linked with objective realities, meets objectively existing needs, and has been grasped by the masses of the people. We are historical materialists, opposed to historical idealism."[154]

Naturally, historical materialism falls into this category of the very best, as depicted accurately by Engels: "Just as Darwin discovered the law of development of organic nature, so Marx discovered the law of development of human history; the simple fact concealed by an overgrowth of ideology that mankind first of all eat, drink, have shelter and clothing before it can pursue politics, science, art, religion etc.; that therefore the production of immediate material means of subsistence and consequently the degree of economic development attained by a given people or during a given epoch form the foundation upon which the state institutions, the legal conceptions, art and even the ideas on religion, of the people concerned have been evolved, and in the light of which they must, therefore, be explained, instead of vice versa, as had hitherto been the case."[155]

To recognize this simple fact and to explain social history from this perspective is called the historical materialist viewpoint. If one uses the simplest words to express this, it is that social existence determines social consciousness. Needless to say, as a conceptual formation, historical materialism is itself a philosophical manifestation of social existence, only it is more concentrated and more universal than others. Thus it has become a truth that has universal application.

At this point, according to the insight of Mao Zedong, one must raise a question: Was Marxism immediately accepted by progressive Chinese simply because it was a superior ideology? Obviously one cannot take that line. If one uses thought alone to discuss thought, it is impossible to give a clear explanation as to why a certain school of "foreign" thought could take roots in the hearts and minds of the Chinese.

As everyone knows, Marx himself was no "sage-prophet." Take, for example, a fundamental position of historical materialism—that the history of human civilization should be seen as a series of class struggles. On the theoretical level, this viewpoint was stimulated by previous thinkers in at least three aspects. The French bourgeois historians—Thierry, Mignet, Guizot, and others—discovered that it was the struggle among classes that led to revolution. The theory of evolution developed by the British naturalist Charles Darwin provided a basis in the natural sciences for the theory of class struggle. Finally, its main philosophical premise should be attributed to the German idealist philosopher Hegel's dialectical historical viewpoint. If we want to trace this idea back even farther, we must recognize as accurate the views of the Italian philosopher Labriola, affirmed by Plekhanov. He believed that many ancient and early modern historians had a clear understanding of the meaning of class struggle, since they saw these struggles for themselves within certain determined contexts.[156]

Marx and Engels themselves admitted on numerous occasions that historical materialism had its own theoretical precursors. But their recognition of this in no way decreases their reputation as the founders of historical materialism. On the contrary, it enables us to understand their great discovery. They not only contributed to and researched the results of the proletarian revolution, but also critically absorbed the crystallization of a variety of valuable insights from human civilization and culture.

Were there any parallel embryonic formations of the historical materialist viewpoint in the historical consciousness of the Chinese people before Marx's great discovery was widely disseminated in China? Logically the answer to this should not be negative. Otherwise it would be hard to understand why it aroused greater and greater resonance among progressive Chinese as soon as it came to the East. Of course, logic cannot take the place of history, so it may be appropriate to try to use some historical sources from before the introduction of historical materialism into China and make a rough preliminary investigation along chronological lines.

2

Some elements of Marxist theory in the West can be traced back to classical Greek philosophers. Likewise in China, at the latest starting from the Warring States period, certain simple facts that are the expression of the historical materialist viewpoint have been explored by a succession of scholars.

Classical Chinese philosophers all sought out the laws or principles that regulated human society. In contradistinction to Lao Zi who proceeded him and Mo Zi who followed, Confucius's views on the manners and morals of the time were probably least convincing. He saw history as a continuous process of decline, and he felt the determining cause of this decline was the fact that people were becoming more and more evil. In his latter years he used the compilation of a history to lay out his personal political views and then used this measure to pass judgment on the rights and wrongs of the political system of the Kingdom of Lu over the recent past. Between the lines he made clear his own indignation and sense of unease over the way in which "vulgar people" (*xiaoren*), in other words nonaristocrats, were overstepping traditional rites, resulting in a disintegration of the pattern of existence of "superior people" (*junzi*), that is, aristocrats. This kind of judgment of the overall historical process based on the motivations of human behavior[157] is said to be the main perspective that he introduced into China's only existing historical compilation of the time—the *Spring and Autumn Annals*. It has been called "the exposure of ulterior motives" (*zhuxin zhilun*). Since the *Spring and Autumn Annals* was respected as the major source of law for the Han dynasty, this rather mediocre perspective became the source of the orthodox historical viewpoint of Chinese feudalism.

Nevertheless, even though Confucius's pen was directed at the intentions of "disorderly officials and their rapacious underlings," one could still say he was aware that people had to eat, and at one point he made the principle of a full national granary one of the three basic principles of good government. By the period of the Warring States, the later disciples of Confucius, all of whom were seeking to establish themselves as his authoritative "successor," no longer had to worry about getting support from the rulers. The result was that most forgot that the nation needed "adequate food." This can be seen in the eulogy to the fifteen expressions of Confucian virtue in the *Book of Rites* (*Li ji, Ruxing*), which might also be called the norms of behavior for the fifteen Confucian sects. Not one of the fifteen glorified an attitude of concern for the provision of the people's livelihood, a fact that is roughly indicative of the situation. At that time the only exception was Xun Kuang.

Xun Kuang was typical of most of the transmitters of the Confucian classical texts and commentaries in the Middle Ages. He was the true godfather of the theories that predominated from the period of the

Western Han. As a Confucian, he had to make use of the term rites (*li*). As the scholar who developed an apologetic for the future advantages enjoyed by the feudal classes, in talking about rites he had to put some new wine in these old bottles. Thus he raised a problem that startled vulgar Confucians: where do rites come from? His answer was an extremely simple one. Rites arise from physical nourishment (*yang*). Is this not the case? All people are born with physical desires, the eyes need to see color, the ears to hear sound, the mouth to taste flavor, the nose to smell odor, the body to rest. If one does not gain satisfaction in these areas, one must seek for it. If one seeks satisfaction but imposes no limit on this, there will certainly be conflicts, and these conflicts will lead to social discord, even to the point where it is impossible for all to coexist. Xun Kuang believed that physical resources are limited but desires are inexhaustible, so it is essential to lay down a hierarchical order as a kind of boundary. In that way human desires can be fulfilled, yet the possibilities of the material environment will not be overstepped; thus resources and desires attain a kind of mutual adaptation and can increase gradually. This is the reason for having rites. From this perspective people first must eat, drink, find shelter, and wear clothes; the social order and hierarchy are the product of economic life. This theory is expressed in Xun Kuang's *Discussion of Rites* (*Li lun*) and *Improving Yourself* (*Zheng lun*).

It is hardly necessary to draw attention to the fact that when the problem touched upon who determined the "rites," Xun Kuang immediately turned his back on materialism and said that "the early kings hated disorder" and so thought out this view. This makes it clear that he was still fundamentally a historical idealist, something easy to understand, given that he lived 2,200 years ago.

Around the same period as Xun Kuang, or a little later, there was another thinker who put forward similar topics under the name of Guan Zhong. He was purported to be prime minister of the Kingdom of Qi in the *Spring and Autumn Annals* period. These discourses were published under the title of the *Guan Zi*. For example, the "Essay on Shepherding the People" (*Mu min pian*) says, "when the granaries are full we know the meaning of rites and ceremony, when we are clothed and fed we know the difference between honor and disgrace." This statement certainly had many biases, since the issue of whether resources for material life are adequate or not is measured by different standards in different periods and different regions, and morality and culture still play a shaping role. Nevertheless, from the perspective of the interconnection between existence and consciousness, was this not an embryonic expression of insight into how the development of the economy determines the cultural level? If we look further at the "Essay on Waste" (*Shi mi pian*), the author of this piece suggested raising consumption to stimulate production and using the strategy of setting great store by currency as a means of regulating the relations between consumption and production, a kind of primitive monetarism. He made the point that "waste" was the best way of changing the customs of the time. Naturally, this was a kind of poetic dream in ancient times, but can one not see here an embryonic idea about the level of economic prosperity determining social development?

In mentioning the source and function of rites *The Records of the Historian* (*Shiji, lishu*) repeats Xun Kuang's viewpoint about rites being a matter of physical nurture more or less point by point. It is difficult to distinguish clearly whether this was the composition of Sima Qian or of Zhu Shaosun. But one point is clear, and that is that Sima Qian approved of Xun Kuang and of the *Guan zi*. Even though the famous "Biographies of Merchants and Artisans" ("Huo zhi lie zhuan") was mocked by Ban Biao and his son Ban Gu as Sima Qian's personal vindication for his love of wealth and disdain for poverty, it was certainly the first recorded attempt in classical China to use historical facts as proof that the search for wealth and power accorded with the pattern of social development. "The desire for wealth is something all human beings possess without having to learn it." Is not the proof to be found in all the writings from the time of Yao and Shun and in all the realities experienced by eye and ear? "Rites come into being with prosperity and disappear with poverty." If ordinary people were not "afraid of poverty" and did not therefore "exert the greatest possible effort to get what they desire," how would commerce flourish, wealth be accumulated, and conquests be made, so that a situation of social stability could be reached? Of course Sima Qian was singing the praise of ordinary people, who became rich through commerce and handicrafts, and he had no sympathy for the slaves who directly carried out tasks of production and were exploited to the point that they had nothing. But he hoped to open up the secret of the forces that brought about social change over the whole period from ancient history up to his own time. He sought evidence to show that commercial development and the appearance of cities was a natural tendency of history. Thus, as early as two thousand years ago, he laid out a rough picture of how the base of society was structured through a depiction of this one aspect.

Sima Qian was the last historian to investigate the actual historical process and he was the last historian before the feudal political tradition became solidified. While he was still alive, the principles of the so-called exposure of ulterior motives of the *Spring and Autumn Annals*, formulated by the feudal autocracy, had already become dogmatic and even theological. As a result, he was rebuked for his historical views by feudal rulers of the time. The method whereby the history of economic structure set the overall tone, which he had pioneered, had already become a tradition of historical compilation and had accumulated much systematic material for research into feudal relations of production. Nevertheless, within a short few hundred years, there was practically no one left who dared to admit the historical function of evil desires.

Xun Kuang had revealed, however, that the contradiction between material resources and desires had an objective existence, and that this contradiction becomes particularly acute when the tendencies to corruption of the ruling class increase—this is something no one can avoid seeing. In the late eighth and early ninth centuries, the Tang dynasty rulers had for a long period had been perplexed by the armed rebellions of warlords and were thus forced to give some importance to economic concerns and to initiate tax reforms. So they put out a huge publication called the *Universal Classics (Tong dian)*. Its author, Du You, was a famous expert in finance, yet his vision was not narrowly focused on money or the silk handkerchiefs used as currency. It encompassed the whole feudal system—its past and its future. Naturally he gave suggestions that would enhance the security and stability of Tang rule. And the end point of his advice was to strengthen the dike of the feudal Confucian ethical code. Yet experience had taught him that if the state treasury was empty, no sermons on morality, no matter how high sounding, could prevent the imperial throne from being shaken. The fundamental method for filling up the imperial storehouses was to allow the small farmer to have something that could be expropriated.

Experience was transformed into theory, with the result that the first volume of the *Universal Classics* made the following pronouncement: "The foundation for moral transformation is in adequate food and clothing." By foundation he meant something like the roots or trunk of a tree. Du You attempted to argue that it was only necessary to solve the problem of food and clothing—to make sure the people had no worries about having enough to wear or to eat. Then one could talk about "carrying out moral transformation," in other words, making sure the people would submit to the law of the land and accept the principles of the hierarchical social order.

From there one could proceed to the ideal political conditions of an orderly feudal system. He made these precepts into a systematic approach to compiling history and so founded a school of classical Chinese history that saw the solution of economic problems as the starting point for historical change.

Even though Du You "saw the enrichment of the nation and pacification of the people as his duty" and he was once supported for prime minister by the reformist clique of the "two Wangs and the eight prefectural officials," he still failed to move the country toward good government. The reasons were complex, but the fact that he felt the crux of good government lay in persuading the rulers to restrain their greed and scrupulously abide by the Confucian ethical code was undoubtedly an important factor. Of course, the notion that human desires are a force that hinders historical progress was regressive if compared with the theories of his predecessor Xun Kuang. Nevertheless, he recognized the importance of problems of food and clothing in contrast to the idealist theories of Han Yu, his contemporary and the author of *What Is the True Way?* (*Yuan Dao*). Anyone who touches on problems of the pattern of historical development would have no difficulty in seeing this distinction.

3

After the collapse of the Tang dynasty, Chinese feudal society developed at an even slower pace, a fact that is well known. The reasons for this still need to be researched, but one point is certain: on the feudal body that was becoming more and more decrepit could only grow a feudal head that was daily more dull-witted. Therefore, it was not at all surprising that Song neo-Confucian beliefs about "preserving heavenly principles and repressing human desires," which stifled the vitality of the Chinese people, dominated intellectual circles for eight hundred years. Thus once Zhu Xi's position had practically reached a higher level than that of Confucius, it was again not in the least surprising that such crude historical ideas as that the patriarchal feudal system had already reached its finest manifestation, found in the *Outline of the Comprehensive Mirror* (*Tongjian gangmu*) and the *Aid to the Outline of the Comprehensive Mirror* (*Gangjian yizhu lun*), should become the be-all and end-all of orthodox historiography. Needless to say, in the midst of this utterly decadent scholarly atmosphere, any historical viewpoints that had even a hint of historical materialist thought could only be fated to condemnation as heretical.

Nevertheless, beginning at the latest in the fifteenth and sixteenth centuries, there quietly emerged a strand within the Chinese feudal system that went against the forces of feudalism—this is what we call the seeds of capitalist relations of production. This strand was viewed by neo-Confucians as a vicious tendency for human desires to run amuck, and the early representatives of the urban classes that were coming to life in the cities were the first to practically undermine the feudal ethical code of the three cardinal principles and five constant virtues. After this there was a need for people who could create certain illusions and ideas concerning themselves, in other words, to cause the ruling ideas to adapt to changing economic conditions and the emerging lifestyle of urban people.[158]

Thus we can see that literature that spoke on behalf of an urban population first appeared in the literary circles of this time. And in the intellectual history of this time, some heterodox ideas appeared, which were attacked by neo-Confucian scholars yet practically beneficial to the future of the urban classes. This was the case even though those developing these new ideas probably saw themselves as disgusted by the merchant class, and in many cases they claimed to be continuing or reviving certain feudal theories. Take, for example, some of those who came from the lower classes of society and attached themselves to the Ming neo-Confucianism of Wang Yangming. Under the banner of Lu Jiuyuan's philosophy of the mind they rebelled against being slaves to chapter and verse of the Four Books and opposed being parrots who mouthed phrases from the ancients sages and worthies. This reached a point where Li Zhi openly repudiated the position that what Confucius took as truth must be true. Who was benefited by this stance?

The so-called orthodox historical viewpoint had flaunted the position that Confucian views were equivalent to truth. After the great social upheavals of the late Ming and early Qing, it was inevitable that this should now face serious challenges. What was strange was that this challenge should have started with a final squaring of accounts with the teachings of Wang Yangming. For example, the historical viewpoint of Li Zhi was the common target of attack for thinkers of the Ming-Qing transition period and was even condemned by Wang Fuzhi as "leading all under heaven into depravity and excess." What reasons did he give? To put it simply, this group of thinkers were all eyewitnesses to the social upheavals of the times. They were panic-stricken by the deep contradictions in the feudal system revealed by the peasant uprisings of the late Ming. They were even more indignant about the way in which the early Qing rulers had forced the subjugated Han people to break off all connections with the civilization of the past. By the time the disturbances came to an end with the establishment of the rule of the comparatively less civilized Manchu race, the fear and indignation of the past changed into perplexity and quiet reflection, an urge to research the secrets of the collapse of the Ming and the rise of the Qing.

The old answers provided by the "exposure of ulterior motives" of the *Spring and Autumn Annals*, which explained the cause of disorder in terms of the blindness of individual rulers and the corruption of their officials, were patently inadequate. The Chongzhen emperor could not be characterized as muddle-headed, and the various scholars of the Donglin sect whom he appointed to official positions were far from being corrupt. They searched far and wide and came up with the answer that the disaster had its sources in the empty words that harmed the nation emanating from the later currents of Ming neo-Confucianism. This had led to the penchant for bad habits of empty talk in both the court and among the people, allowing the Qing rulers to take advantage of the resulting vacuum and impose an autocratic system. Thus they all expressed their grievances against the unfortunate Li Zhi. This was naturally unfair, yet it had its sense. Ming neo-Confucianism, with its characteristic tendency to subjective idealism in dealing with both ancient and contemporary issues, always followed the method of "using the six classics for self expression" and paid no attention to facts. If one takes this kind of approach in dealing with history or with contemporary events, in the final analysis one's words will be irresponsible. One example of this is Li Zhi's praise for Qinshi Huang (the founding emperor of the Qin dynasty) as the "one and only great emperor in a thousand years." Because of this, Ming neo-Confucianism, which had consistently raised challenges for orthodox Song neo-Confucianism, was exposed and criticized. This became the starting point for a solid criticism of the feudal historical viewpoint, a development quite in accordance with logic.

In the Ming-Qing transition period, Wang Fuzhi's attacks on the Ming neo-Confucianism of Wang Yangming were the most intense; it was also he who put the greatest effort into historical research. In his *Reading Notes on the Comprehensive Mirror (Du tongjian lun)* and *Discussion of the Song Dynasty (Song lun)*, he lashed out at Song and Ming scholarship with its tendency to use history specifically as a means of passing judgment, while having no qualms about distorting the facts in order to use the past as a means of satirizing the present. He emphasized that there was no eternal principle separate from the changes of history, that one must be aware of the way history constantly adapted, that order only existed in the process of constant change and one had to understand this point before one could draw lessons from history. Clearly, he not only touched on some of the complex phenomena of history, but also considered the very nature of history in some of its aspects, and in his breadth of knowledge he was superior to Gu Yanwu.

What is even more fascinating about Wang Fuzhi was his recognition that not only is history changing, but it is changing in a new direction each day. In his *Reading Notes on the Comprehensive Mirror*, he once expressed disdain for the scholars of earlier dynasties and their debates over Qinshi Huang's abolition of feudalism and establishment of the system of prefectures and counties. He called this "an unprofitable argument" for the reason that those who attacked Qinshi Huang were stubborn in their opposition to him, while those who defended him did not realize that the displacement of the feudal system by the system of prefectures and counties was an "inevitable tendency of the times" and not a matter that could be decided by the personal will of the emperor or of his prime minister, Li Si.

How, then, did he view the overall trend of history? A small volume entitled *Thoughts and Questions* (*Si wen lu*) provides an answer. In this book he argues: "Human beings have evolved from wild animals; contemporary human beings have evolved from savages; these changes can be categorized as changes in 'nature' (*zhi*) or in 'culture' (*wen*), with flesh and blood representing the nature of human persons, while rites and ceremonies represent the 'culture'; what brings about change is the change in the content of what people eat and the character of their clothing; when their food changes, their flesh and blood is different, and when their clothing changes, their rites and ceremonies diverge." In this book there is a coherent argument suggesting that the difference between animals and human beings lies in the fact that animals do not possess the "nature" of human beings, and the difference between savages and civilized human beings lies in the fact that savages do not possess the "culture" of civilized people. His conclusion is that human history generally tends to progress from savagery to civilization, yet there are also latent possibilities for the opposite to happen. If savagery overcomes civilization, civilized people may be forced to adopt the customs and manners of savages and the whole race may regress. You can see that the terms he used were still a matter of the "interaction between nature and culture," and in his conclusion he opposed the practice of "drawing on the barbarian to transform the Han," as if in his theoretical framework he had not moved beyond the stagnant pool of the traditional Confucian teachings. But there is one aspect of his content that probably no one can deny belongs to a kind of evolutionary view of history, one point that goes far beyond all the various historical theories that had been posed about human development from the time of Mo Zi, Zhuang Zi, and so forth. He made a firm rebuttal of all the rigid and dogmatic views about society never changing, and so his work gave special encouragement to Tan Sitong and Zhang Binglin several hundred years later when they were seeking to break through the trammels of feudal thought.

If one says that Wang Fuzhi's theories concentrated their energy on explaining the past history of the human race and made a start at clearly explaining the interconnection between human activities and the changing environment in the past, then his contemporary, Huang Zongxi, concentrated on seeking a way of good government for the future through explaining the secrets of order and disorder, prosperity and weakness over the history of the most recent three dynasties.

Huang Zongxi wrote *A Plan for the Prince* (*Ming yi da fang lun*). This small book, which discussed in a specialist vein the past and future of the feudalist state system, fascinated the bourgeois reformers of a period two hundred years later through the way it reflected the hazy aspirations for democracy of the newly emerging urban classes. But what interests us here is the historical reasons he gave for demanding reform in the state system. The main reason was the irrationality of the autocratic system he was criticizing. He felt that autocracy was not only a negation of real equality between rulers and people in the period of the ancient worthies Yao and Shun but was the product of increasingly acute conflict between rulers and ruled. "The issue of order or chaos in the universe is not simply a matter of the success or overthrow of one person, but it is a question of the distress or happiness of the people as a whole"; and the feudal autocracy had simply inverted this relationship, "making their own private gain essential for the good of the universe."

Thus the relationship between rulers and officials that arose from the division of labor had been mistakenly interpreted as analogous to the natural relationship between father and son by feudalist neo-Confucian scholars, resulting in a situation where officials had no sense of responsibility to the people as a whole, but had become family slaves and concubines to the ruler. The "laws for the peace of the country," which had been produced over three dynasties to solve the problems of food and clothing, had become "the laws of one family," which served the private gain of the rulers. As a result, able officials had no alternative but to submit to this kind of "law which was no law." Therefore, the arenas in which officials, army personnel, intellectuals, and people had formerly met to discuss public questions of right and wrong had now become simply "schools set up for training scholar-officials," and as a result, people were forced to submit to the personal will of the ruler alone. "What the emperor praises, the people accept as a rule without question, and the rules that the emperor dislikes the people disregard." The people thus lack any real education and the nation is not secure. This was the vein of his thinking, and there were very few problems relating to the feudal state system that Huang Zongxi did not expose or refute through historical evidence.

If research into history produced only negative conclusions, this would be a kind of historical nihilism. *A Plan for the Prince* does not fall into this category. Clearly, the author's reason for giving evidence of what should be negated in feudal autocracy was that it had itself negated a reasonable system that predated it—what has been called up to now the primitive democratic system. So his rebuttal was for the sake of affirmation, an affirmation of the need to limit the power of the ruler in future, the need to establish a legal system, the need to respect the wishes of the people, even the need to limit the number of the emperor's wives and concubines in order to guard against a dictatorship of eunuchs. In this respect, his manner of description was a traditional one, from the specialist terminology used to the examples drawn upon, never freeing itself from the influence of the five Confucian classics. The content was fresh, however, and it caused people to feel the justifications given to them by orthodox historiography to prove that the ruling autocracy was something everlasting and unchanging not only were invalid but actually proved the opposite. They could only become historical evidence that such antiauthoritarian systems as constitutional monarchy or a three-way division of powers were destined to emerge.

Needless to say, an evolutionary perspective is not the same as historical materialism, and to speak on behalf of the future good of the urban classes could even less be seen as understanding the pattern of history. Subjectively, Huang Zongxi still took Wang Yangming's ideal-ist theories as truth, and Wang Fuzhi did not ever overtly touch upon the problem of the reasonableness of autocracy even though the fact that he so hated what he called the "solitary Qin and vulgar Song" demonstrates that he had thought about the problem. Other scholars seem to have been even farther from the mark. Take, for example, Gu Yanwu, who had equal fame with Wang Fuzhi and Huang Zongxi. He praised *A Plan for the Prince*, yet his massive *Daily Record of Knowl-edge* (*Ri zhi lu*), which he himself claimed "had a practical application to human affairs," shows that he did not understand the hazy intima-tions toward a democratic system that were expressed in this book. What is important here is simply the understanding of social history that these scholars gleaned from their life and practical experience. If Wang Fuzhi had not had the experience of living in hiding for a considerable period in a relatively backward minority region after the failure of resistance to the Qing, if Huang Zongxi had not had the perceptual knowledge that came from living in the southern coastal region where the social relations of capitalist production took form at a relatively early period, would they have reached that level of historical conscious-ness? Surely not. Even if they had studied every word of the hundred schools until they had it off by heart, it would have been difficult to find anything of value in their historical perspectives.

4

Just like the road traversed by history itself, history's conceptual ex-pression does not move forward in a straight line. Much of seventeenth-century China was passed in a state of war. History had not yet provided adequate conditions for the rebuttal of feudal thought. It did, however, provide the opportunity for yet another historical law to mani-fest itself, that is, the law that conquerors of a relatively low level of civilization are themselves conquered by the relatively higher culture of those they have subjugated.[159] Taking advantage of the fact that a new peasant government was not yet firmly established, and making a hard push in order to plunder the fruits of revolution, the Qing ruling group began this process once they had occupied the whole country with the cavalry of their Eight Banners. Nevertheless, on the surface it appeared as if their starting point was to force the subjugated races, whose level of civilization was somewhat higher, to accept Manchu social customs.

This led to a whole series of rebellions and their repression, misunderstandings and hostilities, suspicions and jealousies.

The Qing ruling apparatus quickly caught on to the fact that the Song neo-Confucian teachings about the three cardinal guides and five constant virtues were a useful tool for enslaving the hearts and minds of the Han race. Thus with the emperor leading the way, they put all their efforts into promoting it, not realizing that in the very process they were themselves being subjugated by Han feudal culture, and indeed by a feudal culture that was extremely decadent. As a result of the cultural policy that Dai Zhen characterized as "using principles to kill people," it was inevitable that intellectual circles should be depressed and stifled. The writings of Wang Fuzhi were consigned to oblivion. Huang Zongxi was taken up as the master of orthodox Qing historiography. Gu Yanwu's critical views about the Qing were distorted, and it was only his methods of textual criticism on the classics and history that received extraordinary reverence from scholars who were seeking shelter from the political vicissitudes of the time. All in all, the new historical consciousness that had emerged in the Ming-Qing transition period disappeared from historical memory until the late eighteenth century. Even the fact that the earth was round, something known by Kangxi himself, was forgotten as the minds of high officials in this period reverted to a view of the earth as square. The whole historical viewpoint was determined by such dogmatic and ossified notions as that of "preserving heavenly principles and repressing human desires," and "the heavens do not change, neither does the Way."

In the middle years of the Qing dynasty, however, depicted by Gong Zizhen as "a time when ten thousand horses were muted," social contradictions that lay concealed were beginning to sharpen and find expression in public crises; could thinkers remain silent in this situation?

Dai Zhen was recognized by all as a "great master of textual criticism." He could not tolerate seeing the autocratic Yongzheng at every opportunity citing phrases from the Song neo-Confucians about "preserving heavenly principles and repressing human desires" as a reason for killing people and had to initiate some debates. His small volume on philosophy, the *Textual Criticism on the Meaning of Terms in the Mencius* (*Mengzi ziyi shuzheng*), which he himself said was the most important thing he had written in his life, censured "contemporary people who do not debate good and evil, but dress their own views up in a misleading way as 'principles' and so bring disaster on the people.'' He wanted to use genuine "principles" to expose the false "principle.'' What is notable here is that what Dai Zhen called truth was no different than the old theories we are already familiar with: "sympathizing with the needs of the people and fulfilling the people's desires." The people's "desires," from his point of view, were the daily material needs of human beings for food and drink. "To neglect these in order to talk about principle was not the 'principle' that was discussed by the ancient sages and worthies." This distinction was a matter of simple reality, as Xun Kuang had already discovered at an early period, yet by the 1760s not only did it need to be argued all over again, but the argument had to be camouflaged within the theory of the innate goodness of human nature of Mencius, the "secondary sage" (*yasheng*), before it could be presented publicly. This shows how difficult it was to speak a few words of truth in the period of feudal autocracy.

Half a century later, Gong Zizhen attacked the feudal historical viewpoint from another perspective. Under the banner of a revival of the Gongyang scholarship of the Western Han on the *Spring and Autumn Annals*, this sensitive poet and philosopher gave voice to his own romantic and colorful historical views on political theory. He had already predicted in a rather mysterious way the coming tempest of peasant warfare, and he had already daringly expressed his views that great social changes could not be avoided. He carefully observed all the various indications of the decline of the feudal system. With a heart full of grief he also prepared an overall strategy for resisting the invasion of foreign capitalism.

What interests us even more, however, are the historical reasons he established for the inevitable process of social change. Dong Zhongshu's statement that "the heavens do not change and so the Way also does not change" had always been the superstitious foundation for the eternal existence of the feudal system, but Gong Zizhen showed that it could be proved that "no order under heaven had lasted more than eight hundred years, yet the Way had not been changed in tens of thousands of years." This seems at first glance to be a repudiation of principle, but if one looks more closely it is not. It seems that, in his view, the Way is the central law that regulates history, and the so-called prosperity or decline of an "order under heaven" actually referred to the success or weakness of a particular system, for example, such concrete historical changes as dynastic successions. This thus refuted Dong Zhongshu's errors in mixing universal regularities with specific social systems and so enabled people gradually to realize that the eternal laws of history were actually evident in the constant succession of changes in societies, and so for this reason "from ancient times to the present there have been no laws that do not change."

Just as Dai Zhen dreamed about being able to use the method of directly speaking the truth to persuade feudal rulers to give up their habit of "killing people on the basis of opinion," Gong Zizhen and his friend Wei Yuan also hoped at one time to use the method of recollection of historical success and failure as a way of persuading the rulers to initiate reforms themselves. Facts have proven them wrong. Since they adhered to a kind of conceptual determinism, they remained fundamentally attached to the idealist view of history. Yet they supported the pursuit of truth and the search for universal laws determining history. Thus they made it possible for the materialist view to be applied to social phenomena, and inhibited the tendency to explain social history according to personal inclinations. There can be no doubt about this.

5

In criticizing the outcome of the Opium Wars, Marx commented: "All these dissolving agencies . . . received their full development under the English cannons in 1840, which broke down the authority of the Emperor, and forced the Celestial Empire into contact with the terrestrial world. Complete isolation was the prime condition of the preservation of old China. That isolation having come to a violent end by the medium of England, dissolution must follow as surely as that of any mummy carefully preserved in a hermetically sealed coffin, whenever it is brought in contact with the open air."[160]

That is precisely how it was. Even though the corrupt rule of the Qing dynasty was not immediately overthrown, due to the fact that it quickly gained support from the foreign capitalists who invaded the country, still the process of the dissolution of the structure of Chinese feudal society was greatly speeded up over the previous several centuries. The capitalist relations of production were now no longer embryonic, but had become a kind of force capable of destroying the feudal economy. The first generation of industrial workers appeared, as did the first early modern capitalists. Even though they were few in number they represented classes that had not existed before this. A group of intellectuals also emerged, who had new ideas or were half forward-looking and half traditional. They were able to use new terms to criticize the old ways. Naturally, there also emerged some strange creatures who were called by everyone false foreign devils. They appeared on the surface to be as different from the old crazies with their wooden brains as fire from water, yet, in fact, they opposed the Chinese democratic revolution from the opposite perspective. Actually it would have been quite strange if this intense battle between old and new had not ensued.

The changes in China's intellectual circles, however, came later than had been predicted, in contrast to Japan. In the 1850s the Japanese began to learn from the West, and they took Wei Yuan's *Blueprint for Maritime Countries* as their primer. In a matter of forty years, the weak feudal Japan had already become a rich capitalist aggressor nation gazing covetously at and about to bite the hand of the nation that had been its teacher for a thousand years. Meanwhile, China's Kang Youwei had only just managed to persuade the emperor to learn from the changes in the Meiji Restoration period and support the project of making Confucius the savior of the universe in order to reveal the weaknesses of the capitalist classes! This is without doubt an irony of history, and I don't plan to discuss the reasons for it at this point. One thing is clear: the unhealthy development of the Chinese capitalist class finally led to the self-conscious struggle to create a social environment that would enable them to survive. Naturally, the thinkers among them turned their eyes to the theory of evolution.

It has been noted earlier that China had the concept of evolution at an early period, including a concept of historical evolution. But this could be called a classical concept of evolution, as it lacked the rigorous evidence of natural history. For this reason it could not overcome the metaphysical arguments for no change that took as their pillar the concept that "heaven does not change" and that held predominance. Once the progressive intellectuals who were seeking reform discovered that a scientific theory of evolution was already being disseminated in the West, one can easily imagine their intense eagerness to understand it.

The introduction of the theory of evolution by Chinese can be traced back to the 1860s or 1870s. The Jiangnan Arsenal, run by the Westernizers, published two scientific classics: Herschel's *Outlines of Astronomy* (*Tan tian*) and Lyell's *Manual of Elementary Geology* (*Dixue qianshuo*). The Chinese translations were made respectively by Li Shanlan and Hua Hengfeng, both famous mathematicians of the early modern period. *Outlines of Astronomy* was written by the famous British astronomer John

Herschel, and it used the Kant-Laplace nebular hypothesis to explain process of evolution of heavenly bodies. The *Manual of Elementary Geology* was the work of the famous British geologist Charles Lyell, and it proved that the earth and its surface formations had gone through a gradual process of change, so that the animal and plant life now on the earth's surface had also developed through gradual change. Everyone knows that the theories of Kant, Laplace, and Lyell were highly regarded by Engels, who felt that from different perspectives they had managed to attack the ossified belief that nature is absolutely unchanging, and also the theory that God created the universe.[161] What sort of responses did these two works on the heavens and the earth elicit from progressive Chinese? To answer this question, one only has to point to several kinds of books that appeared just before and after the 1898 Reform Movement, such as Kang Youwei's *Lectures on the Heavens* (*Zhu tian jian*) and Zhang Binglin's *Reflections after Reading the 'Guan Zi'* (*Du 'Guan Zi' shu hou*) and *Theories on the Heavens* (*Shi tian lun*), and one can get an idea.

Nevertheless, no book received a more overwhelming response than Yan Fu's *Theory of Evolution* (*Tian yan lun*). This small book was based on the famous British scholar Huxley's *Evolution and Ethics*. Even before it was published it was passed around for perusal among such leaders of the reform movement as Kang Youwei and Liang Qichao. After it was published in 1896 it became even more fashionable, attracting tremendous interest from such progressive young people of the time as Lu Xun and giving a great impetus to the 1898 Reform Movement. This was the first introduction to China of Darwin's theory of evolution and of Spencer's organic theory of society. The theory of evolution proved that human development is a historical process, and the organic theory of society suggested that human society is an expression of the struggle for social existence, resulting in the overall principle of the so-called survival of the fittest. Darwin's theory belongs to the level of natural science and was praised by Marx as "a natural-scientific basis for the class struggle in history."[162] Spencer's theory undoubtedly belongs to the idealist historical perspective and was only "fit to be used as a handle for aggressors in the recent period," to use the critical comment made by Li Dazhao on the eve of the May 4th Movement. Nevertheless, at the time of the 1898 Reform Movement, the progressive elements who were seeking to reform China's "accumulated weaknesses" found that its reverse side provided a handle to refute the feudalist diehard group. They warned that if China did not reform itself and seek to become strong, it would be hard to avoid becoming a public example of the "law of the jungle."

Chinese classical philosophers all saw humanity as interconnected with nature, and they saw natural phenomena as portents of human disaster or good fortune. The historical viewpoint was no exception to this. Since Darwin attacked the metaphysical view of the natural world very forcibly, when the theory of evolution was introduced to China, even if Yan Fu himself had not used it to criticize the ossified feudal historical viewpoint, it would still have attacked the superstitions of autocracy being eternal and unchanging. No wonder, therefore, that he made no attempt to conceal the fact that what he wished to refute was the concept of an "unchanging way." It is not surprising that the half-idealist "theory of evolution" stimulated people in this way. Nor is it surprising that the theory that "the material world competes and heaven selects" became the pet phrase of all the new social groups of the time, both genuine and false.

The theory of evolution was a kind of bridge to the theory of classes. But natural science does not in the end wait on the social sciences, and the most important formula of evolutionary theory, the "struggle for survival," even as a law of development for the organic world, was not perfect. Much less could it be shifted across to become a formula solving the contradictions of society. Engels made a trenchant critique of this point.[163] Thus the bridge had itself to be reconstructed. Not long after the *Theory of Evolution* was published, the first attempt at this reconstruction emerged in the form of Zhang Binglin's *Theory of Bacteria (Jun shuo)*.

The *Theory of Bacteria*, which appeared in 1899, was written in even more traditional and abstruse language than the *Theory of Evolution*, yet its evolutionary concepts were much more radical than those of Yan Fu. Zhang Binglin attempted to give a clear depiction of the natural historical process of development from bacteria to human beings. His starting point was all the material of the natural world, and there were no absolute boundaries distinguishing kinds of matter, since contradictions existed within all things and were the basis for all changes. He argued that the reason bacteria become animals and monkeys become human beings lay in a kind of order from lower to higher levels, from simple to complex, an order of interconnections and interdistinctions. Each link had boundaries that were relatively fixed, but that was precisely because these boundaries were set against one another. Therefore they were constantly broken through by the internal demands of the evolution of life. Within the organic world there was both competition and cooperation, both conflict and harmony. In the reciprocal interaction of these contradictions was manifested the mystery of evolution, a mystery that Zhang Binglin saw himself as expounding. He was very nearly able to use this notion to explain social change, but he failed. Even though he emphasized the connectedness of change in the environment and change in human life, and even though he criticized the "law of the jungle" as going against this principle of interconnectedness, he still believed a society's level of intelligence and ability to unite were the critical reasons for progress. Like Yan Fu, he lost his way and slipped into the marsh of belief in a world determined by opinions.

6

It was in 1899 that the Chinese first heard of someone in the West called Marx, who had discovered a "new scholarship for pacifying the people," that is, the theory of socialism. This was disclosed through a journal published by American missionaries, the *Review of the Times* (*Wanguo gongbao*), which carried an article written jointly by a British missionary, Timothy Richards, and a Chinese, Cai Erkang. Probably few people noticed it. Three years later, when Liang Qichao, who had been a secretary to Timothy Richards, referred again to Marx in the journal he edited, the *Xinmin congbao*, he used a different transliteration of Marx's name. Clearly, none of these people appreciated Marx's new theory. Liang Qichao even made the nonsensical remark that Marx was only concerned about "the past" and had no interest in the "future."

In that period, however, Liang Qichao could certainly be regarded as "one of China's new people." He enthusiastically publicized the need to develop a whole new approach to historical research based on evolutionary theory, and in the first years of this century he published the *Narrative Account of Chinese History* (*Zhongguo shi xulun*) with its fierce criticism of famous Chinese historical works as simply "genealogies of the emperors," as if China had never had a history. In the next year he published the *New Historiography* (*Xin shixue*), calling for a "revolution in historical circles" that would transform feudal history into a history of national development. He maintained that history should investigate all the progressive movements of human society, "that is, all the experiences of the nation and their interconnections and from this seek the common principles that have governed human progress.'' We all know that Lenin once pointed out that historical materialism dispelled two important faults of previous historical theories, the first being the fault of past history neglecting the activities of the masses of working people.[164] Even though Liang Qichao instinctively disapproved of Marx, since he insisted on using an evolutionary perspective to look at history, and since he stood amidst the progressive movements of his time, he could hardly help coming near to the historical materialist perspective on this one important question. This may seem contradictory, but it is a fact. Liang Qichao could be regarded as the first to find himself caught in this kind of ridiculous contradiction in early modern history, but he was certainly not the last.

In the early part of the century, some changes became evident in China's translation efforts. As the number of persons sent to study abroad increased, people like Yan Fu, who had become thoroughly familiar with the West as well as China, were no longer as rare as phoenix feathers or unicorn horns. The practice for several hundred years of relying on foreigners who knew the Chinese language, or of having Chinese who knew a foreign language dictate to a scholar unable to read a foreign language, but able to write well, was replaced by translations of the quality of Yan Fu's *Theory of Evolution.* Since the number of Chinese scholars in Japan was the greatest, the number of Western works that were translated from the Japanese was the greatest. This kind of translation from a translation may have led to the loss of the genuine flavor of the original works, yet it was at least more accurate than translation that depended on oral dictation and recording; furthermore, the translators now had the power to select what they wished. One should not underestimate the importance of this change for the dissemination of the writings of Marx in China. Convincing evidence of this can be found in the fact that several books introducing and translating Marx's work appeared simultaneously in China between 1902 and 1903.

We are particularly interested in two of these: *Socialism of Modern Times (Jinshi shehui zhuyi),* translated by Zhao Bizhen, and a translation of *The Marrow of Socialism* made by the Chinese Translation Society for Transmitting Knowledge (Zhongguo dashi yishe), which was in fact a group of revolutionary youths who published *Zhejiang Tides (Zhejiang chao).* The authors of both books were Japanese, Fukui Junzo and Kotoko Shusui, the latter one of the famous and relatively early Japanese scholars to promote Marxism.

In the first of these two books not only do we find the life of Marx and an outline of *Capital,* but there is a much more detailed account than is found in Zhu Zhixin's *Biography of German Revolutionaries* (*Deyizhi gemingjia xiaozhuan*), which was published four years later; there is also a summary of Marx's historical theory of the five types of social formation, which runs to over 1,500 characters in length.

In the second book we see the first Chinese depiction of the historical materialist viewpoint, which reads as follows: "The first teacher of socialism, Karl Marx, revealed for us the true fact of the way in which society is organized with the words: 'since history began, no matter in what region or time, all social organizations had to be based on the foundation of the method of production and exchange. In no matter which period, politics and history cannot be explained apart from this.' " It is not difficult to see that this introduction was quoting from some main ideas of Engels, even though Kotoko Shusui's Japanese translation may not have been so clumsy.

The fact that the number of translations suddenly increased is not in itself proof that progressive Chinese responded warmly to Marx's theories. Rather, we should look for evidence at two articles that the Chinese themselves wrote which were published in 1903: "The Theories of Two Giants on Materialism" and "A Comparison Between Socialism and Evolutionary Theory." The two "giants" of the first article were Darwin and Marx, and the main argument is that "if we want to save the yellow races from disaster, the only way is to strongly promote materialism." The second articles compares similarities and differences between Darwin's evolutionary theory and Marx's socialism. The author of both articles was Ma Junwu.

Ma Junwu's fame as the first translator of Darwin's *Origin of Species* has tended to obscure the historical fact that at a very early period he had joined the ranks of a revolutionary party under the leadership of Sun Yat-sen. For this reason, few people have noted that he had already given his views that Marx's theories were superior to evolutionary theories. In his article "A Comparison Between Socialism and Evolutionary Theory," his notes and references indicate that he had drawn upon *The Communist Manifesto*, *The Poverty of Philosophy*, *The Critique of Political Economy*, and *Capital*, and he had also used for reference Engels's *The Condition of the English Working Classes*. Probably he had based his work entirely on Japanese introductions, since he mistakenly attributed Engels's books and theories to Marx. Nevertheless, all of these works were classics of Marxism and, even if he had only read synopses of them, he would still have had a relatively good grasp of the general picture of Marxist theory.

From the perspective of today, Ma Junwu not only stopped short of a full understanding of Marx but made some serious mistakes in interpreting him. For example, he regarded Marx's thinking as a kind of utopian socialism, and he castigated socialists for negating the "benefits of competition," saying that this would only slow down the development of society. This kind of comment revealed his prejudice, yet if we take a historical perspective, this young scholar of eighty years ago had the best of motives in introducing and criticizing Marx's theories. It was only through him that the Chinese people learned many things: that Marx advocated "class struggle as the key to history"; that the gap between workers and peasants was slight in China, and this was evidence that social development was behind that of the West by a whole historical period; that socialist theory was much superior to capitalist reality; that "all nations which earnestly seek progress have without exception welcomed socialism, and once socialism is implemented, the masses experience great progress in morals, knowledge, material resources and all that pertains to their livelihood." For this reason he once asserted that if socialism were implemented, then Darwin's so-called natural selection, the theory of the survival of the fittest, would have lost its basis for existence. You can see that this early intention to make an attempt at using the historical materialist viewpoint in explaining Chinese history found rather clear expression.

There is no need to deny that Marxism was just one of many schools of thought that were beginning to be disseminated in China in the early twentieth century, and that its influence could not compare with that of Rousseau's theory of the social contract, Locke's theory of natural rights, Darwin's theory of evolution, or even Spencer's organic theory of society. Yet, for this very reason, we cannot help feeling surprised that, when it was first disseminated, it gained the sympathy of progressive Chinese, and that it continuously stirred up reverberations among revolutionaries.

After the Revolutionary League (Tongmenghui) was set up in 1905, we find echoes of it in the historical opinions of some of the revolutionary intellectuals, for example, Chen Tianhua's *Discussion of Chinese Revolutionary History* (*Zhongguo gemingshi lun*), which affirmed peasant revolutions; and Zhang Binglin's *Morality of Revolution* (*Geming zhi daode*), which used people's socioeconomic status as a measure to determine which classes would have attitudes of support for or opposition to democratic revolutions—even to the point where some who were in favor of revolution encouraged class struggle, and so forth. All of this would be difficult to explain if we did not take note of the fact that Marx's theories had already begun to be disseminated.

Still, if we try to take the historical materialist view that social existence determines social consciousness to its logical conclusion, that is, if we regard historical materialism itself as a kind of ideological formation, then wherever this simple fact exists—the fact that mankind eats, drinks, has shelter and clothing—concealed by an overgrowth of ideology, will be found the embryonic formation of certain parts of the historical materialist viewpoint making its appearance in intellectual history. There is nothing surprising about this, especially in a country like China with its ancient civilization and long-term respect for cultural traditions. We need only admit that the historical materialist viewpoint is not without its sources in China's history, but that it had been groped after in a hazy form by a considerable number of thinkers over the generations who struggled yet were unable to get a whole and clearly articulated understanding. It then becomes easy to understand why the historical materialist viewpoint discovered by Marx, "or more correctly the consistent continuation and extension of materialism into the domain of social phenomena,"[165] was accepted by the people rather quickly once it was introduced into China. In less than twenty years it was recognized by revolutionaries as the only scientific historical viewpoint.

8 | China's Lost Renaissance

1

Well before the May 4th Movement, a group of students at Beida (Beijing University) who supported the new culture movement compared it to the European Renaissance. They organized a society called New Tides (Xinchao) and inaugurated a journal by the same name, consciously using this term as a translation of the English word Renaissance, a point later confirmed by their mentor, Hu Shi. Ever since that time, many scholars who commemorate or do research on the May 4th Movement have taken note of this point and have discussed the May 4th Movement and the European Renaissance in a comparative way.

But there is another, related fact that has been neglected up to the present. Another group of students at Beida at the same period organized a journal entitled *National Antiquities* (*Guogu*), which began publication soon after *New Tides* and its godfather, *New Youth*, and made them a target for debate. This group of students had Liu Shipei as their mentor. He had had a rather bad reputation for his political platform in the late Qing and early Republican period. Now that he took it upon himself to promote ''a reordering of national antiquities,'' thus spearheading the criticism of the literary revolution, he was naturally hated even more. In fact, however, if China was really promoting a European-style Renaissance, Liu Shipei should be recognized as one of the pioneers of this movement. Even though he supported the contributors to *National Antiquities* in their arguments with the young people associated with the New Tides Society, in his scholarship he never actually went beyond the views of his earlier years.

It is essential that we take note of this latter point in our attempt to understand the history of the May 4th Movement. At the very least it shows that even though seventy years have passed since the movement, we need to continue exploring the process of its unfolding.

2

May 4th was both a political and a cultural movement. It is complex enough to try to study its development purely from the perspective of culture, not to mention the fact that in early modern China culture and politics were always intertwined. In this essay I intend to depict in a simple way the origins of the illusion that gripped people of that period about trying to bring about a Renaissance in China.

From the mid-nineteenth century, the disintegration of Chinese society began to proceed at an even more rapid pace than before. After the failure of the Boxers' attempt to use religious martial arts to protect their persons and fend off the cannons of the foreign invaders, a whole range of intellectual currents from the West flooded into China in a way that really was like a rising tide. The history of how the various countries in Europe and North America had taken the road to modernization was given careful attention and studied by Chinese reformers. The Italian Renaissance, the German Reformation, the French Revolution, and the American War of Independence all became models that the reformers tried to emulate.

But what route should the Chinese reforms take? Most people of that period overestimated the importance of spiritual strength, imagining that if only people's thinking could be changed, the traditional powers would lose their base and the old system could be exchanged for a new one. But when the question arose as to which particular model should be followed, there were divergences of views among the different groups.

On the most general level, we might say the reformers who advocated reforms within the Qing dynasty government, from Kang Youwei to Tan Sitong, were most closely agreed in their views. They took a Lutheran-style Reformation as the model to be emulated. Kang Youwei put forward the idea of "establishing the Confucian religion," and Liang Qichao and Tan Sitong both hoped that he would become the Martin Luther of Confucianism, something that showed clearly what they were looking for. The failure of the Hundred Day Reform (1898), however, showed that their hopes for China to follow the road of religious reformation were no more than a grand illusion.

As for the group of revolutionaries who promoted the overthrow of the Qing government, they had little in common in their ideals except for the shared desire to establish a republican government. Those who do research on the history of the 1911 Revolution have all noted the divergence of opinion between Sun Yat-sen and Zhang Taiyan, but they fail to pay attention to Zhang Taiyan's admiration for the Italian Renaissance.

Zhang Taiyan was the chief theorist for the revolutionary group in the period of the Revolutionary League (Tongmenghui). The ideas and sources he used to construct his own theoretical system were complex. Nevertheless, at the same time as he was loudly proclaiming that "the revolution was already completed," he was calling for the "use of the national essence (*guocui*) to stir up the nature of the Chinese race." In this he was clearly inspired by the Italian Renaissance: "The predecessor of the resurgence of Italy was a literary movement to revive antiquity."[166]

Many people censured Zhang Taiyan's views on "reviving the national essence" both at the time and later. I don't plan to discuss these criticisms here. The national essence that Zhang Taiyan explained and referred to was not, however, a Confucian religion with Confucius as the savior figure, but rather the history of the Chinese race, what could be termed its cultural tradition in contemporary language.

3

In the matter of emulating the Italian Renaissance, Zhang Taiyan made some practical achievements, which is more than can be said for his other famous proposal that "religion be used to stimulate the people's confidence," or for Kang Youwei's establishment of a "Confucian religion," both of which were mere illusions.

The Italian Renaissance, which took place between the fourteenth and sixteenth centuries, made an important contribution to Western civilization in a number of ways: it revived and made use of the ancient cultural heritage; it established the point that "the development of the freedom of every individual is the essential condition for the freedom of all mankind" (Engels once used this quote in his claim that Marx was a new Dante); it initiated an interest in the natural world which led to tremendous progress in the natural sciences; it brought an end to the humiliating situation in which philosophy and the other human sciences were servants to theology, and so forth. Most historians would agree on these points.

When it comes to concrete achievements, Zhang Taiyan may not match up to such giants of the Renaissance as Dante, Michelangelo, and others, but he had undoubtedly pondered the history of the Renaissance in some depth, and for this reason he put forward tremendous practical efforts.

At this point there is no need to go any further into Zhang Taiyan's scholarly achievements. He left his mark on the fields of philosophy, the human sciences, and social sciences, as everyone knows.

There are three aspects of his work, however, that are of significance for this essay. The first point is that the work he did in his early years in criticizing and repudiating Confucius and the classical tradition should be recognized as the direct antecedent to the May 4th call to "overturn the stall of the Confucian clan." The second point is that Zhang Taiyan's friends and students in his early years were the core of the group that organized the new culture movement, friends such as Chen Duxiu and Cai Yuanpei, and students such as Qian Xuantong, Lu Xun, and Zhou Zuoren. Even Hu Shi himself could be included in this group. The third point is that a group of scholars and literary figures whom he supported in his early years had already made genuine, if unsuccessful, efforts in their scholarly writing and poetry to experiment with a "literary restoration of antiquity." They included Huang Jie, Liu Shipei, and Ma Xulun of the *Scholarly Journal on National Essence (Guocui xuebao)*, also Liu Yazi and others of the Southern Society (Nan she).

Thus if we speak about the promotion of a Renaissance in China, Zhang Taiyan would have to be recognized not only as a theoretician who wrote on the subject, but also as someone who took action to support it. And this took place before the 1911 Revolution. The Chinese-American scholar Chow Tse-tsung, in his English-language history *The May Fourth Move-*

ment, states that the term "Chinese Renaissance" was first put forward by Huang Yuanyong in 1915 and claims that the Chinese Renaissance took the form of a kind of "concept of liberalism" only three years later. Even though he mentions Zhang Taiyan in a number of places, he never takes into account the facts about Zhang Taiyan that I have listed above. This is certainly an oversight on his part.

4

Perhaps because the term "national essence" held bad connotations after May 4th, the very existence of the *Scholarly Journal on National Essence* has hardly been mentioned, even by intellectual historians up to the present. In fact, it was not only unique among the new-style journals of the era before the 1911 Revolution, but it had considerable influence and survived for longer than either the *Xinmin congbao* or the *Min bao*. No matter how we evaluate this historical fact, we cannot simply brush it aside.

This journal was published in Shanghai, and its contents mainly related to history, particularly the cultural history of the Han people. A certain flavor of Han chauvinism was not hard to detect, as it was in fact the resounding voice of the revolutionary thought of the period. The group around Zhang Taiyan originally called the revolution they sought to bring about a "recovering" (*guangfu*), meaning by that a "recovering of old things." This slogan was directly inspired by the Italian Renaissance, as was clearly stated in the *Scholarly Journal on National Essence*. From the Renaissance movement initiated in Italy it was necessary to go back to the beginning of the call to revive the antiquities of Greece and Rome in order to stimulate in turn the growth of a civilized people with a civilized language and the distinctive maturation of each. This may not have been stated as clearly as I have put it here, but this was precisely what was said by the group that called themselves the "Restoration Society" (Guangfu hui) in their *Scholarly Journal on National Essence*. If we remind ourselves that the Qing empire of the time constituted a situation in which a minority race forcibly exerted rule over the Han race and other minority peoples, then we may be able to understand how what was called a restoration of old things carried similar connotations to the revival of antiquity in the European Renaissance. Both implied an urgent effort to nurture a modern, civilized people. Naturally, the meaning of this could only become evident in the future.

Needless to say, what this group meant by national essence contained both traditions long dead and strange fabrications. For example, the *Scholarly Journal on National Essence* promulgated article after tedious article disseminating the theory that the Chinese peoples had come from the West, simply a conjecture concerning the history of the Han race that originated from the sacred texts of the Society of Jesus, whose members came to China in the seventeenth century. However, the fact that this type of conjecture became fashionable in such slogans as "initiate the character of the race" (*xu zhong xing*) and "think of our homeland" (*si zu guo*) early in the century showed clearly that the "literary revival of antiquity" practically went beyond the temporal and spatial limitations of what was called "national essence."

Any research done on the history of intellectual and cultural movements in early modern China must give some attention to the process of their development, and most especially to each critical point in this process. Similar slogans may have quite a different historical significance at different critical points. There is plenty of historical evidence for this. Take Liu Shipei as a case in point. Before the 1911 Revolution he called for the preservation of national essence, while before the May 4th Movement he was promoting a reordering of national antiquities. While these slogans were similar, they had an opposite meaning at different times. Before the 1911 Revolution, he was pressing China to carry out a Renaissance, while before May 4th he was attacking the new youth who were calling for China's Renaissance. Nevertheless, the qualitative change in intention behind the slogan does not prevent the content of the slogan from having its own relative historical sense. There was at least one person at the time of May 4th who detected this, and that was Hu Shi, who was himself attacked by the *National Antiquities Monthly Journal (Guogu yuekan)*.

5

Hu Shi insisted on calling the new culture movement China's Renaissance and admitted that his theory of literary revolution came from the lessons of Chinese literary history and the European Renaissance. Obviously he thought about China's need for a Renaissance in the same way as Zhang Taiyan and others had done before the 1911 Revolution.

It was very strange how, at the very height of the movement, on August 16, 1919, he wrote in a letter to a member of the New Tides Society that "there are now many reasons why we must put in order our national antiquities.'' He also made the famous remark that was later to call for endless essays censuring him: ''There is a certain equality to scholarship, whether one discovers the ancient meaning of one character or one discovers a fixed star, both are a great achievement.''[167]

In the critical articles written since the 1950s, nearly all have emphasized that this shows that Hu Shi had already retreated from his stand on the literary revolution and had gone back to a reactionary position supporting the reordering of national antiquities. But all of these critics seem to have neglected two points: First, the patent rights for the ''reordering of national antiquities'' belonged to Liu Shipei, and what Hu said was simply in response to Liu. Second, Hu Shi's first exposition of his view that the literary revolution called for the promotion of a Chinese Renaissance was made on the August 1, 1919,[168] that is, just two weeks before the letter mentioned above. Is it possible that in two weeks he had already forgotten what he had written with such seriousness? Would it make sense to imagine that he only read one little article by student opponents defending the slogan of ''reordering national antiquities'' and quickly lowered the flag to them?

The real situation was that Hu Shi did not feel there was any irresolvable contradiction between promoting a Renaissance and reordering national antiquities. On the contrary, he affirmed that the task of ''using scientific methods in doing research on national antiquities'' was an important responsibility of the Chinese Renaissance.

Whether or not Hu Shi's view of scientific method, that is, the so-called method of pragmatism which he emphasized over and over, could in fact be considered scientific is another issue. However, the way he took the examples of the scholars of the Han learning in the Qing dynasty and claimed that there were among them some great discoverers of the study of national antiquities, the way he insisted that their work coincided with scientific method and that to take on the task of reordering national antiquities called for the conscious adoption of what had been the unconscious method of the Han scholars, all was a kind of response to Liu Shipei and his school. It was not a matter of giving in before his opponents, nor was it a retreat from his original position.

Hu Shi was clearly familiar with the history of the European Renaissance. It has already been noted that one of the great contributions of the European Renaissance lay in the revival and use of the ancient cultural heritage. Engels once described this achievement in the following way: ''In the manuscripts saved from the fall of Byzantium, in the antique statues dug out of the ruins of Rome, a new world was revealed to the astonished West: that of ancient Greece; the ghosts of the Middle Ages vanished before its shining forms; Italy rose to an undreamt-of flowering of art, which seemed like a reflection of classical antiquity and was never attained again.''[169]

Hu Shi's evaluation of research and compilation done by the Han scholars of the Qing dynasty on the classical literature, linguistics, and history of ancient China never reached the level of this founder of Marxism in his evaluation of the European Renaissance, even though he called the Han learning of the Qing dynasty one of China's Renaissances. Still, Hu Shi clearly included the task of reordering China's antiquities as part of the proper work of the Renaissance and did not turn away from his original views of the so-called Renaissance. As to whether the Han learning of the Qing dynasty could be seen as another Renaissance, that is a different question.

6

Of course, it would be preposterous to suggest that the new youth of the May 4th period equated the Renaissance with the reordering of national antiquities. Yet, even though most of Hu Shi's fellows disagreed with his support for systematizing national antiquities, he never allowed himself to be restricted by this.

It has been noted earlier that another great contribution of the European Renaissance to modern society lay in its insistence on making the development of the freedom of each individual the condition for the development of the freedom of all humanity. On this point let me again draw upon the words of Engels: This was ''a time which called for giants and produced giants—giants in power of thought, passion, and character, in universality and learning. The men who founded the modern rule of the bourgeoisie had anything but bourgeois limitations. On the contrary, the adventurous character of the time unloosed them to a greater or lesser degree. . . . For the heroes of that time had not yet come under the servitude of the division of labor, the restricting effects of which, with the production of one-sidedness, were so often noted in their successors. But what is especially characteristic of them is that they almost all pursue their lives and activities in the midst of the contemporary movements, in the practical struggle; they take sides and join in the fight, one by speaking and writing, another with the sword, many with both. Hence the fullness and force of character that makes them complete men."[170]

No more needs to be said. You only have to look at the main personages on the editorial board of the journals *New Youth* and *New Tides* and what they pursued and practiced in the May 4th Movement to see it was precisely like this. They called for the liberation of individuality and they sought individual liberty. They dared to criticize, oppose, and struggle against every kind of authority, all forces that they saw as preventing China's progress toward implementing democracy and science, whether it be that of the dead or of the living, of warlords or of bureaucrats. They not only took on the struggle against the "Tongcheng fallacies" and the "lingering evils of selective studies," but they also attacked the "shop of the Confucian clan" and the traditional ethical code. They not only lashed out in words against a dark society that was becoming ever more corrupt, but they used action to resist a violent and cruel autocracy. From the point of view of the individual, all of them—Chen Duxiu, Li Dazhao, Hu Shi, Lu Xun, Qian Xuantong, Liu Bannong, and even such younger members as Chuan Sinian and others—had their weak points; none could be called perfect. But before they became divided into different groups, they brought about a shaking of the foundations of Chinese society more fundamental than that of either the Hundred Day Reform or the 1911 Revolution.

For this reason, once the May 4th Movement had become history, and that group of young people had already become objects of historical research, no matter how each of them was criticized or repudiated individually for his ideas, scholarly attainments, and character, they were recognized as the pioneers of the Chinese people's striving for democracy and freedom. As such they made up a component of modern Chinese history.

7

Nevertheless, in spite of all the efforts of the two generations of people from the 1911 Revolution to the May 4th Movement, the so-called Chinese Renaissance has already proved to have been only an illusion. After the storms of the May 4th Movement had calmed, Chinese society remained in a state of civil war, chaos, and poverty. A certain amount of stability emerged between the late 1920s and the early 1930s, but the Japanese invasion and war pushed China back into a sea of fire. In the 1940s, as the sounds of internal gunfire gradually retreated, the Chinese people heard the solemn announcement that the great revolution had already triumphed, and that it was in the process of revitalizing the great culture of China. People were filled with hope, as they awaited the Renaissance of a new period to appear quickly on China's old territory. Yet, up to the fifty-fifth anniversary of May 4th, in 1974, this wait led people to feel an even more somber sense of loss. Finally they could wait no longer and rose up with angry shouts, compelling the ten-year-long Cultural Revolution to end in failure. In the end, China moved onto the difficult road to reform. Reform needs time, as everyone knows. Nevertheless, as we now reach the seventieth anniversary of the May 4th Movement, it is almost impossible for people not to wonder about those pure hopes seventy years ago. Was it inevitable that they should only bring in their train the sense of loss that accompanies a great illusion?

APPENDIX

The Strange Ideas of Philosophers as One Historical Period Supersedes Another

> Dispersion leads in turn to accumulation. This is something that ordinary men do not think of.[171]

The title for this section comes from an explanation of the "Dispersion" ("Huan") figure in the *Book of Changes* (*Zhou yi: Huan guo*). In simple language, it means that when scattered individuals are brought together they will do things beyond the imagination of ordinary people. China's intellectuals are not united; each has his or her own thoughts. But if we took the strange ideas of each individual and collected them together, we would discover that from as early as the beginning of the seventeenth century, China had many ideas beyond normal human imagination. Since ordinary people could not understand them, I have called them "the strange ideas of philosophers."[172]

Xu Guangqi

Xu Guangqi asked Matteo Ricci many questions about Western political ideas and wanted to go to Europe to make an investigation in person. That this did not happen was not his fault. If he really had gone to Europe and returned, would the intellectual history of the late Middle Ages have taken a different form?

Li Zhizao

In early seventeenth-century China, Li Zhizao translated Aristotle's *Logic* into Chinese. Had he already realized that the Chinese tradition of thought did not include formal logic? No one knows. But we do know the *Logic* was translated into Chinese.

Liu Xianting

Liu Xianting did not want to be an official, and he wandered throughout the country. He knew many dialects, and he also knew numerous foreign languages. He was said to be engaged in linguistic comparisons. Sad to say, he only left behind his *Scattered Notes on Broad Experiences* (*Guangyang zazi*), which included all kinds of fantastic ideas in embryonic form. Otherwise we might be able to work out whether or not he could be regarded as the founder of comparative linguistics in China.

Pan Pingge

Who would have thought that Pan Pingge, a primary school teacher of the early Qing, would cause the great scholar Gui Zhuang to adopt him as teacher, and Wan Sitong to accept his views after one debate with him? The result was that Huang Zongxi himself wrote numerous letters of thousands of characters each to his favorite pupil in order to refute these arguments, strongly implying that Pan Pingge was "Shaozhengmao" (a rival teacher of Confucius). Why was this? It was because he suddenly proclaimed that "Zhu Xi is a Daoist and Lu Jiuyuan a Chan Buddhist," in fact that the whole group of great Confucian scholars from Song to Ming were simply a bunch of Buddhist monks. No wonder Huang Zongxi was so annoyed with him and Lü Liuliang also refuted his ideas. Yet, half a century later, Li Gong made copious quotations from his *Record of the Search for Humaneness* (*Qiuren lu*), seeing the knowledge and experience expressed here as superior to that of Zhu Xi or Lu Jiuyuan.

Zhang Lüxiang

While Zhang Lüxiang also was Liu Zongzhou's student, he took the opposite position to that of Huang Zongxi, feeling that his teacher's critique of Wang Shouren was right to the point. His fellow townsman, Lü Liuliang, admired Zhu Xi, and no doubt he had been directly influenced by him. Yet in spite of the fact that he was admired by Zeng Guofan and others as the second of the four great transmitters of Confucianism in the early Qing, his most profound ideas supported the unity of physical labor and book learning. He wanted to abolish the division of labor as a means of remedying the decadent habits of the literati. Nevertheless, in the end he had to depend on teaching and taking in students to make his own livelihood, showing that this solution was not viable.

Lu Shiyi

Lu Shiyi, a diehard of a past dynasty, was arrested in the early Qing because of his association with the Southern Ming government. Although he opposed the Wang learning and had serious doubts about the Cheng-Zhu school of Song neo-Confucianism, in the waning years of the Qing he was taken by such hardliners as Zeng Guofan as the third of the four transmitters of Confucianism. Those who investigate this question are puzzled and enter into all sorts of debates, but they don't realize that he was ''Zeng Can'' to Fang Bao, the founder of the Tongcheng sect. When Yongzheng died, Qianlong had to arrange a funeral for his father. Through Wei Tingzhen, the minister of rites, Fang Bao suggested that the traditional funeral rites be restored. There was fear over this, and Wei actually lost his official position as a result. Fang Bao's plan had in fact been derived from Lu Shiyi. Since Zeng Guofan considered himself a direct transmitter of the Tongcheng school, why should he not venerate Lu Shiyi?

Yan Yuan

Anyone who has read *The Scholars* will remember the description in it of the filial son who undergoes hardships and dangers in order to find his father's corpse. This rather ludicrous caricature was modeled after Yan Yuan. Yan Yuan had read the *Zhou Rites* (*Zhou li*) and had set himself to carry out in practice all of the regulations concerning ''how the Confucian uses virtue to gain the hearts of the people.'' Yet those neo-Confucian philosophers who were always making a lot of noise about ''practicing what one preaches'' never intended actually to carry any of this out.

Li Gong

To carry out the teaching of his master, Yan Yuan, that the humane person should think and act with absolute consistency, Li Gong wrote a diary every day, faithfully recording both his words and his actions. The result was one entry in the diary that reported, "Last night I had sex with my wife one time." Most people could not help laughing aloud at this, but could those who did not find this laughable adopt the same principle of "not cheating the bedchamber"?

Gu Yanwu

Everyone knows that Gu Yanwu persisted in opposition to the Qing after the fall of the Ming. Yet his nephews, the "three Xus,"[173] all became high officials under the Qing—if not ministers then prime ministers—and he often went as a guest to their homes. It is true that he sometimes criticized his nephews, yet his most severe criticisms were along the lines of telling them not to let their banquets go on into the middle of the night as this was not good form. So in the end, people really did not know what he was thinking.

Huang Zongxi

Like Gu Yanwu, Huang Zongxi firmly refused the invitations of the Qing rulers and was unwilling to take part in the examination for mature officials. Yet he was extraordinarily concerned about the *Ming History*, which was being compiled in the Qing, and sent his very best student, Wan Sitong, to participate practically as a writer; he also sent his son, Huang Baijia, to follow the trends of what was happening in the project. It is even said that it was he who made the final decision on the layout of the history. Can he truly be said not to have cooperated with the Qing?

Lü Liuliang

Zeng Jing, a Hunan teacher, read Lü Liuliang's books, decided earnestly to follow them, and sent a disciple with a letter to a Han governor advising him to take up arms against the Qing. This case in the early period of Yongzheng shook the whole country and made his name widely known. In the late Qing he was revered by revolutionary parties as a people's hero. But do you know what the level of his knowledge and experience really was? It was certainly no higher than that of Huang Zongxi, once a close friend but later cut off by him, and in fact he sincerely believed Zhu Xi's teaching about making strict distinctions between barbarians and Chinese, and so forth. Yet he was not very happy to be one of the remnant faithful to a past dynasty, and he thought of the idea of writing comments and notes on eight-legged essays as a means of making his political views known to the literate and young first degree holders (*xiucai*). The result was that forty years after he died, his various collections of eight-legged essays, such as *Comments on the Four Books* (*Sishu jiangyi*), were still on sale in the street stalls. Zeng Jing read one and became captivated by it, saying, "Lü Liuliang should have been the emperor of the late Ming." Given this situation, how could he not be punished by having his coffin exhumed and his corpse beheaded?

Wang Fuzhi

In making judgments about the three great loyalists of the later Ming, Zhang Taiyan said, "Of these Ming loyalists, Wang was regarded by the peasants as most pure." Yet if one looks at the inscription he wrote for his own tombstone, the last phrase reads "Remnant official of the Ming and traveler Wang Fuzhi," which makes one think of his *Veritable Records of the Yongli Reign* (*Yongli shilu*). Since he had once been the minister for foreign affairs of the Southern Ming Gui emperor's government, of course he was not ignorant of the fact that the whole government, from top to bottom, had been converted to Catholicism, nor was he ignorant of the fact that the Queen Mother, who held all real power, used her baptismal name of Mary. He was also aware that an imperial counsel held by Queen Mary once decided to send eunuchs to the Vatican to ask for support for the Gui emperor's government. Yet not a trace of any of this appeared in the "veritable record." So was he really "most pure"?

Shunzhi

Shunzhi's personal name was Fulin; his temple name, Qing Shizu. The romantic story about him and Dong Xiaowan once gained the sympathy of literary writers. Historians have already proved this story to be fictitious. Although this is disappointing, nothing can be done about it. Nevertheless, writers seldom note that this emperor's most esteemed adviser was the Westerner, Adam Schall von Bell, and that the teacher to whom he was most attached was the great Chan master, the monk Muchen, also that he himself had not the slightest interest in Confucianism.

Lu Longqi

Lu Longqi was the first famous official after the Qing adopted Confucian temple ceremonies who was an adherent of Song neo-Confucianism. The secret of his success lay in the viewpoint he formulated that

Zhu Xi had already fully explained the teachings of Confucius and Mencius, and all people have to do is take Zhu Xi's *Collected Annotations on the Four Books (Sishu jizhu)* as the truth and follow it word for word. Where did this view come from? Lü Liuliang. But he was not as foolish as Lü Liuliang, recognizing that many things could be said that would never be carried out. He rejected Lü Liuliang's call not to serve as an official under the Qing and compared himself to Shan Tao, hinting that Lü Liuliang could be Ji Kang and he could allow his son to be Ji Shao.[174] So after he became an official he kept repeating over and over that he was a serious believer in the teachings of Zhu Xi, and he made a lot of noise about such notions as the "great ultimate" (*taiji*) and the "regulation of vital energy" (*liqi*). No wonder after he died he was given the special honor of being classed with Confucius, Mencius, Zhu Xi, and the Cheng brothers and offered sacrifices of cold pork, while Lü Liuliang's recompense was to have his whole family exterminated.

Zhang Boxing

"Zhang Boxing's personal integrity makes him first among Qing officials." This judgment was made by Kangxi in his latter years in settling a dispute between the governor general and his second in command in Liangjiang. Even though he was sheltered by Kangxi in this way, however, the ugly reputation of this unscrupulous official of the Qing kept getting out. There was so much opposition to him that Kangxi finally had to agree to have him dismissed from office and punished for his crimes. His scholarship was absolutely inferior, yet he loved to write books and have them published. The *Complete Writings from the Hall of Righteousness (Zhengyi tang quanshu)*, which he edited, amounted to five hundred chapters and was commended by Lu Longqi and Lu Shiyi, supporters of the transmission of the Way (*daotong*). Zeng Guofan and his followers revered him as the rearguard of the four transmitters of Confucianism, causing great puzzlement to those who try to explain the situation. In fact, one only has to look at the way Gali impeached him for defending Fang Bao and all is clear.

Shi Runzhang

The Strange Stories Written in the Liao Studio (Liaozhai zhiyi) often refers to Shi Yushan, and that was Shi Runzhang's studio name. This poet lived in the time of Kangxi and was as famous as Song Wanqi—

it was said that "the south had Shi and the north had Song." He had been an official at both prefectural and county level and had been a Hanlin expositor. Apparently he supported the Qing rulers. Yet his *Song on the Cock Crowing (Jiming qu)* has the unexpected line "One endless night continues into another, both people and ghosts cry out together." His *Journey of an Old Woman (Laonu xing)* surprisingly pays no attention to the Confucian ethical code and asks, on behalf of a servant-girl: "The nights of pleasure for my master never end, yet how long will I have to sleep alone in an empty room?"

Chen Menglei

A fellow townsman of Li Guangdi, Chen Menglei also took the *jinshi* examination in the same year. He never expected that just when he took time off to return to his native village, the rebel feudatory leader Geng Jingzhong would force him to enter his secretariat. He also never expected that even though he strongly advised Li Guangdi to be patriotic and sent secret intelligence to him to be passed on to the emperor, this would end in bringing about his own ruin and cause him to be sent away for penal servitude for sixteen years. Even less did he expect, when he was finally forgiven, returned to Beijing, and given the position of a retainer to the emperor's third son, Prince Cheng, that a three-thousand-folio collection which he had devoted himself to writing for twenty-three years would just have been published and snatched up by the newly ensconced emperor, Yongzheng. Yongzheng had its name changed to *A Collection of Old and Contemporary Books (Gujin tushu jicheng)* for circulation, yet he himself had the old case of his helping a traitor forty years earlier investigated and was sent off again to a distant place for penal servitude. He was thus once again sacrificed to the plotting of the imperial court. A rough and bumpy road for fifty years was the cost of this unprecedented encyclopedic collection, which might be called one of the wonders in the world history of libraries. Was it worth it? That depends on what perspective one uses in making a judgment.

Yang Wenyan

Yang Wenyan was drawn by Chen Menglei into close personal service in the court. As a literary adviser to the emperor along with Chen Menglei, he had a case framed against him by Yongzheng at the time of his accession to the throne. Yet his reputation for having a thorough knowledge of Western astronomy and mathematics was widely celebrated not only because he had been commended by the Kangxi emperor, but even more because the structure of the version that was handed down of the *Treasury of Mathematical Principles* (*Shuli jingyun*) originated from his work, and this volume made a name in history. Political trickery is a fearful thing, yet it also is judged by history, even when it was the emperor himself who played tricks on him.

Mao Qiling

Mao Qiling's second name was Dake, and he was one of the strange characters among Qing classical historians. He had not the slightest faith in the sacredness of the Confucian classics, yet after Yan Ruoju put out his *Studies on the Old Text Book of History* (*Guwen shangshu shuzheng*), he put out his *Grievances on Behalf of the Old Text Book of History* (*Guwen shangshu yuanci*), in which he purposely defended the fake classics. He did not make clear his reason for doing this, yet if one realizes that before his death Yan Ruoju had become an honored guest to the fourth son of the Manchu emperor, later to become the Yongzheng emperor, one may be able to understand the real reason why he made this intentional show of defiance.

Sha Zhangbo

Those who do not pay close attention to poetry during the Qing dynasty certainly would never imagine Sha Zhangbo's influence during the Kangxi era. He firmly maintained that poetry was a kind of *Spring and Autumn Annals* in rhyme, and he made it clear that he referred to using poetry to criticize or commend contemporary or past events. He wanted to rival Du Fu, that sage of poets, yet on the level of technique at least he could not be compared. Still, in terms of doing poetic history, perhaps he should be researched. "You don't see: Year in and out the middle plains are a battle ground: in a thousand miles of desolation, there is not one tree." Who would believe that this was an image depicting the situation at the height of Kangxi's rule of prosperity?

Zeng Jing

Yongzheng personally edited the record of Zeng Jing's interrogation. In the *Record of Resolving Delusion* (*Dayi juemi lu*), which was promulgated throughout the nation, his influence was used in a way both laughable and pitiable, the epitome of a minor fool who had no under-standing of the complexity of things. Yet Yongzheng never anticipated that Zeng Jing's *Record of New Ideas* (*Zhi xin lu*), that is, his reading notes on studying Lü Liuliang, would also be disseminated in a secret version. In these he made some surprising comments: "Between Han and Manchu there can be no relation of official and ruler." "Only a true Confucian scholar should be emperor. This position should not go to a people's hero, let alone to a crafty old scoundrel who might well be called a ruffian." When one sees this type of comment, who still be-lieves that Yongzheng's record of Zeng Jing's confession was not a forgery?

Yuan Mei

Yuan Mei's poetry, his menus, and the fact that he accepted women students have all been given enormous attention. Yet no one has noticed that he said "I have little faith and many doubts with regard to the classical learning." He certainly had many doubts and said that if the Old Text version of the *Book of History* (*Shang shu*) could be doubted, then the New Text version could also be doubted. So could the *Rites and Ceremonies* (*Yili*) and the *Book of Rites* (*Liji*). If one could have doubts about the six books handed down by the seventy disciples of Confucius, then one could also doubt the words of Confucius or Mencius in the *Analects*. He further criticized the "transmission of the Way," saying this was something like Daoist monks' trickery about receiving pills of immortality from God. Nevertheless, Zhang Xuecheng stole his views and then criticized him for having no sense of shame. I shall never understand how people can echo these views of Zhang.

Wang Fu

Wang Fu, a Weizhou scholar who came from a family of porcelain kiln workers in Jingdezhen, had spied out every area of learning and written a pile of books as high as himself. He can be seen as the mentor of all who attain fame through self-study. Yet people always forget that his model was Lu Longqi. After he died his ancestral tablet was finally accepted into the Ziyang Academy together with that of Jiang Yong, and so his desire to enjoy the same sacrificial meals as Zhu Xi was realized. Yet, in the final analysis, he also could not avoid some verbal jibes from the writer of the *Outline to the Four Treasuries* (*Siku tiyao*), who said that his classical attainments could be compared with those of Lu Longqi at best. When the maid tries to ape her mistress, this is generally the result.

Jiang Yong

Jiang Yong was the founder of the Wan School within Han learning. Later his disciple Dai Zhen became more famous than he and referred to him in contempt as "Jiang Shenxiu, the old Confucian of my home prefecture." Yet of all the great teachers in the Wan School, he was the only one who made no attempt to conceal the fact that his own learning had been inspired and enhanced by "Western learning" (*xixue*). This is yet one more example of how the mind and emotions of a founder tend to be broader in sympathy than those of his followers.

Dai Zhen

Dai Zhen was ambitious to use reasoning to gain power and influence and to explain the true "principle" of Confucius and Mencius to the autocrats, to prevent them from "killing people on the basis of mere opinion." What was the result? The emperor Qianlong took note of him, but not of his teaching about "understanding the people's feelings and satisfying the people's desires." Rather, he used his views concerning the false "principle" of the Cheng brothers and Zhu Xi to heap scorn upon those who were not happy with the policy of "using the Manchus to drive the Han" (*yi Man yu Han*), saying they all had a "false Confucianism." For this reason Qianlong conferred on him the title of *jinshi*. This might be called "using the Han to control the Han" (*yi Han zhi Han*).

Ji Yun

Outstanding, yet a strange character, Ji Yun was in charge of editing the comprehensive index for the *Complete Library of the Four Treasuries* (*Siku quanshu*), which was the synopsis of the grandest and most extensive book collection of the Middle Ages. Yet he himself left to posterity only a notebook in which he wrote about devils and strange occurrences. People only take note that it was a clumsy copy of *The Strange Stories Written in the Liao Studio* (*Liaozhai zhiyi*), but they don't realize that he was explaining human suffering as a recompense causally related to an earlier life, a high-minded way of trivializing pain.

Zhao Yi

"In every generation China has produced talented people, and over the centuries leaders of literary excellence have emerged." This sentence has appeared in countless introductions to essay collections, which all claim that Zhao Yi opposed the restoration of antiquity. Good, but how then does one explain "Suppose I could hold ten thousand scrolls and daily spend time with the ancients"? Are not *The Reading Notes on the Twenty-two Books of History* (*Nianershi zhaji*) and *The Reading Notes on General History* (*Gaiyu congkao*) also his writings?

Qian Daxin

Qian Daxin is said to be the prototype of the textual critic who does criticism for its own sake. If one looks at the *Variant Readings on the Twenty-two Books of History* (*Nianershi kaoyi*), this certainly seems to be the case. Yet if one opens up the *Collected Essays from Qianyan's Studio* (*Qianyantang wenji*) and reads the essay in which he says Qin Gui was not a traitor to the Han, one will get a big surprise. Did he not in fact use textual criticism as a way of pandering to the preferences of the Qing rulers?

Wang Mingsheng

Wang Mingsheng's *Discussion on the Seventeen Books of History* (*Shiqi shi shangque*) and *Variant Readings on the Book of History* (*Shangshu kaoyi*) are of course celebrated books on the history of the classics. Yet if one looks at his biography, it says that whenever he went into the houses of those with wealth and power, he made a gesture of tucking his hands together and said he was gathering in the atmosphere of wealth; it also says he had no compunction about accepting bribes. Yet what has been passed on to the world is his books. This cannot help making people lose their respect for him. It seems that his way of thinking was very similar to that of certain literary hacks of later generations.

Wang Baitian

The *Life Chronology of Master Zhu Xi* (*Zhuxi nianpu*), which Wang Baitian spent over twenty years in writing, is known for being correct and to the point. Nevertheless, Zhu Xi's interaction with Chan Buddhists, the fact that he was given to Daoist techniques for fabricating pills of immortality, the fact that he changed his name to "Zhou Xin who called himself the Daoist master of emptiness" (*kongtong daoshi Zhouxin*) to write the *Variant Readings on a Daoist Text* (*Cantong qi kaoyi*), the fact that he openly framed up a case against an old friend and fellow official who fell in love with one of the official prostitutes—all these sorts of heterodox activities and abnormal jealousies, which have been demonstrated by conclusive evidence—he not only omitted to investigate, but also failed to record. No wonder Yongzheng, whose behavior was similar, felt that he had excellent common sense, called him in to give special guidance, made an exception in promoting him, and even bestowed on him a set of ''Master Zhu's Writings.''

Cai Shangxiang

At the advanced age of eighty-seven, Cai Shangxiang completed his *General Investigation into the Life Chronology of Wang Jinggong* (*Wang Jinggong nianpu kaolue*), exhausting all his energies to disprove the slander against the reformer of seven hundred years earlier—Wang Anshi. From that time onward, people have been prepared to talk about the modernizing political reforms of the time and dared to recognize Wang Anshi as a pioneer. But was this really his intention in writing this book? The *General Investigation* proves that his genuine interest was in refuting the slanders against such philosophers of the mind school as Lu Jiuyuan and Li Fa who had said good things about Wang Anshi, and who had been attacked by the neo-Confucian philosophers who took on the task of transmitting the ''orthodox beliefs'' of Zhu Xi.

Ling Tingkan

Ling Tingkan considered himself a student of Dai Zhen, yet he was not satisfied with him. He held to his intention of debating the meaning of principle with the Song neo-Confucian philosophers when there was no need to do this at all. He asserted in a simple and straightforward way that Song neo-Confucianism (*lixue*) was no different from Buddhist meditation (*chanxue*), and that the study of Wang Yangming's teachings was no different from the study of Zhu Xi's teachings. He went on to say that only Xun Kuang's idea of rite contains the true meaning of the sages, so the highest responsibility of scholars is to devote themselves to rites. If one said that Qing dynasty Han learning became the study of rites or of the Master Xun, he could be seen as the initiator of this trend. Yet he firmly asserted that all scholarship under heaven inevitably changed with the times, so what one sees cannot be true Song learning, nor is there any true Han learning. There are simply differences in scholarly views. How can one explain these self-contradictions? The answer can only be found outside of his discussions of rites.

Xu Zongyan

Xu Zongyan, a famous *jinshi* who passed the examination in the year that Qianlong died, is said to have combined excellence in knowledge of the classics, poetry, and essay writing. Yet he himself despised all three of these. "If Confucius had been born in these times, he would go back no earlier than the period from Ming to Song and then close his ears; he would not seek back beyond three generations in the past for unfounded statements and use them as a guide for society, when not one is of any use." I ask you, can he be considered a neo-Confucian philosopher, a philosopher of Han learning, or a classicist?

Fang Dongshu

There are many condemnatory views among those who refer to Fang Dongshu's *Deliberation on Han Learning* (*Hanxue shangdui*). Yet he was a private secretary to Ruan Yuan, who was known as a defender of the Han learning, and he even dared to dedicate this book to Ruan Yuan, although within it he had attacked the book Ruan Yuan edited by name, the *Explanations of the Qing Classics* (*Qingjing jie*). Looking at this nowadays, it is nearly beyond imagination.

Gong Zizhen

Was Gong Zizhen China's Dante? Dante once said, "The stones of the wall around Rome are worthy of our respect, yet we should turn our eyes to the land on which this ancient city is built, which is even more valuable." In contrast Gong Zizhen said, "How can I boast that I am a healer of the nation, when my medicine shop sells only the old pills which have long been known?"

Wei Yuan

It is said Wei Yuan was the first person to open his eyes and really look at the world outside, a view that inevitably goes against history. Nevertheless, after the shameful humiliation of China's defeat by the British navy, he dared to tamper with the tradition of "using the barbarian to control the barbarian" and put foward the proposition of "learning valuable techniques from the barbarian" He can thus be seen as one of those persons of theoretical courage after the Opium Wars.

Wang Tao

One of the new intellectuals who was misunderstood both by the landlord class and by the peasants, Wang Tao had no alternative but to escape to the British colony of Hong Kong. There he ran his newspaper and published his views on how to reform China's condition.

Dai Wang

Although a scholar who stood at the crossroads between the New Text scholarship of the Qing dynasty and the reformist movements, over the last hundred years very little attention has been given to Dai Wang. This may be the real reason why Zhang Taiyan wrote the *Mourning for the Later Dai (Ai Hou Dai).*

Wang Kaiyun

This "old man of Hunan" (*Xiangji laoren*), Wang Kaiyun was still alive and very old at the time that Yuan Shikai restored the monarchy, and in his last years he dared to take his Nurse Zhou right into the president's palace. How can one believe that someone who belittled traditional social mores in such a way was truly one of the great classical scholars?

Yu Yue

Who could believe that Yu Yue, a textual critic of a century earlier, the great teacher who brought the old text classical school to its height, would revise and edit the *Popular Tales of Martial Heroes (Qixia wuyi)*?

Sun Yirang

Sun Yirang's thinking was fresh and modern yet the means he used were traditional, a contrast clearly reflected in his person. If one only read the *True Meaning of the Zhou Rites (Zhouli zhengyi)* and *Textual Criticism on the Mo Zi (Mo Zi jiangu)*, one would not imagine that the writer of these volumes could be an enthusiastic supporter of the democratic movement in the late Qing.

Tan Sitong

Tan Sitong was so fed up with the Chinese tendency to fix their eyes on the point "three inches below the navel" that his *Study of Benevolence (Renxue)* contained the absurd idea that "if male and female sex organs were located on the forehead in the first place, so that sexual intercourse were as open and public as kissing is in the West, the feudal sexual consciousness would never have come into existence.''

Kang Youwei

Do you know that at the very time Kang Youwei was opposing the revolution he wrote a book called *Materialism as a Way of National Salvation (Wuzhi jiuguo lun)*?

Afterword to the First Chinese Edition

It has long been an aspiration of mine to explore the many topics relating to China's move out of the Middle Ages from the perspective of cultural history.

But aspirations are one thing, and actually making a start at this task has been quite another, leaving me often with the feeling that I am standing up against a brick wall.

Everyone admits that China had an exceptionally lengthy Middle Ages, and most people agree that China led the way into the Middle Ages in world history. Many difficulties appear, however, once the problem is seen within the historical domain.

When one speaks of China "leading the way," where should the beginning line be placed? How is one to ascertain where the boundary should be placed for this beginning? What kind of measure should be used to determine this beginning point?

When we speak of China's Middle Ages being "lengthy," there are even greater problems. Where should the end of the Middle Ages be placed? Was it true that China came close to the end and then went backward again? Were there different phases in this lengthy process? If there were different phases, then how is one to establish the dividing line among them? The common view for many years has been to cut the Qing dynasty in two as a marker between the Middle Ages and the early modern period. But if we examine the situation from the perspective of logic and the continuity of history, we may come to a different conclusion. Naturally, there are many and varied commentaries and expositions in China and abroad, but these are so complicated that they can only be described in terms of "different people having different views."

There is nothing wrong with different people having different views. The main purpose of scholarship is to seek out the truth, and Marx pointed out long ago that the truth is ascertained through the process of debate. When it comes to historical research, however, while debates are an essential process in ascertaining truth, there should be a commonly recognized rule in the competition among various contending positions: we must respect historical facts.

History belongs to the past. All the various events of the past have already become reality, and since each can have only one reality, they cannot be changed into something different to fit the canons of logic. Thus, to know the truth of history, we must first ascertain historical facts before we can give any clear explanation of the reason for them. History is also a process. It is only by examining thoroughly all the phenomena that emerge in the historical process, both true and false, superficial and deep, oblique and full face, that we can hope to make judgments about the objective historical process—the reality of history—that will approach the truth. No one could have expressed it better than Marx when he said that the facts of history are clarified through the exposition of contradictions.

I believe that the only way we can attempt to solve the riddle of China's move out of the Middle Ages is by following the method of Marx, that is the historical materialist method, which was restated by Engels in his speech at the grave of Marx.[175]

Nevertheless it has been this very attempt that has made me feel as if I were up against a brick wall.

In my opinion, China went through the tortuous process of coming out of the Middle Ages in the period from the late Ming to the late Qing, that is, in the three hundred years between the late sixteenth and the early twentieth century. Even though I spent many years reading the writings of classical scholars and the books written by early modern scholars before reaching this understanding, it is still merely an impression, one that I myself feel to be rather crude. For this impression to become genuine knowledge, I will have to work carefully through all the historical materials once again and clarify historical reality, taking one topic at a time.

As Zhuang Zi once said, "Human life has its limits but knowledge has no limits. How difficult it is to use what is limited in seeking out the unlimited." In recent years, as I tried to pursue my aspirations, taking the limited fragments of time left over from my teaching and editing work to research the process of China's coming out of the Middle Ages, I could not help feeling more and more the truth of Zhuang Zi's words.

This little book that I am offering to readers is evidence. The book's title—*Coming Out of the Middle Ages*—is rather high sounding. Yet its contents are meager indeed, just a collection of rather capricious essays and notes on cultural and intellectual history from the late Ming to the late Qing, written as fillers for scholarly journals or to stir up the dust at scholarly conferences. Given that they are not systematic but fragmentary, the book cannot avoid the suspicion of being unworthy of its title.

I am thus the first one to feel astonishment that this random collection of essays has become a book. On second thought, however, I think differently. When Confucius became fifty years old, he knew he had been mistaken for the previous fifty years.

Although I have already passed the age when I should know the will of heaven, I still cannot bring myself to emulate this sage. I feel that human persons cannot avoid making mistakes. What is important is that we do not start out with the intention of making mistakes, and that we are prepared to correct our mistakes once we recognize them. Then there is no need for posturing or for going so far as to repudiate everything that has happened in our past. The essays in this small book have largely come from the records I made of thoughts that occurred to me in my reading. My original intention was simply to jot down points that became clear to me, and to explore different facets of problems that were still unresolved. I had never thought they would be collected into a book and published. For this reason, even thought they are not systematic, at least I don't fall into the category of "those who have treated and handed down the sciences," whom Bacon so scorned: "For they put them forward before men's eyes with such ambition and affectation, and so fashioned and as it were masked, that they seem to be quite perfected and carried through to the end."[176]

For the work of editing and compiling this small volume, I owe thanks first to Ni Weiguo of the Shanghai People's Publishing House. He was so good at chasing after the manuscript, coming to my little house in the hottest days of summer and the coldest days of winter to urge me on, that I could not refuse to hunt out these random jottings and essays, go over them again, either to cut out parts or fill in other parts, and produce something like a book.

In the process of editing, Lu Yongling gave me tremendous assistance. Though she had already moved to Nanjing to take up a teaching post, she still helped me to collect old essays, check historical sources, and patiently copy out the whole manuscript. So I must express deepest appreciation to her for this work.

In addition, the stimulus of intellectual exchange with other scholars and the encouragement of friends and former students, including close friends abroad who kept in constant contact by letter, helped me to curb my own moods and complete the manuscript.

If my book can catch readers' attention so that they either seek to prove or refute my investigation, or perhaps offer criticisms of their own, I will be most appreciative.

Notes

1. F. Engels, "The Peasant War in Germany," in *The German Revolutions*, ed. Leonard Krieger (Chicago: University of Chicago Press, 1967), p. 34.

2. Arnold Toynbee, *The Study of History*, vol. 9, concluding section, translated from the Chinese edition of 1974.

3. First preface to *Capital* (Moscow: Progress Publishers, 1984), 1:21.

4. "Sui gan lu," in *Lu Xun quanji* (Renmin chubanshe, 1981), 1:344.

5. Zhou Yutong, ed., Zhu Weizheng, comp., *Zhongguo lishi wenxuan* (Shanghai guji chubanshe, 1981), 2:270–74.

6. Marx, *Capital*, 1:59, n. 1.

7. *The European Messenger* quoted by Marx in *Capital*, "Afterword to the Second German Edition," p. 27.

8. Two scholars from the Federal Republic of Germany have recently written a series of two articles on China in the eyes of Central and Western European political thinkers, the first covering 1570–1750, the second 1750–1850, both based on excellent historical research. There are forthcoming in *Zhongguo wenhua*.

9. Engels, "The Peasant War in Germany," p. 34.

10. According to the *Zizhi tongjian*, one day Emperor Taizong was playing with his beloved little sparrow when he saw Wei Zheng coming, and he quickly hid it in his robe. Wei Zheng was aware of this and purposely brought many issues to his attention, going on at great length. By the time Wei Zheng had finished and left, the little bird had been suffocated to death in the emperor's robe.

11. Marx, *Capital*, 1:81.

12. Ah Q is of course the famous counterhero of Lu Xun's "True Story of Ah Q."

13. *The New Science of Giambattista Vico*, trans. from the 3d ed. (1744) by Thomas Goddard Berger and Max Harold Fisch (New York: Anchor Books, 1971), p. 334.

14. Jean Jacques Rousseau, *A Discourse on Inequality*, trans. Maurice Cranston (New York: Penguin Books, 1984), p. 160.

15. Ibid., p. 134.

16. A quotation from the poet Ding Diaoyuan.

17. Rousseau, *Discourse on Inequality*, p. 134.

18. Vico, *The New Science*, p. 334.

19. Three famous scholars of the Northern Song (eleventh century): Su Xun, the father, and his two sons, Su Shi and Su Che.

20. Zhu Weizheng, "Chuantong wenhua yu wenhua chuantong," *Fudan xuebao* (Social science edition), no. 1 (1987).

21. Rousseau, *Discourse on Inequality*, p. 134.

22. Gao Ming, *Pipa ji.*

23. *Hanshu, Yu Dingguo zhuan*: "His father Yu Gong solved his case; for this reason Jun Zhong set up a shrine for the living and called it the Yu Gong shrine." Wang Xianqian adds: "Zhou Shouchang said that the custom of later generations setting up shrines for the living began at this point."

24. *Hanshu, Jiaoji zhi.*

25. Only the emperor, of course, could be wished ten thousand years (*wansui*).

26. The "*Chang* official" refers to the fact that Wei Zhongxian was head of the Dongchang. In grasping power, Wei Zhongxian used the pretext of attacking famous members of the Donglin party to take on all who opposed him, and he had the following books edited and produced successively as a kind of blacklist: the *Jinshen bianlan* by Gu Bingqian and Wei Guangzheng, and the *Dianjiang lu* by Wang Shaozheng in 1624. He also took the advice of Cao Qincheng and had the *Sanchao yaodian* compiled in 1626.

27. *Shiji, Zhongni dizi liezhuan.*

28. Francis Bacon, *The New Organon*, ed. F. Anders (New York: Bobbs Merrill, 1960), p. 81.

29. Zhu Weizheng, ed., *Zhou Yutong Jingxueshi lunzhu xuanji* (Shanghai renmin chubanshe, 1983), pp. 32–33, 338–39.

30. Liang Qichao, "Qingdai xueshu gailun," in *Liang Qichao lun Qingxueshi er zhong*, ed. Zhu Weizheng (Shanghai: Fudan University Press, 1985).

31. These were the words of Pi Xirui. See his *Jingxue lishi*, ed. Zhou Yutong (Shanghai zhonghua shuju, 1963), p. 193.

32. See for reference the new and old *Tang Shu, Li le zhi.*

33. *Han Feizi, Xianxue.*

34. "To take the public position that one is going to reform the system is an important step that is likely to frighten people. Therefore, why not take precedents from the ancient kings, as these will not shock people and one can avoid disaster." See *Kongzi gaizhi kao, Kongzi gaizhi tuogukao.*

35. See the preface and annotation to "Kongzi gaizhi kao" in *Zhongguo lishi wenxuan*, ed. Zhou Yutong, rev. Zhu Weizheng (Shanghai guji chubanshe, 1980), 2:309–11.

36. "Ding Kong" was first included in *Qiushu* and later modified and included

in *Jianlun*. See Zhu Weizheng, ed., *Zhang Taiyan quanshu* (Shanghai renmin chubanshe, 1984), 3:134–36, 523–27. "Lun Zhuzi xue" was originally published in 1906. See *Zhang Taiyan xuanji*, trans. Zhu Weizheng and Jiang Yihua (Shanghai renmin chubanshe, 1981), pp. 352–99.

37. See *Zhang Taiyan xuanji*, pp. 361–65.

38. See Zhang Binglin's letter to Liao Zhizheng in *Shidi xuebao* 1, 4 (August 1922): "When I was young and engaged in study, I believed devoutly in the Old Text versions of the classics, thus going counter to the views of Kang Youwei and his group. Subsequently I developed a deep dislike of his idea of a 'Confucian religion,' going to the extreme of attacking Confucius. In my middle years, my faith in the Old Text classics remained, but I no longer attacked Confucius. As I probed the issue more calmly, I developed a deep understanding that the Way of Confucius was not as Kang Youwei and his supporters maintained it was. Yet I had already broadcast my earlier position, and although I later retracted my hastily expressed views, they stuck with those of lesser learning." See also Zhang Binglin, "Zishu sixiang bianqian zhi ji," in *Zhang Taiyan xuanji*, pp. 586–93.

39. See the letter to Liao Zhizheng in *Shidi xuebao* 1, 4 (August 1922).

40. For Liang Qichao's words, see "Qingdai xueshu gailun," in Liang Qichao, *Lun Qingxueshi erzhong*, ed. by the author (Shanghai renmin chubanshe, 1983). For Yi Baishi's words, see "Kongzi pingyi," part 2, in *Zhongguo xiandai sixiangshi ziliao jianbian*, ed. Zhu Weizheng (Zhejiang renmin chubanshe, 1982), 1:96–102.

41. Qian Xuantong, "Lun 'Shisuo' ji qunjing bian wei shu," in *Gushi bian* (reprint; Shanghai guji chubanshe, 1982), 1:52.

42. Yigu Xuantong, "Lun 'Chunqiu' xingzhi shu," in *Gushi bian*, 1:276.

43. This phrase comes from the famous novel *Dream of the Red Chamber* (*Hong lou meng*).

44. Marx, *Capital*, afterword to second German edition, 1:28.

45. See, for reference, Zhu Weizheng, " 'Lunyu' jieji zuoshuo," *Kongzi yanjiu*, inaugural issue (1986): 40–52.

46. For the original essay, see Zhu Weizheng, ed., *Zhou Yutong jingxueshi lunzhu xuanji*, pp. 292–323. See also Zhu Weizheng, "Zhongguo jingxueshi yanjiu wushi nian," in ibid., pp. 843–45.

47. In this kind of periodization the persons and events selected are merely suggestive, with one period containing early indications of what was to develop in the next. Even while Confucius was alive, Zi Gong had publicized him as the one whom heaven allowed to come to earth and become a sage. *Xun Zi, Fei shi er zi* had already given Confucius the title of sage king (*shengwang*). The term "uncrowned king" (*suwang*) can be found in *Zhuang Zi, Tianxia*; thus, this term was already in use in the Warring States period. As for the point that Confucius was not merely a Han dynasty giver of the laws but actually prophesied the demise of the dynasty, Gai Kuanrao hinted at this in the period of Han Xuandi. In the period of Yuandi of the Western Han, such classical scholars as Yi Feng and Jing Fang were even bolder. The New Text scholars of the Western Han had an "internal scholarship" all along, which was secretly passed down from the masters to their most promising disciples. In this period the secret texts of divination were passed down. Many recent scholars think that the books of divination originated in the period between Ai Di and Ping Di of the Western Han, which is a serious mistake. Since this is not the subject of this volume, I will not go into it in detail here.

48. See the estimate made in Materials Room of Fudan University's History Department, ed., *Zhonguo jindai lunwen ziliao suoyin* (Shanghai renmin chubanshe, 1985), 2:598–618. This volume lists 530 articles and does not include articles on the five classics or so-called *chuanji* (traditional records).

49. See *Zhou Yutong jingxueshi lunzhu xuanji*, pp. 705–10. This article first appeared in *Xueshu yuekan*, no. 7 (1962).

50. Lu Xun, "Kanjing yougan," in *Fen* (Beijing renmin wenxue chubanshe, 1973), p. 164.

51. This was a privately compiled history based on official archival records.

52. Alfons Väth, S. J., *Johann Adam Schall von Bell: Missionär in China Kaiserlicher Astronome und Ratgeber am Hofe von Peking. 1596-1666. Ein Lebens und Zeitbild* (Köln, 1933). The Chinese version, translated by Yang Bingchen, is entitled *Tang Ruowang zhuan* (Shanghai: Commercial Press, 1949), 2 vols. The introduction promises that the notes and references will appear in a third volume, but apparently they have never come out.

53. This name is taken from the *Mengzi, Li Lou*. See Fang Hao, *Zhonghua Tianzhujiao shi renwu zhuan, Tang Ruowang* (Hong Kong xianggang zhujiao zhenli xuehui, 1970), 2:2, for an explanation of how both of Schall's names were taken from this passage in the *Mengzi*.

54. In this essay, the Chinese traditional calendar is followed for the months, except where reference to the Western calendar is made specific.

55. Jiang, *Donghua lu*, 2d year of Shunzhi, 7th month. See also *Tang Ruowang zhuan*, pp. 220–23, 234–38.

56. Ibid., pp. 238–41.

57. Ibid., p. 243. This was not just a Manchu superstition; the Han rulers of the medieval period thought the same.

58. A Manchu title bestowed on sons of imperial princes.

59. Actually he was the second son, but because his elder brother by the same mother, Chu Ying, died at an early age, people later always called him the eldest son of the empress.

60. *Tang Ruowang zhuan*, pp. 263–66, records this story, which has the flavor of a Tang or Song legend: On a certain day in the third month by the lunar calendar of 1651, suddenly three young women appeared inside Schall's residence, saying that a certain concubine close to the emperor had sent them, because her daughter was gravely ill and she did not trust the doctors but wanted to get an opinion from Schall. Schall asked about the nature of the illness, felt it was not serious, and gave them a sacred tablet, saying that if they hung this tablet it would protect them from all kinds of illnesses. Five days later the three women came to express their gratitude. After making some inquiries, Schall learned that this concubine was actually the present empress dowager, that the one who had been ill was her niece, and that it had already been decided that she would formally marry the Shunzhi emperor in September of that year.

61. Ibid., p. 277.

62. Ibid., pp. 289–91.

63. Ibid.

64. Ibid., pp. 268–69. "The emperor was from outside the church and found it very difficult to understand and take seriously the celibate life of the missionaries. Therefore he had to make a thorough investigation in order to be clear about it. The guests he sent in the middle of the night to Schall never once found any

evidence they could point to. Once the emperor had satisfied himself about the truth of Schall's absolutely celibate life, he then chose him as his teacher and friend, also as his closest and most trusted adviser. He also met all of Schall's wishes, as far as this was possible."

65. Ibid., pp. 289–91.

66. Ibid., pp. 291–92.

67. Wang Shizheng, "Tingzhi runyue," in *Chibei Outan.* See for reference *Mingshi, Wen Tiren zhuan,* Wang Taizheng, *Shi xinlu,* quoted in *Qingdai renwu zhuangao* (Beijing zhonghua shuju, 1984), sec. 1, 1:300, for the materials drawn on here.

68. This material is based entirely on the essays included in *Bu de yi.*

69. *Tang Ruowang zhuan,* p. 388. "Because of Schall's position of high prestige, all kinds of people came to see him from morning to night in his official residence. These visitors came and went constantly in an endless stream. From early morning to late at night, at any time, a message might come from the emperor calling him to go to the palace at top speed. So under these conditions, the normal rules of the Church and of the order actually did not regulate his life."

70. Aleni came to China in 1613 and died in 1649. There was one Portuguese missionary who had come to China earlier and died in the same year, Gaspar Ferreira, but he did most of his missionary work in Guangdong and wrote very little, so that his influence in the church was far less than that of Aleni.

71. *Tang Ruowang zhuan,* pp. 435–36, lists points in Furtado's notice: (1) The duties of the head of the Imperial Astronomical Bureau could not be harmonized with those of the faith, because the almanac and the reports to the emperor contained words and phrases that implied superstition and divination. (2) Because he had taken up the position of head of the Imperial Astronomical Bureau, Schall's words and actions in many ways transgressed the Old and New Testament and the teaching of the Church fathers. (3) Therefore Schall was in serious danger of being impeached and brought before the Roman inquisition. (4) If Schall refused to give up his position as head of the bureau, then the Church would have to excommunicate him. (5) The Society of Jesus's oath forbade members to accept any position of president or director outside of the Church. (6) Schall's way of managing the Astronomical Bureau aroused the disapproval of the missionaries. (7) In carrying out this responsibility, Schall could easily put his life at risk, because if any of his reports to the emperor were not reliable, he could be acccused of the crime of being a traitor to the country and beheaded. (8) Because Schall was carrying out the duties of an official, he could easily commit the sin defined by Church rules as "being an obstacle." Since he was an official of the court, he could not avoid exposing the misdeeds of disloyal officials who had been removed from office; but once he had made this exposure, he would share in the collective responsibility for the condemnation of a man to death, and this went against the merciful purposes of the Church. So this could be an obstacle to the missionaries. (9) Because of his position, he could cause the Society of Jesus to be under suspicion of making it convenient for him to carry out superstitious activities of astrology and divination that were forbidden by the Church. (10) Taking into account all of these nine points, Schall's position as head of the Astronomical Bureau was an obstacle to the good reputation he had in entering the Society of Jesus.

72. *Tang Ruowang zhuan,* pp. 463–65. This is from the ruling made by the four professors on January 31, 1664.

73. Shunzhi bestowed on Schall the title of "teacher versed in metaphysics," and in the fourteenth year of his reign (1657) he bestowed on Schall's church a headboard with the name *tongxuan jiajing* (beautiful place of metaphysical reflection) carved on it, also an imperial stele stating that "the Western scholars are very good at calculating the calendar" and that Schall was the most outstanding among them. Yet in looking at the church with its sacred statutes and Bibles, it was not possible to understand them. "What I admire is the way of Yao and Shun, Duke Zhou and Confucius, and what I emphasize is the Way of the Mean and the most pure principle. As for all the other sacred books such as the *Dao de jing* and the *Leng yan jing*, although I have looked at these, I can't understand the main ideas in them. How much less have I read Western books and Roman Catholicism, so how could I possibly understand their theories?" See Wang Bailu, *Zhengjiao fengbao*. The language indicates this was written by a Han literary official, yet it reflects Shunzhi's tendency to make a distinction between Western scholarship and Western religion.

74. Simon de Cunha was a Portuguese missionary who had taken the position of inspector for the Japanese and Chinese church regions.

75. According to *Tang Ruowang zhuan*, pp. 474–75, Buglio had composed a volume entitled *Tianxue zhenquan* and published it in Beijing in 1662. Its contents refuted Yang Guangxian's *On Exposing Heterodoxy*. In 1639 Huang Mingqiao of Fujian had written a book entitled *Tianxue chuangai*, and no other book by this title has survived in China. No source is given in *Qingdai renwu chuangao*, sec. 1, 1:301, where it says the *Tianxue chuangai* of Buglio, Magalhães, Li Zubai, and others was published in 1661. However, see Paul Rule, *Confucius or Kong-tzu* (London: George Allen and Unwin, 1986), for a copy that seems to have survived in Taiwan.

76. *Tang Ruowang zhuan*, pp. 474–75.

77. Ibid., p. 475. In his *Bu de yi*, Yang Guangxian quotes similar statements, though they clearly had been even further exaggerated.

78. The eight people mentioned in this accusation included four European missionaries—Schall, Verbiest, Buglio, and Magalhães—and four Chinese Christians—Li Zubai, Xu Zhijian, Pan Jinxiao, and Xu Baolu. Later Yang Guangxian accused numerous other persons as well. It seems all the missionaries in China whose names he knew were pointed to at one time or another.

79. *Tang Ruowang zhuan*, p. 485.

80. Ibid., pp. 494–96, has a detailed record of what happened. Yet according to Verbiest's later admission, his calculation was actually five minutes early, but because the high-ranking ministers and officials were overexcited at the time, they did not notice the small error.

81. *Shiji, Kuli lie zhuan, Du Zhou zhuan*, vol. 10, juan 122, p. 3152 in the Zhongguo shuju edition.

82. *Tang Ruowang zhuan*, p. 500.

83. The whole document is found in ibid., pp. 511–12.

84. Ruan Yuan's *Zhou ren zhuan*, vol. 45, says Tang Ruowang died in the 17th year of Kangxi (1678), which is a mistake.

85. The third character in this name is different in Chinese, though the names of the two brothers are identical in pinyin.

86. *Qing Shengzu shilu*, vol. 27.

87. Ruan Yuan, *Zhou ren zhuan*, vol. 45, biography of Verbiest.

88. See Jiang, *Donghua lu,* 10th month of the 7th year of Kangxi, and 2d month of the 8th year of Kangxi.

89. Ibid., 8th month of the 8th year of Kangxi. See for reference *Qing sheng zu shi lun,* the record for the same year.

90. The title now read *tongwei jiaoshi* rather than *tongxuan jiaoshi.* The term *xuan* (metaphysics) was changed to *wei* (abstruse learning), since Xuanye was Kangxi's name so *xuan* could not be used.

91. Dai Zhen, *Mengzi ziyi shuzheng.*

92. There are different views on when the suppression of Catholic propagation began in the Qing dynasty. In an imperial edict of August of the 8th year of Kangxi (1669) concerning the rehabilitation of Adam Schall von Bell there is already this sentence: "With the exception of the normal activities of Nan Huairen (Verbiest) and his group, all provincial Catholic activities are forbidden." (See Jiang, *Donghua lu,* vol. 9.) Yet in the 34th year of Kangxi (1695) there was also an imperial edict allowing the European missionaries to go to the hinterland and preach. (See Joachim Bouvet [Baijin], "Kangxi dizhuan," in *Qingshi ziliao,* ed. Qingshi yanjiushi, Zhongguo shehui kexue yuan Lishi yanjiu suo, 1:24.) In April of the 56th year of Kangxi (1717), Kangxi approved the Ministry of War's response to the Guangdong military commander Chen Ang's memorial, reiterating the edict of 1669 that forbade the propagation of Catholicism in all provinces. (See Jiang, *Donghua lu,* vols. 2 and 3.) In the 59th year of Kangxi (1720), after receiving the Patriarch Mezzabarba, the second imperial envoy sent by Pope Clementine 11th, and in some written comments on the Papal edict brought by Mezzabarba forbidding Chinese Catholics to worship Confucius and their ancestors, Kangxi reaffirmed the ban on "Westerners disseminating their religion in China." (See *Kangxi yu Luoma shijie guanxi wenshu,* ed. Gugong Bowu yuan, 14th edition, appended imperial rescript.) Therefore, if one says that the repression of Catholicism began after Yongzheng came to power, as is stated by the authors of chapter 7 of volume 10 of the *Cambridge History of China* (for the Chinese translation, see *Jianqiao Zhongguo shi, shangjuan* [Chinese Academy of Social Sciences, 1985], p. 587), this is inaccurate.

93. *Deyizhi yishi xingtai* (The German ideology), Chinese ed. (1961), p. 1.

94. *Kangxi yu Luoma shijie guanxi wenshu* has already made public the archives of the Qing court on this subject. Luo Guang's *Jiaoting yu Zhongguo shi jieshi* (Taiwan chuanji wenxue chubanshe, 1969) also relies on the evidence the author has seen in the Vatican archive, in seeking to outline the sequence of events. Yet there are contradictions in the year, month, and day of the two records. According to Luo Guang, the first time the Kangxi emperor received the special envoy from the Holy See, the Patriarch De Tournon, was December 31, 1705, that is, the 44th year of Kangxi's reign, the 16th day of the 11th month, but this is not found in the *Qingshi lu* or the *Donghua lu.*

95. See *Makesi Engesi xuanji* (Selected works of Marx and Engels) (Beijing renmin chubanshe, 1971), 4:501.

96. In the *Kechang* case the officials supervising the *juren* examination in Nanjing and Beijing were accused of allowing cheating, after the notes of the examination candidates had been investigated. The examination had to be repeated, and the main victims of the case were scholars from the Jiangnan region. In the *Zouxiao* case, the Qing government used the pretext of unpaid taxes to punish around thirteen thousand scholars and officials from the four Jiangnan prefectures

of Suzhou, Songjiang, Changzhen, and Zhenjiang. In the Mingshi case, an unofficial history of the Ming dynasty written by Zhuang Tinglun was attacked and the author's corpse was exhumed and humiliated. All who had helped to write, print, and sell the book were arrested and put to death—a total of seventy people, all from the Jiangnan region.

97. The words of Zhang Taiyan. See "Qiushu, Qingru," in *Zhang Taiyan quanji*, ed. by the author (Shanghai renmin chubanshe, 1984), 3:155.

98. In the Jiaqing period Bao Shichen, in a letter to a friend, discussed the eight great literary figures of the Tang and Song period, saying that their style was strongly influenced by "Han Feizi" and "Lushi chunqiu," yet "because they looked down on them, they were unwilling to admit they had learned from them." ("Zai yu Yang Jizi shu," in *Yizhou shuangji, Lunwen.*) This was not necessarily the attitude of such people as Han, Liao, Au, and Su, but it reflects the attitudes of Han scholars of Bao's time and earlier. In their attitudes toward Western learning, did they not also reject it on the surface yet actually accept it on a deeper level? At the very least, this needs to be researched before anyone has the right to write about it.

99. Some of the writings in *Huang Qing jingjie* were first published in the Jiaqing era yet really belonged to the Han learning of the Qianlong era.

100. See "Qiushu, Qingru," in *Zhang Taiyan quanji*, 3: preface, 158; also Liu Shipei, "Qingru deshi lun," *Min bao*, no. 14 (June 1907).

101. See *Zhou Yutong jingxueshi lunzhu xuanji*, ed. by the author (Shanghai renmin chubanshe, 1983), p. 319.

102. There are so many views concerning this process that it is impossible to discuss them all. See the author's "Jingxueshi: Rushu duzun de zhuanzhe guocheng," in *Shanghai tushuguan sanshi zhounian jinian lunji wenji* (1982).

103. See chapter 7 of this book, which first appeared in *Makesi zhuyi zai Zhongguo de shengli* (A collection of essays) (Fudan daxue chubanshe, 1983).

104. This is based on Engels's summary in *Ziran bianzhengfa* (The dialectics of nature) (1971), p. 198.

105. Zhang Taiyan put forward this view in the late Qing. See "Qiushu, Wangxue" in *Zhang Taiyan quanji*, 3:145–50.

106. See the introduction to "Mingru xuean," in *Zhongguo lishi wenxuan*, ed. Zhou Yutong, rev. Zhu Weizheng (Shanghai guji chubanshe, 1980), 2:168–69.

107. "The Song Confucians lectured on Confucian ethics, the Ming Confucians did not talk about the Confucian ethical code, which is the main gap between the Confucians of Song and Ming." "The Song leaders overemphasized Confucian ethics, so that the Ming discarded them." See *Shen bao*, May 15, 1922, "Zhang Taiyan jiangxue diqiri xuji." In speaking of the Ming Confucians here, Zhang Taiyan was referring to Wang Shouren and his followers, including He Xinyin and Li Zhi.

108. See Chen Di, "Songxuan jiangyi. yili bian," in *Yi zhai ji* (Qing, Daoguang 28th year, Chen Douchu edition).

109. See Rong Zhaozu, *Mingdai sixiang shi* (Kaiming shudian, 1941), chap. 8, pp. 276–78.

110. See Huang Zongxi, *Nanlei wenyue*, chap. 3. Of Huang Zongxi's essays that show clearly thorough and systematic research into the Western theories introduced by the missionaries, in addition to "Shangdi," there is also "Hunpo" and "Xili hui hui li jia ru." Liang Qichao once contrasted his *Mingyi daifang lu* to

Rousseau's *Social Contract* and said that Huang Zongxi was even earlier than Rousseau. See *Liang Qichao lun Qingshi erzhong*, ed. by the author (Shanghai: Fudan University Press, 1985), p. 145. It would be more appropriate to compare Huang's writing with his contemporary Montesquieu's *Spirit of the Laws*, with its analysis of the three-way division of power. Also, the fact that Huang had already written the book in the first two years of Kangxi's reign (1662–1663) and did not get his inspiration from the European missionaries is a point worth researching.

111. Yan Yuan was from Zhili. In his later years he made a "southern journey" to Henan, during which he saw the bad practices in the loud promotion of Confucianism in scholarly circles and was extremely turned off by it. He claimed it was from this point that he decided "to make a clear distinction between Confucius and Mencius on one side and the Cheng brothers and Zhu Xi on the other," and that "one has to get the Cheng brothers and Zhu Xi out of the way before one can get near to Confucius and Mencius." See *Xizhai xiansheng nianpu*, ed. Li Gong, arr. Wang Yuan, vol. 2.

112. The year-long Jiangsu examination hall riot in the fourteenth year of Shunzhi (1657) was dealt with by Shunzhi personally. In 1659 Coxinga led a military expedition to Jiangsu, breaking into Zhenjiang, subduing Wuhu, surrounding Jiangning, and defeating the Qing army, frightening the Shunzhi emperor. According to Adam Schall von Bell, at that time Shunzhi "had thoughts of wanting to escape back to Manchuria." After Coxinga withdrew from Jiangnan, the Qing government investigated every locality where officials had given taxes to Coxinga, killing several tens of thousands. See Historical Research Center of People's University, ed. *Qingshi biannian, vol. 1 (China People's University Press, 1985), the materials relating to the 14th and 16th years of Shunzhi's reign.*

113. See *Qing Shizu shilu*, Shunzhi's 18th year, the 7th day of the New Year.

114. For example, Tang Bin, Wei Xiangshu, Wei Yijie, and others were all disciples of Sun Qifeng. Wei Yijie once suggested to the Qing court a policy of destruction for the Southern Ming.

115. In 1694 Xiong Cili offered the *Transmission of the Way* to the emperor and Wang Hongxu and Gao Shiqi requested that it be printed as a textbook for the civil service examinations. Kangxi sent an edict to the grand secretaries commenting that "I see this book has too many stratagems," and "Confucian philosophy is just an empty term, used for all kinds of manipulation." He refused permission. See Jiang, *Donghua lu*, 5th month, 33d year of Kangxi.

116. See Zhu Weizheng, "Zhang Taiyan yu Wang Yangming," in *Zhongguo zhexue* (Sanlian shudian, 1982), 5:313–45.

117. "The scholarship of our contemporary period consists solely of respect for the Master Zhu. The will of the Master Zhu is the will of the sages, and whatever is not his will cannot be the will of the sages." Lu Longqi, *Songyang jiangyi*, chap. 3.

118. See *Zhang Taiyan xuanji, bei xian dai*, ed. Zhu Weizheng and Jiang Yihua (Shanghai renmin chubanshe, 1983), pp. 404–407.

119. This has been neglected by scholars until recently. At an October 1986 international conference on Huang Zongxi in Ningbo, many papers discussed it.

120. In the *Qingdao wenziyu dang*, ed. by the documents section of the former Beiping Gugong Museum, there is a systematic reflection of this. See the 1986 reprinting of this book, which contains documents on Qianlong's literary inquisition, done by Shanghai shudian.

121. The founders of Han learning in the Qing dynasty, recognized in scholarly circles, include Gu Yanwu, from Kunshan county, Jiangsu province; Yan Ruoju, whose family came from Taiyuan in Shanxi province but who placed his household register in Shanyang county, Jiangsu; Hu Wei, from Deqing county in Zhejiang province; and Yao Jiheng, from Xiuning county in Anhui, whose household register was in Renhe county, Zhejiang. If one includes also those in historical scholarship such as Huang Zongxi and Wan Sitong (who were from Yuyao and Yin counties in Zhejiang respectively), then with the exception of Zhang Erqi (from Jiyang county in Shandong, who was regarded by Zhang Taiyan in *Qing Ru* as the pioneer of the study of ritual in the Qing), all were from Jiangnan.

122. Xu Guangqi was from Shanghai in Jiangsu; Li Zhizao and Yang Tingyun were both from Renhe county in Zhejiang. In the late Ming they were called the three great pillars of belief in Western learning and thorough knowledge of the Western learning.

123. The words of Dai Zhen. See Jiang Fan, *Hanxue shi chengji*, folio 3.

124. "Yu Shi Zhongming lun xueshu," *Dai Dongyuan ji*, chap. 9.

125. "Yu mou shi," ibid., chap. 9.

126. See for reference Zhu Weizheng, "Zhongguo jingxueshi yanjiu wushi nian," in *Zhou Yutong jingxue shi lunzhu xuanji*, pp. 850–59.

127. See Duan Yucai, *Dai Dongyuan xiansheng nianpu* and *Dai Dongyuan ji*.

128. Zhao Lian, *Xiaoting zalu*, chap. 9, gives an emotional account of this.

129. See Fang Dongshu, *Hanxue shangdui, Chongxu*.

130. See the author's "Chuantong wenhua yu wenhua chuantong," *Fudan xuebao*, no. 1 (1987).

131. The late Ming scholar Xu Guangqi could be seen as typical of those who were influenced by Western learning. Yet Xu Guangqi's social and political views seem to have remained within the boundaries of neo-Confucian teaching, as can be seen in such writings as his *Paoyan*. See Shanghaishi wenwu baoguan weiyuanhui, ed., *Xu Guangqi zhuyi ji* (1984).

132. It is possible to get a general picture of the arguments among categorizers of the Southern kingdom over whether there should be four sections or seven sections. See Qian Daxin, "Jing shi zi ji zhi ming he fang," in *Zhongguo lishu wenxuan*, comp. Zhu Weizheng, vol. 2.

133. The French missionary Joachim Bouvet's (Bai Jin) *Kangxi dizhuan* has a detailed record of this. This book was translated into Chinese by Ma Xuxiang. See Qing History Research Room, History Research Center of the CASS, ed. *Qingshi ziliao*, vol. 1.

134. Hu Shi, "Kaozhengxue fangfa de laili."

135. Wang Mingsheng, "Shiqi shi shangque, xu."

136. Dai Zhen, "Yu mou shu," *Dai Dongyuan ji*, vol. 9.

137. "Lunshi jueju."

138. *Min bao*, no. 14 (June 1906).

139. This fact is recorded both in Chinese and foreign documents. See Alfons Väth, S. J., *Johann Adam Schall von Bell, Missionär in China*.

140. See Bouvet, *Kangxi dizhuan*, and Luo Guang, *Luoma jiaotingshi jieshi*.

141. See Jiang, *Donghua lu*.

142. These were the 8th and 9th sons of Kangxi. Yongzheng had their names changed to Aqina and Saisihei, which mean dog and pig in Manchu.

143. This has been proven by Chen Yuan. See *Chen Yuan xueshu lunwenji*,

vol. 1, "Yong-Qian jian feng Tianzhujiao zhi zongshi."

144. *Capital*, 1:105, note.

145. See "Jing jingu wenxue" and "Hanxue yu Songxue," in *Zhou Yutong Jingxueshi lunzhu xuanji*, as well as the editor's afterword to this volume.

146. See my comments on this in chapter 5.

147. See Zhou Yutong, comp., Zhu Weizheng, ed., *Zhongguo lishi wenxuan* (Shanghai guji chubanshe, 1980), 2:168; Zhu Weizheng, "Zhang Taiyan yu Wang Yangming," in *Zhongguo zhixue*, vol. 5, and chapter 5 of this volume.

148. Anshi refers to Xie An, an aristocratic leader of the Eastern Jin dynasty in the fourth century A.D.

149. Sun Wanguo, "Yetan Zhang Taiyan yu Wang Yangming—jianlun Taiyan sixiang de liangge shijie," in *Zhang Taiyan shengping yu sixiang yanjiu wenxuan* (Zhejiang renmin chubanshe, 1986), pp. 296–368.

150. Sun Wanguo's words in the essay cited above criticizing the author.

151. These two articles were published in the *Huaguo yuekan* in 1924.

152. Marx, "Theses on Feuerbach," in *Selected Works of Marx and Engels*, 2:405.

153. Marx and Engels, *The Holy Family or the Critique of Critical Critique* (Moscow: Foreign Languages Publishing House, 1956), p. 125.

154. Mao Zedong, "The Bankruptcy of the Idealist Conception of History," in *Selected Works of Mao Tse-tung* (Beijing: Foreign Languages Press, 1961), 4:457.

155. Engels, "Speech at the Graveside of Karl Marx," in Marx and Engels, *Selected Works*, 2:167.

156. "In his excellent essay 'In Memory of the *Manifesto of the Communist Party*,' Professor Antonio Labriola has very correctly observed that already the historians of antiquity, and in modern times Italian historians of the Renaissance, were well aware of the class struggles raging before their eyes within the close limits of the urban republics. No less correct is Labriola's remark that the class struggle, which has assumed a far greater sweep in the modern state, was even more evident during the first half of the nineteenth century." Georgi Plekhanov, *Selected Philosophical Works* (Moscow: Progress Publishers, 1976), 2:430.

157. F. Engels, "Ludwig Feuerbach and the End of Classical German Philosophy," in Marx and Engels, *Selected Works*, 2:392.

158. "The division of labor manifests itself also in the ruling class. . . One part appears as the thinkers of the class (its active, conceptive ideologists, who make the formation of the illusions of the class about itself their chief source of livelihood), while the others' attitude to these ideas and illusions is more passive or receptive; because they are in reality the active members of this class and have less time to make up illusions and ideas about themselves." Marx and Engels, *The German Ideology* (Moscow: Progress Publishers, 1976), p. 68.

159. "The barbarian conquerors . . . (were) . . . , by an eternal law of history, conquered themselves by the superior civilization of their subjects." Marx, "The Future Results of British Rule in India," in Marx and Engels, *Selected Works*, 1:353.

160. Marx, "Revolution in China and Europe," in Marx and Engels, *Collected Works* (New York: International Publishers, 1979), 12:95.

161. Engels, "Introduction to the Dialectics of Nature," in Marx and Engels, *Selected Works*, 2:68-69.

162. "Marx to F. Lasalle in Berlin," in Marx and Engels, *Selected Correspon-*

dence (Moscow: Progress Publishers, 1955), p. 123.

163. See "Engesi zhi Bi-la-lafuluofu," in *Makesi Engesi quanji*, 34:161. "All substances in the natural world—whether dead or alive—in their interaction include both mutual adjustment and conflict, both struggle and cooperation. Therefore if a so-called natural scientist wants to include all aspects of historical development, with its many variations, under the biased and impoverished formula of the 'struggle for survival,' then this approach already passes judgment on itself, since the use of the formula in the natural world still merits debate."

164. "The earlier theories did not embrace the activities of the masses of the population, whereas historical materialists made it possible for the first time to study with scientific accuracy the social conditions of the life of the masses, and the changes in those conditions." V. I. Lenin, "Karl Marx," in *Marx, Engels, Marxism* (Moscow: Progress Publishers, 1965), p. 23.

165. Ibid.

166. See his *Geming de daode*.

167. *Xinchao* 2, 1.

168. *Changshi ji, zixu*.

169. Engels, "Introduction to the Dialectics of Nature," in *Selected Works of Marx and Engels* 2:63.

170. Ibid.

171. "Huan/Dispersion," *The I Ching*, trans. C. F. Baynes and H. Wilhelm (Princeton: Princeton University Press, 1967), p. 229.

172. This introduction was written by the author especially for the English version of the text.

173. Xu Qianxue, Xu Yuanwen, and Xu Lihu.

174. After the demise of the Wei Kingdom in the third century, and the rise of the Western Jin dynasty, Shan Tao and Ji Kang were two of seven famous intellectuals who remained loyal to the Wei. Shan Tao later decided to cooperate with the Western Jin and Ji Kang wrote him a letter cutting of all relations, because of his failure to remain loyal. As a result, Ji Kang was put to death, and his son, Ji Shao, came under the tutelage of Shan Tao. When he asked Shan Tao whether or not he should become an official, Shan Tao replied that all things change, so why should people not adapt?

175. Marx and Engels, *Selected Works*, 2:167.

176. Francis Bacon, *Novum Organon*, trans. G. W. Kitchin (Oxford: Oxford University Press, 1855), p. 66.

Index

Zhu Weicheng is Professor of History and Director of the Research Section on the History of Chinese Thought and Culture, Department of History, Fudan University, Shanghai.

Ruth Hayhoe is an associate professor in the Higher Education Group, The Ontario Institute for Studies in Education, Toronto.